The Promise and Limits of Private Power
Promoting Labor Standards in a Global Economy

This book examines and evaluates various private initiatives to enforce fair labor standards within global supply chains. Using unique data (internal audit reports and access to more than 120 supply chain factories and 700 interviews in fourteen countries) from several major global brands, including Nike, Hewlett Packard, and the International Labor Organization's Factory Improvement Programme in Vietnam, this book examines both the promise and the limitations of different approaches to improving working conditions, wages, and working hours for the millions of workers employed in today's global supply chains. Through a careful, empirically grounded analysis of these programs, this book illustrates the mix of private and public regulation needed to address these complex issues in a global economy.

Richard M. Locke is Class of 1922 Professor of Political Science and Management, Deputy Dean of the Sloan School of Management, and Head of the Political Science Department at the Massachusetts Institute of Technology (MIT). His current research focuses on improving labor and environmental conditions in global supply chains. Working with leading firms such as Nike, Coca-Cola, and Hewlett Packard, Locke and his students have been showing how corporate profitability and sustainable business practices can be reconciled. Locke is the author of *Working in America* (with Paul Osterman, Thomas Kochan, and Michael Piore, 2001), *Employment Relations in a Changing World Economy* (with Thomas Kochan and Michael Piore, 1995), and *Remaking the Italian Economy* (1995, 1997). He was awarded the Jamieson Prize for Excellence in Teaching in 2008 and the MIT Class of 1960 Teaching Innovation Award in 2007. Locke was named a 2005 Faculty Pioneer in Academic Leadership by The Aspen Institute.

Cambridge Studies in Comparative Politics

General Editor

Margaret Levi   *University of Washington, Seattle*

Assistant General Editors

Kathleen Thelen   *Massachusetts Institute of Technology*
Erik Wibbels   *Duke University*

Associate Editors

Robert H. Bates   *Harvard University*
Gary Cox   *Stanford University*
Stephen Hanson   *The College of William and Mary*
Torben Iversen   *Harvard University*
Stathis Kalyvas   *Yale University*
Peter Lange   *Duke University*
Helen Milner   *Princeton University*
Frances Rosenbluth   *Yale University*
Susan Stokes   *Yale University*
Sidney Tarrow   *Cornell University*

Other Books in the Series

Continued after the Index

The Promise and Limits of Private Power

Promoting Labor Standards in a
Global Economy

RICHARD M. LOCKE
Massachusetts Institute of Technology

CAMBRIDGE
UNIVERSITY PRESS

CAMBRIDGE UNIVERSITY PRESS
Cambridge, New York, Melbourne, Madrid, Cape Town,
Singapore, São Paulo, Delhi, Mexico City

Cambridge University Press
32 Avenue of the Americas, New York, NY 10013-2473, USA

www.cambridge.org
Information on this title: www.cambridge.org/9781107670884

First published 2013

Printed in the United States of America

A catalog record for this publication is available from the British Library.

Library of Congress Cataloging in Publication Data
Locke, Richard M., 1959–
The Promise and limits of private power : promoting labor standards in a global economy /
Richard M. Locke.
     p.   cm. – (Cambridge studies in comparative politics)
Includes bibliographical references and index.
ISBN 978-1-107-03155-5 (hardback) – ISBN 978-1-107-67088-4 (paperback)
1. Industrial relations.   2. International business enterprises – Management.
3. Globalization.   I. Title.
HD6961.L63   2013
331.12′042–dc23   2012044106

ISBN 978-1-107-03155-5 Hardback
ISBN 978-1-107-67088-4 Paperback

To my mother, Franca Franzaroli, who taught me about the value of work and the dignity of Labor.

Contents

Acknowledgments

Throughout the world, millions of people, both young and old, work long hours, under harsh conditions and for low wages, to make the goods most readers of this book consume every day. These workers' citizenship rights are frequently violated, and their health, because of long work hours and hazardous working conditions, is often compromised. This book seeks to understand what, if anything, can be done to promote labor justice for these workers. Through an analysis of several private voluntary initiatives promoted by global corporations, lead suppliers/contract manufacturers, labor-friendly nongovernmental organizations (NGOs), and international organizations such as the International Labor Organization (ILO), this book sheds light on both the promise and the limitations of private power in enforcing labor standards for the millions of people employed in global supply chains. The central finding of this book is that working conditions and labor rights can only be promoted in our global economy through a mix of both private and public regulation. Private voluntary regulation is important in redressing labor abuses in global supply chain factories, but it is not enough. Without the support and legitimacy of government regulation, these private initiatives will produce only limited and often unsustainable improvements. In the chapters that follow, I illustrate how this is already taking place, notwithstanding significant resistance by powerful interests operating at different points of most global supply chains.

This book has a long history. It began ten years ago, through a series of conversations with my then MIT colleague Dara O'Rourke, while I was working on a teaching case about Nike and alternative conceptions of corporate responsibility. Although I had done work on labor politics before, I had never studied global supply chains and private voluntary regulation. Dara was an excellent mentor, and his enthusiasm for the topic was infectious. Trying to convince global corporations such as Nike to work with me, share their factory audit reports, and facilitate visits to their suppliers was not easy. It took years and many conversations and visits to corporate headquarters. But the time and effort paid off and as a result, what began as a case study evolved over the years into a full-fledged research project involving the collection, coding, and analysis of thousands of factory audit reports; more than 700 interviews with company managers, factory directors, NGO representatives, and government labor inspectors; as well as field research in 120 factories in 14 different countries. As such, the project evolved from a study of one company (Nike) in a particular industry (athletic footwear) to a research project covering several global corporations competing in different industries, with different supply chain dynamics, and operating across numerous country boundaries.

Throughout this trajectory, I was fortunate to work with a terrific group of graduate students and wonderful colleagues who diligently (and patiently) commented on the various constituent pieces of this larger research project. I was also fortunate to collaborate with a number of company managers, NGO representatives, union leaders, and even government agents who opened up their offices and factories and shared incredible amounts of original data. Without this generosity and openness, this book could never have been written.

Let me first thank the amazing group of students who worked with me as research assistants for this book. These include Matt Amengual, Akshay Mangla, Monica Romis, Alberto Brause, Fei Qin, Hiram Samel, Ben Rissing, Timea Pal, Jonathan Rose, Jennifer Andrews, Dinsha Mistree, Rushan Jiang, Salo Coslovsky, Alonso Garza, Gustavo Setrini, Greg Distelhorst, and Seth Pipkin. I hope that these students learned as much from me as I did from them. Several of these students (Matt, Akshay, Monica, Greg, Alberto, Fei, Timea, Hiram, and Ben) did more than simply assist me in the research but also collaborated as intellectual partners and coauthors on several papers that were written as part of this larger research project. Three of these papers have been published, and sections of these papers, with the permission of the different journals, appear in Chapters 2, 3, and 5. I would like to thank the *Industrial and Labor Relations Review, Politics and Society*, and the *Review of International Political Economy* for both publishing the original papers and allowing me to use excerpts of those papers for this book.

This project also benefited from the tireless support and patient feedback from a truly special group of colleagues, both at MIT and elsewhere. Special thanks to Lucio Baccaro, Kristin Forbes, Simon Johnson, Don Lessard, Eleanor Westney, Bob McKersie, Paul Osterman, Judith Tendler, Michael Piore, Ed Steinfeld, Ben Ross Schneider, Kathy Thelen, Jens Hainmueller, Bob Gibbons, David Singer, Rebecca Henderson, John Sterman, Susan Silbey, Mari Sako, John Ruggie, Michael Hiscox, Chuck Sabel, Hau Lee, Peter Gourevitch, Dara O'Rourke, Archon Fung, Khalid Nadvi, Stephanie Barrientos, Gay Seidman, Jonathan Zeitlin, Roberto Pires, Andrew Schrank, Tim Bartley, Gary Herrigel, Gary Gereffi, Jill Ker Conway, Layna Mosley, and David Weil. I would like to offer special thanks to Suzanne Berger, Josh Cohen, Tom Kochan, and Margaret Levi, who read and commented on multiple drafts of the manuscript and encouraged me along the many years of this project, especially when I could not see how the various pieces fit together into anything resembling a coherent whole. Thank you for your help, your friendship, and especially for showing me how academics can make a real difference in the world.

I would also like to express my appreciation to the many participants at the various workshops, seminars, and conferences where different parts of this project were presented and discussed. These include participants at seminars and workshops at Bocconi University, Brown University, Duke University, Harvard University, MIT, New York University, Oxford University, Rutgers University, Stanford University, the University of Pennsylvania, the University of Wisconsin–Madison, and at the annual meetings of the Academy of International Business (2008), the Society for the Advancement of Socio-Economics (2008, 2010, 2011, 2012), the American Sociological Association (2008), and the American Political Science Association (2010, 2011). I am especially indebted to participants at the Seattle Seminar book workshop held at the University of Washington in January 2012, who provided excellent advice on how to revise the book manuscript. Special thanks to Josh Cohen, Margaret Levi, Aseem Prakash, John Alquist, Jennifer Noveck, and Anne Greenleaf for their close reading of and advice on an earlier version of this book manuscript. Thanks also to the anonymous reviewers who read the earlier manuscript for Cambridge University Press and to Lewis Bateman and Margaret Levi for their patience and support as I revised the manuscript and transformed it into the book it is today.

In addition to my academic colleagues and friends, I would like to thank various managers of the companies I studied, as well as leaders of several NGOs, who together both facilitated access to the hundreds of factories my students and I visited throughout the world as well as helped us make sense of the reality of working conditions in global supply chains: Maria Eitel, Hannah Jones, Dusty Kidd, Kelly Lauber, Caitlin Morris, Mark Loomis, Jeremy Prepscius, Charlie Brown, Catherine Humboldt, Mike McBreen, Steve Castellanos, Marcela Manubens, Judy Glazer, Scott Nova, Auret van Heerden, Ed Potter, Jorge Perez-Lopez, Dan Rees, and Linda Yanz. Financial support for this research was provided by the William and Flora Hewlett Foundation, the Alfred P. Sloan Foundation, and the MIT Sloan School of Management Dean's Innovation Fund. I would also like to thank Anita Kafka and Adriane Cesa for their help with preparing the final manuscript and Nausicaa Renner and Jim Haba for their help copyediting the manuscript.

Aside from the academic, financial, and organizational support I received from various colleagues and institutions throughout the many years of research and writing of this book, I could never have completed this project without the support of my family – my children, Juliana and Nate, who tolerated endless lectures about factory conditions and labor standards in developing countries; and my partner Zairo Cheibub, who patiently acquiesced to many working weekends and canceled vacations and also encouraged me throughout the process by reading drafts, asking hard questions, and prodding me to finish the book. Finally, I would like to thank my mother, Franca Franzaroli. Although she still complains that I did not become a doctor or even a businessman, her own career and life have been an inspiration for me. I dedicate this book to her.

The Rise of Private Voluntary Regulation in a Global Economy

Introduction

When an electronics worker in Suzhou, China, sought compensation for the chemical poisoning he suffered at work, he appealed neither to his employer nor to the government agencies responsible for supervising local workplace standards. Instead, he addressed the global brand that purchased the product he was working on: "We hope Apple will heed to its corporate social responsibility."[1]

This incident reflects a broader trend in global supply chains. Throughout the world and in many industries, global buyers have acknowledged a degree of responsibility for workplace conditions in supplier factories. They have pledged efforts to ensure that the goods they eventually market are not made under abusive, dangerous, environmentally degrading, or otherwise unethical production conditions. They have committed, in short, to using private, voluntary regulation to address labor issues traditionally regulated by government or labor organizations.[2] For the most part, they have acted on these commitments.

But how effective are these private initiatives at improving labor standards? In this book, I explore both the promise and the limits of private voluntary regulation in today's global economy. Through a detailed examination of initiatives undertaken by several global brands (e.g., Nike, Hewlett-Packard) – either alone or in collaboration with other firms, nongovernmental organizations (NGOs), and even international organizations such as the International Labor Organization (ILO) – this book sheds light on the conditions under

[1] David Barboza, "Workers Sickened at Apple Supplier in China," *The New York Times*, Feb. 23, 2011, p. B1.
[2] Charles Duhigg and Steven Greenhouse, "Electronic Giant Vowing Reforms in China Plants," *The New York Times*, March 29, 2012; and Poornima Gupta and Edwin Chan, "Apple, Foxconn Revamp China Work Conditions," Reuters, March 29, 2012, p. A1.

which private, voluntary programs can successfully promote labor standards among their globally dispersed suppliers. Although it describes some successes, this book is principally an argument about the limitations of these private initiatives and the need to bring the state (public regulation) back into the picture. Bringing in the state in this case does not mean a return to traditional command and control regulation. The limits of that approach are well known. Nor does it imply that we simply ignore or bypass the myriad private regulatory efforts currently in place. Rather, I argue that the most effective and sustainable approach to ensuring labor standards and workers' rights in global supply chains will require a mix of novel forms of private and public regulation.

The chapters that follow use unique data collected from global buyers and their suppliers, operating in different industries and across multiple countries to document and evaluate alternative strategies and experiments aimed at promoting labor standards. Have private compliance programs – with codes of conduct and audits of suppliers – revealed their limits, and if so, what are the roots of these limitations? Should private corporations, either alone or with the help of international organizations and NGOs, promote "beyond compliance" initiatives aimed at developing the managerial and technical capabilities of suppliers so that they can meet labor standards on their own, or are policing and deterrence programs more effective? Can national governments develop new regulatory programs that protect workers' rights without undermining the competitiveness of local producers or descending into protectionism? These and other questions are addressed in this book.

In the process of addressing these questions, I also document novel forms of private and public regulation that effectively improve labor standards in global supply chains. Even in a world lacking global regulation and characterized by wide variation in national socioeconomic and political circumstances, a range of realistic possibilities for promoting labor justice already exists and can be further strengthened and diffused. I argue that notwithstanding significant limitations manifest in the various private initiatives analyzed in this study, a new form of labor regulation in a world shaped by global supply chains is possible. This new form of regulation blends elements of private compliance programs with technical assistance, capability-building initiatives, and innovative government regulatory efforts in a dynamic and complementary way – one that is both adaptive to local circumstances and that builds on (and reinforces) the respective strengths of both private and public systems of regulation. This new form of labor regulation requires changes in existing practices within individual firms (between, say, purchasing and compliance managers), across firms (among large-scale retailers, global buyers, and their suppliers), and within the myriad workplaces that produce goods we consume every day. These changes in existing practices are not merely technical but also distributional, requiring a reallocation of both the costs and the rewards among all actors – consumers, retailers, buyers, suppliers, factory workers – engaged in these value chains. As such, this new form of labor regulation requires novel institutional arrangements and political coalitions that transcend traditional boundaries between consumers and producers, buyers and suppliers, NGOs and corporations, and advanced and developing economies. As this book documents, fragments of these new institutional arrangements and political coalitions already exist within various industrial and national settings. Whether these fragments can be stitched together into a more coherent and stable system capable of reshaping practices within and across global supply chains and who could do the stitching remain open questions.

Yet, if history is any guide, we should learn from previous reform efforts aimed at addressing other difficult social and environmental issues (e.g., environmental standards, health and safety regulations, antidiscrimination and equal opportunities policies). All of these successful reforms occurred through analogous shifts in organizational practices, institutional arrangements, and the constellation of interests. These changes were by no means easy, and the processes that led to them were filled with conflict and uncertainty. But in the end, they succeeded in creating a more just and safe working environment for millions of workers. The hope is that this book will convince readers that history can repeat itself and that labor justice in today's global economy is possible.

We Live in a World of Global Supply Chains

Globalization,[3] with its volatile mix of economic opportunity and social disruption, is redefining the boundaries of the firm; changing the dynamics among consumers, global corporations, and their suppliers; and shaping the working conditions of the millions of individuals employed in today's global supply chains. The world of global supply chains links thousands of firms, large and small, across multiple cultural and political boundaries. The diffusion of global supply chains in an array of different industries – apparel, electronics, footwear, food, toys, and so on – has provided developing countries with much-needed investment, employment, technology, and access to international markets. As such, the integration of producers located in developing countries into global supply chains is having a catalytic and transformative effect on local economies, allowing poor countries finally to achieve their long-sought goal of

[3] This book focuses on global supply chains and various outsourcing practices by global brands and large retail chains. Another important dimension of globalization, the rise of foreign direct investment by developed-country-based multinational corporations in developing countries (either by opening up their own subsidiaries or investing in joint ventures with local firms) is not covered in this book. For more on the labor implications for these alternative globalization strategies, see Layna Mosley and Saika Uno, "Racing to the Bottom or Climbing to the Top?: Economic Globalization and Collective Labor Rights," *Comparative Political Studies*, 40, no. 8 (August 2007): 923–48; and Layna Mosley, *Labor Rights and Multinational Production* (New York: Cambridge University Press, 2011).

development (Collier and Dollar 2002; Moran 2002). At the same time, however, the social and environmental consequences of this particular pattern of economic development have provoked significant controversies over the role of global brands and their local suppliers, often seen as exploiting developing countries' low wages and weak social and environmental regulation to produce low-cost goods at the expense of local workers' welfare. In fact, child labor, hazardous working conditions, excessive working hours, and poor wages plague many workplaces in the developing world, creating scandal and embarrassment for the global companies that source from these factories and farms (Verité 2004; Pruett 2005; Connor and Dent 2006; Kernaghan 2006).

To get a better sense of this phenomenon, let's take a closer look at how two everyday products are manufactured in today's global supply chains. In her 2005 book, *The Travels of a T-Shirt in the Global Economy*, Pietra Rivoli traces a T-shirt's supply chain journey from the cotton fields of Texas; to the spinning, weaving, and garment factories of China; back to consumer markets in the United States; and finally to the used clothing and rag markets in Africa. Each of these stages involves multiple firms and complex transactions. In many stages of this supply chain, workers toiled under difficult and precarious conditions. Borrowing from Rivoli's approach, I now turn to an examination of the supply chain dynamics of two common products (athletic running shoes and mobile electronic devices) and their consequences for workers. In subsequent chapters, we examine these two industries in greater detail. For now, I simply want to illustrate the complex nature of most global supply chains as well as the many opportunities, along different stages of these production networks, for workers rights and employment conditions to be compromised.

Athletic Footwear

Early athletic footwear was manufactured in vertically integrated facilities located primarily in Europe and North America. Some of the first athletic shoes to be marketed in the United States (in the early 1900s) were manufactured in the United States. For example, the United States Rubber Company introduced Keds in 1916, using rubber originally produced for bicycle tires for the soles of what became a classic athletic shoe (BBC n.d.).

The production of athletic footwear today, in contrast, requires a much longer supply chain, involving dozens of component parts and materials from around the world, which are manufactured, assembled, transported, and distributed by companies and workers across many national borders. Although many brands maintain their national identity, more and more production is taking place in developing countries with lower production costs. These trends show no signs of slowing down. According to Global-Production.com, a consulting company that analyzes developing countries as locations for global production, emerging economies increased their share of world footwear exports from 76.4 to 78.2 percent between 2002 and 2006. Much of this production is concentrated in Asia, which is the source for 85 percent of the world's low-cost shoe exports.[4] In fact, an astonishing 86 percent of all footwear sold in the United States in 2009 was made in southern China (Dubin 2009). Workers at just one company, Yue Yuen, a Chinese subsidiary of the Taiwan-based Pou Chen Group, produce one out of every six shoes sold globally (Consumers International 2009)!

In their book *Stuff: The Secret Lives of Everyday Things*, John Ryan and Alan Thein (1998) document the many components from which a typical pair of Nike cross-trainers is made and the many locations from which these components and their raw materials are sourced. In tracking the journey of a particular shoe, they found that it was "manufactured" by a Korean-owned factory located in Tangerang, Indonesia, an industrial district outside of Jakarta. The shoe was made up of dozens of component parts, almost all of which were manufactured elsewhere and then shipped to Indonesia for final assembly. First, designers based at Nike's headquarters in Oregon sent product specifications for the shoe to a design firm located in Taiwan. The design company in Taiwan, in turn, sent the more developed plans on to engineers in South Korea. The Korean company then outsourced the actual production of the shoe to Indonesia.[5]

The cross-trainer in question had three main sections: the upper, the midsole, and the outsole. The upper for this particular shoe was made primarily from leather, which came from cows slaughtered and skinned in Texas and then shipped to South Korea for tanning. Tanning itself is a thirty-stage process. The tanned leather was then shipped to the factory in Indonesia. The midsection of the shoe was made from synthetics parts, including EVA (ethylene vinyl acetate) foam made from Saudi Arabian petroleum, refined and transformed into EVA foam in Korea, and subsequently shipped to the factory in Indonesia. Another component that provides cushioning under the heel was manufactured in the United States. The outer soles of the shoes were made of rubber, again a by-product of petroleum, refined in Korea, processed into large sheets of rubber by another company in Taiwan, and eventually shipped to the assembly plant in Indonesia to be cut, shaped, and finally attached to the shoes.

All of these many parts were assembled in the Tangerang factory. Journalist Elizabeth Grossman recently picked up the shoe's story, visiting a similar Korean-owned factory in Tangerang that employs 18,000 people and produces about 300,000 shoes per week. Each shoe is assembled in pieces. First, workers (more than 80 percent are female) assemble the "uppers" of the shoe, made from fabric, synthetics, and leather. Pieces are stitched together using

---

[4] See "Footwear: trends in global production and trade." Retrieved from http://www.global-production.com/footwear/trendstudy/index.htm.

[5] Ryan and Thein describe how South Korea used to be a leading exporter of athletic shoes in the 1980s. By the 1990s, rising wages and labor unrest propelled many companies to shift their manufacturing base elsewhere, primarily to China and Southeast Asia. An estimated 400,000 Koreans employed in the shoe industry lost their jobs between 1990 and 1993.

specialized machines. Other, smaller pieces, including Nike's trademark "swoosh," are sewn either by machine or by hand. The upper sections of the shoes are then placed on a conveyer belt, from which other workers apply glue and then attach the uppers to the soles of the shoe. Next, workers trim excess material from the shoe; this work is done by hand, using small electric tools. Finally, the shoes are polished and fitted with laces and insoles. All in all, factory management estimates that approximately 200 people are involved in making just one pair of shoes (Grossman 2010). The shoes are then stuffed with tissue paper (made from Indonesian trees) and packed into boxes that were originally manufactured by a paper mill in New Mexico (Ryan and Thein 1998). From there, the shoe begins its journey back to markets in the United States, Europe, and elsewhere.

Footwear is a fashion-sensitive sector that poses a particularly difficult set of challenges to companies and workers at all points along the global supply chain. Products have short life cycles and change quickly from season to season; the diversity of styles adds additional complexity to the manufacturing process. A 2009 study by eleven consumer advocacy groups, organized by International Consumer Research and Testing and presented by Consumers International, examined the working conditions in factories that produce running shoes for companies such as Adidas, Reebok, Puma, New Balance, and Mizuno. Although the majority of these factories were located in southern China, similar conditions are found in factories in Indonesia, Vietnam, and Eastern Europe. The core issues identified in the study include forced overtime, lax health and safety standards, union repression, harsh disciplinary practices, and sexual harassment (Consumer International 2009). The fast-paced, quick-changing nature of the footwear market means that factories face tight deadlines, often met by forcing factory operators to work long hours. Excessive overtime is a common problem among athletic shoe suppliers.

Mobile Electronic Devices

Mobile electronic devices are ubiquitous today. These products, however, come with substantial costs to producers, workers, and the environment, involving a complex flow of materials and products around the world. Raw materials for electronic components are extracted, often under harsh working conditions, from mines in Asia and Africa. These materials are refined and processed in Asia, and then sold to companies (Asian and Western) that manufacture component parts such as chips and circuit boards. These parts are then assembled, primarily in China, in large factories that employ hundreds of thousands of workers. The final products are then shipped back to consumer markets located for the most part in already developed economies. The shelf life of these mobile devices is relatively short, and the e-waste generated by consumers who dispose of their phones and other portable devices in exchange for newer models is, in turn, shipped back to Asia and Africa.

To better understand this complex supply chain and its consequences for workers, let's examine one of the industry's most high-profile producers: Apple.⁶ Some of the most value-added parts of an Apple product – for example its innovative software – are still produced in the United States. Almost everything else, however, comes from overseas. A recent *New York Times* study of Apple's supply chain estimated that more than 90 percent of an iPhone's components are produced outside of the United States in places ranging from Germany and Taiwan (where semiconductors are produced), Korea and Japan (for memory boards, display panels, and circuits), Europe (data chips), and elsewhere in Asia and Africa (where rare metals are extracted and refined; Duhigg and Bradsher 2012). The hundreds of components that go into an iPhone or iPad are assembled in China. A huge industry has sprung up around the production of these electronic devices, providing Apple's suppliers with the parts they need. A former Apple executive explained: "The entire [assembly] supply chain is now in China. You need a thousand rubber gaskets? That's the factory next door. You need a million screws? That factory is a block away. You need that screw made a little differently? It will take three hours" (Duhigg and Bradsher 2012).

The working conditions at Apple's suppliers have come under intense scrutiny, following a wave of suicides by factory workers at Foxconn – one of the largest manufactures of iPhones and iPads. The *New York Times* published a series of articles on the working conditions at these factories, citing sources as varied as labor advocacy groups, anonymous workers, and Apple's own internal assessments of working conditions. To meet the high consumer demand for these Apple products, employees in these factories had to work long days with mandatory overtime and forgo their rest days. Conditions in these factories are harsh; workers are not rotated but rather specialize in narrow tasks and therefore suffer from repetitive stress injuries.⁷ Workers are also exposed to hazardous chemicals and unsafe conditions in the workplace. For example, in 2010, 137 workers were injured after using a toxic chemical to clean iPhone screens. More recently, there were several explosions at iPad factories in Chengdu, southwestern China, in which four people were killed and seventy-seven injured (Duhigg and Barboza 2012).

---

⁶ Apple, of course, is not the only company engaged in this kind of production; Dell, Hewlett-Packard, IBM, Lenovo, Motorola, Nokia, Sony, Toshiba, and many others are engaged in similar practices. Apple, however, is an industry leader in both design and profits. Since 2005, its share prices have risen from about $45 to more than $595 (as of October 31, 2012).

⁷ For a detailed description of working conditions in Foxconn factories in southern China, see Pun Ngai and Jenny Chan, "Global Capital, the State, and Chinese Workers: The Foxconn Experience," *Modern China* 38, no. 4 (2012): 383–410. For a more nuanced view that illustrates both the difficult working conditions young migrant workers employed at these factories experience as well as the freedoms they enjoy living away from their rural villages among thousands of other young workers, see Lesley T. Chang, *Factory Girls* (New York: Spiegel and Grau, 2008).

In response to these scandals, Apple carried out its own internal audits of its suppliers and also engaged with the Fair Labor Association (FLA) to further investigate the working conditions among its lead suppliers in southern China. Together they have inspected hundreds of facilities including both first- and second-tier suppliers. Apple's internal audits found evidence of excessive work hours, failure to pay overtime, inadequate safety precautions, and instances of child labor among some of its suppliers (Apple 2009). Even after several years of intense auditing of their suppliers, Apple's most recent Supplier Responsibility Report found that although most of its suppliers were improving their compliance on key issues such as underage labor, involuntary labor, and antidiscrimination, many of these same suppliers continued to struggle with excessive working hours and low wages (Apple 2012). The FLA report of three of Foxconn's factories in China, all major producers of Apple products, found that "all three factories exceeded the FLA Code Standard and the requirements of Chinese law" relating to working hours, especially during peak production periods. Although 48 percent of the workers employed in these factories reported in the FLA survey that they felt the working hours at Foxconn were "reasonable," 64.3 percent of these same workers also claimed that their salary was not sufficient to cover their basic needs (FLA 2012).

Nor is this situation unique to Foxconn or other Apple suppliers. Over the past few years, the FLA conducted surveys among workers employed in Chinese factories supplying various global brands and found that an estimated 50 percent of workers employed in the garment industry and 80 percent of workers employed in the electronics industry work more than the legal limits of sixty hours per week. Forty-five percent of the 1,766 workers surveyed claim that they need to work more than sixty hours per week because their regular salaries are insufficient to cover their basic needs (FLA 2011).

The anecdotes presented here illustrate some of the salient features of most global supply chains – fragmented and globally dispersed production, multiple tiers and actors within each supply chain, suppliers producing for multiple brands, short lead times and tight margins, and the key role lead buyers play in orchestrating this entire process and even investing in their suppliers. As the foregoing anecdotes also revealed, these underlying features create real challenges for the millions of workers employed in supply chain factories, who struggle every day with poor working conditions, long working hours, low pay, and a variety of other (minor and not so minor) injustices. According to the ILO, the rapid growth of cross-border trade and capital flows since 1990 have not led to improved employment conditions in developing countries. On the contrary, the ILO Global Employment Report found that more than 486 million workers throughout the world do not earn enough to raise themselves or their families above the US$1 per day poverty rate and that another 1.3 billion people do not earn above US$2 per day (ILO 2008). More than half of all workers in most developing countries and more than 70 percent in some parts of South Asia and sub-Saharan Africa find themselves in "vulnerable employment," which is roughly defined as informal employment – employment that is poorly paid and that does not provide workers with fundamental labor rights, a "voice" at work, and job security (ILO 2008: 11, 46).

Of course, not all workers in developing countries are employed in factories or farms linked to global supply chains.[8] Because data on employment and labor conditions are collected by either country or sector, we do not know precisely how many of these workers are actually employed at firms supplying global buyers. However, through various reports, published by the ILO, individual NGOs, and even global corporations, we are able to piece together an image of what working conditions and standards are like for the millions of workers employed in global supply chains. According to the ILO, throughout the world, 215 million children work. Of these, 115 million are engaged in "hazardous work" in sectors such as agriculture, manufacturing, and mining, which are deeply integrated into global supply chains (ILO 2008b). More than 12 million people worldwide are victims of forced labor. Although most companies operating in global supply chains do not themselves employ forced labor, many have become implicated in such practices through their second- or third-tier suppliers and contractors (ILO 2008c). As subsequent chapters show, these findings are echoed in the internal assessments of several global brands working in a variety of industries. Woman workers are especially hard hit because they occupy 60 to 90 percent of the jobs in manufacturing and agricultural supply chains (Oxfam International 2004). What, if anything, can be done to improve working conditions and promote worker rights in these global supply chains?

Private Voluntary Regulation as a "Second-Best" Solution

Throughout most of the twentieth century, labor standards were regulated largely on a national basis, through a mixture of laws, union-management negotiations, and company policies. Internationally, the conventions and technical services of the ILO provided an additional source of moral authority and advice but lacked significant enforcement power. The emergence of global supply chains, however, has rendered these national and international strategies inadequate because authority is dispersed not only across national regimes but also among global buyers and their myriad suppliers. It is in this context that private initiatives have emerged to fill this regulatory void.

A number of scholars have already documented the rise of private, voluntary initiatives aimed at regulating global labor standards, and thus the details of this process need not be repeated here (see Haufler 2001; Elliott and Freeman 2003; O'Rourke 2003; Bartley 2007; Reich 2007; Vogel 2008; Meyer and Gereffi

---

[8] In fact, Mosley (2010) shows how the collective rights of workers employed in the subsidiaries of multinational corporations are significantly better than those of workers employed by local, independent suppliers or subcontractors.

2010). Essentially, a series of separate but interrelated (and self-reinforcing) developments unfolded over the final decades of the twentieth century that led to the increasing inability of both nation-states and international organizations to regulate labor standards in the global economy. These developments include the shift of a substantial fraction of global manufacturing from the advanced industrial states (e.g., United States, Europe, Japan) to several large developing countries (e.g., China, India, Mexico). According to Meyer and Gereffi (2010), by 2000, 50 percent of the world's manufacturing production was located in developing countries. This trend only increased in the decade that followed. Linked to this shift in the locus of global manufacturing were dramatic changes in the organization of production. If in the past most manufacturing was carried out by domestic companies and their suppliers located within the same country or by vertically integrated multinational corporations (MNCs) headquartered in the advanced industrial economies (and thus subject to their regulations) that owned (fully or partially) their subsidiaries located in foreign markets, today, global production is organized primarily around global supply chains in which lead firms (brands, global buyers, large retail chains), although still based in the developed economies, are working with and coordinating the production of thousands of independent suppliers located for the most part in developing countries.

As nicely described by Meyer and Gereffi (2010), these changes in the locus and organization of global production had profound implications for labor regulation. In a world where manufacturing occurred primarily within domestic firms and/or vertically integrated MNCs headquartered in the advanced industrial states, national governments could still regulate labor conditions in most factories. However, with the rise of global supply chains and the dispersion of production across multiple developing countries, these new sites of production escaped the regulatory reach of developed country governments. Moreover, in many cases, the national governments of the developing countries hosting these new factories either lacked the institutional capacities to fully regulate labor, health and safety, and environmental standards within these supply chain worksites or they intentionally chose not to enforce their own domestic laws and regulations for fear of driving up costs and thus driving away these sources of economic development, employment, and taxation. As a result, the factories producing for global supply chains fell into a regulatory void in which labor laws and workplace standards were not being enforced by either host (developing) country governments or by the national authorities governing the large consumer markets absorbing much of this global production.

In an effort to remedy this situation and promote global labor standards among the thousands of geographically dispersed factories supplying global brands, various efforts were launched to include "social" clauses within global trade agreements as well as to use access to the large consumer markets of the developed countries as leverage to compel developing country governments to enforce their own labor laws and thus drive improvements in working conditions within the supply chain factories located within their national boundaries (Charnowitz 2001; Compa and Vogt 2001; Elliott and Freeman 2003; Polaski 2004; Bartley 2007; Reich 2008). Yet these efforts also failed, in this case because they were blocked by developing country governments that argued that linking social and environmental standards to trade (or market access) was nothing short of protectionism. Several developing countries threatened to fight these efforts at the World Trade Organization, which had already signaled its unwillingness to support the inclusion of social clauses in global trade agreements. As a result of both this resistance by the developing countries and the growing popularity of neo-liberal ideas among several influential developed country governments (especially the United States), the appetite for this alternative strategy waned (Bartley 2007; Vogel 2008). Although "social clauses" were included in a few bilateral trade agreements (Polaski 2004, 2006; Doumbia-Henry and Gravel 2006), efforts to create an effective and truly global system of labor regulation through trade arrangements for the most part failed.

An alternative path involved efforts by the ILO and the United Nations to promote core labor standards through the establishment of "decent work" conventions and the Global Compact. But these initiatives also lacked enforcement powers and thus offered little more than moral guidance for already committed governments and corporations.

In the absence of a strong system of global justice (Cohen & Sabel 2006) and given the limited ability (perhaps willingness) of many national governments to enforce their own labor laws, an array of different actors, both private and public, including transnational NGOs (Keck and Sikkink 1998; Seidman 2007), global corporations and industry associations (Haufler 2001; O'Rourke 2003; Ruggie 2003; Bartley 2007; Reich 2008; Vogel 2008) multistakeholder initiatives (MSIs), and even a few developed country governments (Bartley 2007), began to promote (sometimes by themselves, other times in collaboration with other actors) a variety of private initiatives aimed at establishing and enforcing labor standards in global supply chains. Private voluntary regulation has many forms. At times, it revolves around corporate codes of conduct in which lead buyers and brands articulate their own internal standards governing working conditions, wages, working hours, health and safety conditions, and the like and require their suppliers to sign on to these standards. Other times, it entails monitoring programs in which private auditors periodically inspect and assess factories to ensure that suppliers are in compliance with the corporate codes of conduct. In still other cases, private regulation involves certification mechanisms that label products "sweat free" and/or "fair trade," thus signaling to consumers that certain products are allegedly made under fair and/or sustainable conditions. Notwithstanding, and perhaps because of, this variation, private voluntary regulation has emerged as the dominant approach that global corporations and labor rights NGOs alike embrace to promote labor standards in global supply chains.

Given the diversity, and often competing goals, of these various initiatives (O'Rourke 2003; Nadvi and Wältring 2004; Bartley 2007), this model of private voluntary regulation has provoked heated debates over the particularities of the actual programs – how compliance programs and certification schemes are designed and implemented; how factory auditors are trained and selected, how information generated from factory audits is shared – or their relation to other forms of regulation, especially state regulation – does private regulation crowd out or complement government regulation (Esbenshade 2004; Seidman 2007; Reich 2007). In subsequent chapters, we review and analyze these debates. Because the debates are highly polarized, however, the basic question about the effectiveness of private regulation in improving labor standards has not been adequately evaluated. This is one of the central aims of this book.

I argue that regardless of the particular mission, or leadership, or organizational design, or even resources underlying any of these private initiatives, they all inevitably produced limited or mixed results because they all confront a fundamental challenge of reconciling diverse and conflicting interests among the key actors engaged in global supply chains. Most (although not all) of these actors may be genuinely interested in improving labor standards across the thousands of factories supplying global brands, but conflicts of interest typically drive them in different directions about how best to achieve these goals. This is not to say that diverse interests can never be reconciled or that genuine progress toward promoting better working conditions within global supply chains is impossible. As subsequent chapters of this book show, under certain conditions, these conflicting interests can be mediated, and novel institutional arrangements and programs that promote labor standards have, in fact, emerged. But these conditions are rare, and the new institutional arrangements (and constellation of interests underlying them) rarely include only private actors.

Conflicting Interests and Collective Action Problems Inherent in Private Voluntary Initiatives

A quick and overly simplified description of the diverse and competing interests expressed by different actors engaged in global supply chains highlights the fundamental challenges faced by all private voluntary initiatives. Consider first the *global brands and buyers* sourcing their products through these global supply chains. On the one hand, these companies have an interest in obtaining high-quality products as quickly and cheaply as possible. At the same time, most reputation-conscious brands also have a genuine interest in ensuring decent labor practices among their suppliers for fear that harsh working conditions could (if discovered) create scandal and hence risk to their reputation and brand image. As such, they actively engage their suppliers in various private initiatives, be they monitoring efforts or certification schemes (Haufler 2001; Heritier, Mueller-Debus, and Thauer 2009; Meyer and Gereffi 2010). Yet, because these brands and buyers are competing fiercely with one another, they are unwilling to pay extra for improved working conditions because this could erode their margins or lead to price increases that most consumers these days are unwilling to accept.[9] As a result, most companies are unwilling to fully redress workplace problems endemic in supply chain factories on their own, especially because most of these suppliers are also producing for their competitors.[10] Moreover, even when individual buyers or brands do invest in "supplier responsibility" programs – and many of them do – some of their "upstream" business practices (i.e., product development, commercialization, purchasing) drive their suppliers to implement production and work systems that ultimately undermine these very same corporate responsibility efforts. In highly competitive markets, global brands and lead buyers face tremendous pressure to sell an increasing variety of products at ever-lower prices. To do this, they pressure their suppliers to reduce costs, shorten lead times, and produce a variety of products in smaller batches. Suppliers, in turn, respond to these increased demands by paying their workers low base wages, limiting employee benefits, and demanding excessive work hours simply to meet the shorter lead times their buyers require. Thus, even when global buyers do invest in programs aimed at improving labor standards among their suppliers, their own "upstream" business practices inadvertently undermine these efforts.

Suppliers, too, possess diverse and conflicting interests. Like the global buyers they work for, these independent contract manufacturers are also competing fiercely with one another for purchase orders from the large global brands. They have an interest in receiving orders that will utilize as much of their productive capacity as possible, for as much of the year as possible (to amortize their fixed costs) and that generate the highest margins. As such, they seek to win large orders with good markups from high-end brands or large retailers. In an effort to reduce transaction costs and risk, they also attempt to develop long-term, stable relationships with these global buyers. To do this, they need to deliver (quickly and reliably) high-quality products at acceptable prices. They also need to make sure that their production and work practices do not create any reputation risks for their global customers. Yet, given that their margins result from

[9] The research on consumer's willingness to pay more for products made under just working conditions presents a mixed picture, in which some consumers at higher income levels are willing to pay somewhat more for these "ethically sourced" products, whereas other consumers with less purchasing power are not willing to pay more for goods made under "sweat-free" conditions. See Jens Hainmueller and Michael J. Hiscox, "The Socially Conscious Consumer? Field Experimental Tests of Consumer Support for Labor Standards," *MIT Political Science Department Working Paper Series*, no. 2012–15 (June 3, 2012).

[10] For an interesting argument for why firms might take these actions, even if other competing firms do not, see Forest Reinhardt, "Market Failure and the Environmental Policies of Firms: Economic Rationales for 'Beyond Compliance' Behavior," *Journal of Industrial Ecology* 3, no. 1 (1999): 9–21. Reinhardt focuses on environmental standards, but the parallels with labor standards are strong.

the difference between the unit prices buyers are willing to pay for the products they order (less every year) and the total costs entailed in producing these goods (i.e., material costs, labor, overhead, transportation – all of which have risen in recent years), suppliers have a strong interest to contain or even reduce their production costs. As a result, they seek to restrain wage increases, limit overtime pay and benefits, and underinvest in various services (canteens, dormitories, health clinics, recreation halls) for their workers. Moreover, to respond to the growing demands by buyers (both existing and potential new customers) for lower prices, smaller batches, and shorter lead times, suppliers structure their production processes in ways that permit them to ramp up production quickly but without incurring additional fixed costs. This means imposing excessive overtime hours on their workers and relying on migrant or contract workers that they can quickly hire and fire, depending on their production schedules. Thus, even when these suppliers embrace corporate responsibility programs and engage in various private initiatives aimed at improving working conditions within their factories, the pressures they face often drive them to engage in various production and work practices that undermine these efforts.

Both workers and developing country governments also express complex and often contradictory interests. *Developing country governments* have both an interest in asserting their sovereignty and protecting the rights and welfare of their citizens by enforcing domestic laws that regulate workplace conditions, and, at the same time, because of the various economic and employment benefits generated by these new sites of global production, these same governments fear that by enforcing their own domestic laws, they could drive up costs and thus drive away these factories. As a result, even those governments with the institutional capacities to enforce their own laws often refuse to do so, or they do so in a nonsystematic way by granting contract manufacturers exemptions (sometime full; other times partial) from various wage, work-hour, and social insurance regulations in an effort to provide them with a more hospitable "business environment." *Workers* employed at these supply chain factories often come to these workplaces from rural villages (or in some cases, other less developed countries) in search of decent jobs with good wages. These workers often want to work overtime because overtime compensation permits them to supplement their base salaries. Given that these factory jobs are often preferable to whatever work opportunities were available in their home villages, many of these workers are willing to work long hours under stressful conditions (Rivoli 2005; Chang 2008). Yet at the same time, these workers want to be treated fairly. They want to be paid for the overtime work they do at the agreed-on rates (not be cheated), they want to work in environments that do not jeopardize their personal safety and health, and they want to be treated with respect – live in clean, not overly crowded dorms; eat nutritious and well-cooked food; and have their personal dignity respected. Thus, although most supply chain factory workers are willing to repeat the same task for many hours, day in and day out, under stressful working conditions and for low wages, they expect to be treated fairly and with respect. If not, they will either leave their employer as soon as they can or engage in individual or even collective resistance.[11]

In sum, even a cursory examination of only a few of the actors involved in global supply chains reveals their divergent and often conflicting interests. How can any private voluntary initiative aimed at promoting improved working conditions and labor standards reconcile these interests and resolve the coordination/collective action problems this mix of actors and interests creates?

The problem of reconciling diverse and conflicting interests and overcoming obstacles to collective action is not new (see, for example, Axelrod 1984; Bowman 1985; Ostrom 1990; Swensen 1991; Putnam 1993; Farrell 2009; Fukyama 1995). In the context of promoting standards through private voluntary initiatives, a number of mechanisms have been proposed to overcome these collective action problems. Some of these entail tapping into the enlightened self-interest of individual corporations by showing that investments in particular voluntary programs will not only improve standards but also signal to potential buyers, rivals, and even regulatory authorities certain distinctive attributes that will enhance the competitiveness of firms that choose to participate in these initiatives. For example, in a series of studies focused primarily on voluntary environmental initiatives, Aseem Prakash and Matthew Potoski (2006a, 2007) have shown that under certain conditions – the home country of foreign investors or trading partners – increased foreign direct investment (FDI) and trade can lead to the diffusion of process standards like ISO 14001 – a private, voluntary standard aimed at promoting improved environmental practices within individual firms. In their book *The Voluntary Environmentalists* (Prakash and Potoski 2006b), they argue that voluntary regulatory programs such as ISO 14001 can mitigate collective action problems by providing participating firms with shared, group benefits (what they refer to as "club goods") like enhanced standing with stakeholders and improved brand image that are not available to firms that refuse to participate in these voluntary programs.

Can similar mechanisms work in the case of labor, or is labor somewhat different? Unfortunately, the particular circumstances underlying the successful diffusion of voluntary environmental standards do not carry over to the field of labor. Unlike ISO 14001, which has established itself as the world's most successful private initiative for environmental standards, for labor standards, no such dominant initiative exists. In fact, there exist multiple, competing

---

[11] For interesting descriptions of this growing worker resistance, especially in China, see Mary Gallagher, "Changes in the World's Workshop: The Demographic, Social and Political Factors behind China's Labor Movement," unpublished manuscript, W. E. Upjohn Institute for Employment Research 2012; and Eli Friedman, "Getting through the Hard Times Together?: Chinese Workers and Unions Respond to the Economic Crisis," *Journal of Industrial Relations* 54. n. 4 (2012): 1–17. In many ways, these worker protests resemble the social conflicts that emerged among migrant factory workers in Europe in the late 1960s/early 1970s. See Charles F. Sabel, *Work and Politics* (New York: Cambridge University Press, 1982).

voluntary programs, each claiming to be more effective and/or rigorous than the other (O'Rourke 2003; Nadvi and Wältring 2004; Bartley 2010). As a result, individual firms cannot signal anything distinctive about themselves simply by participating in any one (or the other) of these initiatives, and as a result, these voluntary labor initiatives are unable to provide exclusive "club goods" for participating companies in their programs. Moreover, whereas ISO 14001 signals that firms are making significant investments aimed at achieving specific process improvements, over and beyond what is expected of them by national legislation, most voluntary labor initiatives simply require participating firms to respect the local "law of the land," which entails very different levels of commitment to labor rights and working conditions across the same supply chain. Finally, as we saw earlier, the collective action problems facing firms seeking to promote improved labor standards in global supply chains are more complex than those facing "voluntary environmentalists" because they entail not simply collective action among rival firms but also coordination and collaboration challenges between global brands/buyers and their multiple suppliers dispersed across the world. As a result of these supply chain dynamics, promoting global standards through "club goods" have not been as successful in the arena of working conditions and labor rights (Bartley 2010).

If market signaling and segmentation appear unable to overcome the collective action problems plaguing private initiatives seeking to promote global labor standards, perhaps embedding these private initiatives within particular institutional arrangements capable of shaping firm behavior in more constructive ways might help. A number of scholars (Streeck 1987, 1991; North 1990; Knight 1992; Hall and Soskice 2001; Thelen 2004; Farrell 2009) have described various institutional arrangements that in different ways promote "credible commitments," "trust," "redundant capabilities," and particular "equilibria" that promote collective action among private firms by modifying or suspending their individual short-term interests. Wolfgang Streeck (1987, 1991), for example, has written extensively on the institutional conditions required to support what he calls "diversified quality production," a production system that for many years appeared to respond successfully to changing consumer tastes, price pressures, variable batch sizes, and growing international competition while still delivering high-quality goods and empowering (rather than immiserating) the workers employed in these factories. Henry Farrell (2009) has described a somewhat different set of institutions that exist in northern Italy and southern Germany that provide local firms with information about one another so that they can engage in interfirm collaborations that would not be possible given their divergent interests and ambiguous circumstances.

Once again, the lessons for labor standards in global supply chains are not so clear, given the variation in political, economic, and cultural circumstances covered by supply chains. The number of actors – both private and public – and the diversity of interests may simply be too complex (and evolving) to construct institutions that can provide either sufficient and accurate information about and/or redundant resources to the thousands of private firms involved in global supply chains so that they modify their self-interested, market-oriented behaviors in more labor-friendly ways. In fact, there appears to be some evidence that the original national/subnational institutional arrangements that have inspired these models are themselves facing difficulties in the face of globalization (Streeck 2009).

Although it is usually the case that current institutional arrangements and/or market-based voluntary initiatives have not sufficed to reconcile the diverse interests and overcome the collective action problems inherent in global supply chains, this book shows that under certain circumstances, and when combined with novel forms of public regulation, private voluntary programs aimed at promoting labor standards can work.

The Argument in Brief

I argue that private initiatives aimed at improving labor standards in global supply chains can succeed when global buyers and their suppliers establish long-term, mutually beneficial relations and when various public (authoritative rule-making) institutions help to both support these mutually beneficial buyer–supplier relations and resolve a set of collective action problems that private actors cannot overcome on their own. As such, private voluntary regulation can best succeed when "layered" on and interacting with public (state) regulation.[12]

If properly designed, private efforts aimed at promoting global labor standards can succeed by tapping into and shaping the self-interest of global buyers and their suppliers.[13] However, the benefits generated by these private initiatives do not merely revolve around brand image or positive stakeholder relations. Instead, I argue that under certain conditions (long-term relations, frequent interactions, and mutually beneficial economic arrangements between buyers and suppliers), private voluntary initiatives can work in ways that both tap into and align the interests and incentives of private firms (by reducing information and transaction costs, developing new capabilities, promoting process and product innovations that enhance the competitiveness of both buyers and suppliers) while also generating positive results for workers through new work and production processes that improve wages, reduce excessive work hours, and empower operators on the shop floor.[14]

---

[12] For more on the "layering" of private and public regulation, see Trubek and Trubek (2007) and Bartley (2011).

[13] For various illustrations of how private initiatives can be designed in ways that align the self-interest of private forms with the broader goal of enhancing labor standards, see Fung, O'Rourke, and Sabel 2001; Elliott and Freeman 2003; Ruggie 2003. Prakash and Potoski (2006b) make a parallel argument concerning environmental regulation.

[14] This argument builds on research on both collaborative manufacturing (Sabel and Zeitlin 2004; Ivarsson and Alvstom 2009, 2010a, 2011; Herrigel 2010; Herrigel and Wittke 2010) and relational contracts (Baker, Gibbons, and Murphy 2002).

UP

In his study of buyer–supplier relations in the United States, Germany, and Japan, Gary Herrigel (2010) describes a system in which buyers and suppliers learn from one another, experiment together, and distribute the risks and rewards of doing business together. He shows how these patterns of buyer–supplier relations were not culturally or even institutionally determined but rather politically constructed over many years of struggle and compromise among these supply chain actors. In subsequent chapters, I document how several global buyers were able to establish similar collaborative and labor standards-enhancing relations with some (but by no means all) of their suppliers when these relations were based upon mutual gains, joint learning, and long-term commitments. Like most global buyers, these companies engaged their suppliers in various compliance and capability-building programs. But these more collaborative relations were not based solely on policing/deterrence or even capability-building/technical assistance – although both of these elements existed in these particular buyer–supplier relationships – but rather on the mutual recognition that each party had to gain from the collaboration. These more collaborative buyer–supplier relations were based on a fundamental understanding that both the risks and the rewards of doing business together would be distributed more or less fairly between the parties; the gains would not be captured nor the losses borne by one or the other party alone. It was this recognition and the positive spillovers it generated that created the real incentives for private firms to engage in the most effective private voluntary initiatives analyzed in this book.

Although clearly beneficial to both global buyers and their suppliers, these more collaborative arrangements are rare within the supply chains studied in this book. Moreover, because of the conflicting pressures facing both buyers and suppliers, where these mutually beneficial arrangements do exist, they remain unstable in the sense that each actor has a strong incentive to cheat or renege on whatever commitments underlie these collaborations. Even in the most successful of these collaborations, moreover, some labor standards (e.g., the right to associate freely into unions and bargain collectively) are not part of the understanding, but remain outside the pale. In other words, these "enabling rights" do not arise naturally from even these enlightened buyer–supplier relations. The only way these rights can be brought to life is when they are required by law. For this, the state needs to be brought into the realm of private governance negotiations. As a result, we need to bring in the state and embed these private initiatives within a system of authoritative rule making and new forms of regulation that can enable them to promote labor standards consistently and sustainably within global supply chains.

Earlier, I described the decline in the capacity of national governments, especially in the developing economies, to regulate labor standards as a consequence of competition for FDI. Recent research shows, however, that national governments – even in poor countries with few natural resources – have far more ability to impose their will on foreign investors than we have previously believed (see, for example, Wellhausen 2012). As a number of recent studies have shown, even when eager to attract foreign investment and constrained by global competition, national governments have underutilized capacity to protect worker rights and resolve some collective action problems among firms (Amengual 2011; Coslovsky 2011; Pires 2011). Because most private voluntary initiatives promoting labor standards in global supply chains simply require participating firms to adhere to local laws, having strong national labor, environmental, and health and safety laws is crucial to the success of these programs. And because monitoring for compliance with these laws is costly, with suppliers having limited incentives to fully enforce them and NGOs having limited capacity to do so, only national governments have sufficient power and legitimacy to enforce their own laws. Moreover, in the global supply settings analyzed in this book, in which different buyers and suppliers have real incentives to circumvent any regulations that increase their costs, national governments are best positioned to prevent defections by individual firms and ensuring that all producers within the same national or regional economy adhere to common standards. Yet, how does one promote this type of government intervention/pubic regulation in a world of global supply chains?

Building on recent research on "experimentalist governance" (Sabel and Zeitlin 2012) and "responsive regulation" (Braithwaite 2006; Graham and Woods 2006), I argue that government, even in most developing countries, can play a positive role in promoting collaborative buyer–supplier relations and resolving collective action problems among different global buyers as well as between these buyers and their multiple suppliers. In explaining the features of experimentalist governance, Sabel and Zeitlin (2012) describe a multilevel process in which government agencies, in collaboration with the private actors they regulate, engage in a process in which broad goals and metrics are developed and implemented in ways that promote responsiveness to variation in local circumstances, learning and the diffusion of best practices across different private and public actors, and ever-increasing compliance with government regulations. As a result of this framework, European governments have been able to promote enhanced environmental standards both within the EU and among developing countries supplying forestry products to Europe. Potoski and Prakash (2004) describe a similar process within the United States, in which innovative state-level policies (i.e., lenient penalties in exchange for transparency and self-disclosure of problems) have encouraged private firms to enhance their compliance with environmental regulations. These innovations are not limited to the United States and Europe but have also emerged in several developing countries, including Argentina (Amengual 2011), Brazil (Coslovsky 2011; Pires 2011), Cambodia (Polaski 2006), and India (Tewari and Pillali 2005). In each of these cases, using different mechanisms and targeting different actors, national governments were able to promote labor and environmental standards by reconciling the competing interests of, and resolving collective action problems among, private firms that were violating these standards. In all cases, this process involved not traditional command and control (deterrence) government regulation but rather a mix of carrots (in the form of capability building/technical assistance programs) and sticks (in the form of threatening sanctions and closing off "low-road" options for domestic firms). Although this book does not explicitly analyze cases of innovative public regulation, it does show that government institutions and laws are key to the success of private initiatives seeking to improve labor standards in global supply chains.

The book develops this argument by analyzing various compliance and "beyond compliance" initiatives promoted by several global brands alone or in collaboration with other firms, NGOs, and even international organizations like the ILO. Each chapter shows both the possibilities and limitations of these private voluntary programs. At the same time, throughout the book, I seek to document cases, often simply fragments of evidence, of what I see as a new approach to labor regulation in global supply chains. Chapter 2 analyzes efforts by private firms and at times entire industries to enforce labor standards in global supply chains through private compliance programs. After reviewing the various debates and controversies surrounding these programs, Chapter 2 analyzes the specific programs of two major global corporations – ABC[15] and Hewlett-Packard – both seen as leaders in corporate social responsibility and pioneers in developing corporate codes of conduct and private monitoring schemes. Chapter 3 explores these issues in greater detail through a case study of Nike, the world's largest athletic footwear and apparel company. Given the central and highly controversial place Nike occupies in debates over globalization and labor standards, it serves in many ways as a nice contrast to the HP and ABC as well as a "crucial case" through which to explore the effect of private compliance initiatives on labor standards in global supply chains.

Together, these two chapters show the results of years of efforts by each of these companies at developing ever more comprehensive monitoring tools, hiring growing numbers of internal compliance specialists, conducting hundreds of factory audits, and working with external consultants and NGOs. Working conditions and labor rights have improved somewhat among some of their suppliers but have stagnated or even deteriorated in many other supplier factories. After more than a decade of concerted efforts by global brands and labor rights NGOs alike, private compliance programs appear largely unable to deliver on their promise of sustained improvements in labor standards in the new centers of global production. Compliance efforts have delivered some improvements in working conditions, as the data presented in these two chapters illustrate. The point is that these improvements seem to have hit a ceiling: basic improvements have been achieved in some areas (e.g., health and safety) but not in others (e.g., freedom of association, excessive working hours). Moreover, these

---

[15] This is not the real name of this corporation. For confidentiality reasons, I have invented this alternative.

(handwritten margin note: Develop Hitlist NGO to LT)

improvements appear to be unstable in the sense that many factories cycle in and out of compliance over time.

Chapter 4 examines the capability-building efforts of several global corporations, labor-rights NGOs, and the ILO. As the shortcomings of private compliance programs became increasingly apparent, these actors began to promote an alternative (but still private, nongovernmental) approach to combating poor labor standards in global supply chains, built around the concept of capability building. Chapter 4 analyzes an array of capability-building initiatives across multiple industries (apparel, electronics, metalworking) and in different countries (Honduras, the Dominican Republic, Vietnam, India, and China). Notwithstanding significant improvements over traditional compliance programs, Chapter 4 shows how many (but not all) capability-building initiatives suffer from their own shortcomings, especially their inability to address certain distributive issues and overcome various political hurdles necessary to achieve labor rights enforcement. Although capability-building programs generated marked improvements for participating factories in terms of increased productivity and quality, and also for most workers, in terms of improved health and safety conditions and in some cases, greater autonomy and empowerment on the shop floor, these same initiatives – precisely because of their technocratic approach – eschewed more difficult, distributive issues (e.g., living wages) and the enforcement of "enabling rights" so that workers could organize to demand higher wages and better working conditions.

Chapter 5 explores in greater detail why capability-building initiatives produce such mixed results through a structured comparison of two apparel suppliers, both located in Mexico and both producing more or less the same products for the same brand (Nike). Notwithstanding the many similarities of these two factories, working conditions at these two plants are quite different. In one plant, workers are empowered and work collaboratively with management on production targets as well as workplace conditions. At the other factory, workers are disenfranchised and working conditions are harsh. Through a detailed case study of these two "matched" factories, Chapter 5 documents how the particular approach to capability building implemented at these two plants had significant (and very different) consequences for the workers they employed.

Chapter 6 describes why poor working conditions, precarious employment practices, low wages, excessive work hours, and weak labor rights persist in global supply chains by looking beyond the suppliers' factories and more broadly at the "upstream" business practices of large retailers and global brands and their "downstream" effects on suppliers and their workers. Chapter 6 tracks how global brands have responded to a business environment characterized by dynamic consumer demand, shorter product life cycles, and concentrated retail channels by reorganizing their supply chains to optimize efficiencies and minimize financial and reputational risks. Although these techniques have allowed major retail chains and global brands to offer a broader selection of products, introduce new products in a more timely fashion, and reduce inventory of poor-selling items, these same practices create various labor problems (e.g., excessive work hours, low wages, exploitation of migrant (contract workers) at supplier factories. Chapter 6 argues that while better-designed private compliance systems and more capacious capability-building programs would certainly help improve labor standards in global supply chain factories, they could not, in and of themselves, adequately tackle these persistent workplace problems because the root cause of many of these labor issues lies in the structure of relations among large retailers, global brands, lead suppliers, and their factories.

In response to both the limitations of these private voluntary programs, and growing demands for more effective state enforcement of already existing labor and employment laws designed to protect workers employed in the factories and farms supplying global buyers, a number of new or reformed public regulatory initiatives aimed at promoting greater compliance with labor laws, health and safety standards, and the ability of workers to freely organize themselves into independent unions have been launched in recent years. Chapter 7 examines some of these efforts by national governments to enforce their domestic laws and assesses their effectiveness. The analysis presented in this chapter suggests that although the revival of labor inspection and the promotion of innovative regulatory initiatives in an array of different countries have certainly helped improve working conditions and labor rights in these countries, these efforts also suffer various limitations – limitations in their organizational capacities and ability to adequately inspect, let alone redress, violations in all workplaces under their jurisdiction. These organizational limitations might be overcome through complementary interactions with private voluntary initiatives. Chapter 7 illustrates the potential of this complementary private-public regulatory approach through a case study of labor conditions among contract workers in the electronics industry. The concluding chapter steps back from the research and ponders how to stitch together and scale up the fragments of labor-friendly practices and more collaborative buyer–supplier relations documented in this book. I argue that a new form of labor regulation is possible and can be constructed through a sequential process that blends private interests and public intervention.

This book is based on five years of research conducted between 2005 and 2010. More than 700 interviews were conducted with factory directors, workers, NGO representatives, government officials, and union leaders in Bangladesh, Brazil, China, the Czech Republic, the Dominican Republic, Honduras, India, Malaysia, Mexico, Thailand, Turkey, Singapore, the United States, and Vietnam. Compliance, operations, and purchasing managers from several global brands were interviewed in both the companies' regional offices and at their respective company headquarters. In addition, my graduate students and I visited more than 120 supply chain factories in all of these countries, providing us with firsthand data on working conditions. Access to these factories was facilitated in most cases by the global brands, although the ILO helped us gain access to some factories in Vietnam and India. However, to guarantee that the students and I were visiting a representative sample of supply chain factories, I randomly selected which factories we would visit from the full list of active suppliers working with each of the global brands analyzed in this book. In some of these factories, we also observed compliance audits, thus giving us insight into the auditing and monitoring process. This qualitative research was complemented by quantitative analyses of the internal audit reports of each of the major global corporations analyzed in this book. Thousands of individual factory audit reports were collected, analyzed, and coded to identify general patterns of compliance as well as changes in compliance outcomes across the various supply chains studied in this book. This original data set, coupled with unprecedented access to the factories supplying several major brands, created a unique opportunity to assess current labor conditions and labor rights within today's global supply chains, as well as to assess the possibilities for improving these conditions and enhancing the rights for the millions of workers employed in these factories.

2

The Promise and Perils of Private Compliance Programs

This chapter analyzes efforts by private firms – and at times, entire industries – to enforce labor standards in global supply chains through corporate self-regulation. In the wake of several well-publicized scandals involving child labor, hazardous working conditions, excessive working hours, and poor wages in the factories that supply major global brands, numerous multinational corporations developed their own "codes of conduct"[1] and "monitoring" schemes aimed at promoting "compliance" with these codes. In fact, given the limited ability (perhaps even willingness) of many developing country governments to enforce their own laws,[2] private compliance is currently the principal way both labor rights nongovernmental organizations (NGOs) and global corporations address poor working conditions in global supply chain factories. The underlying assumption of this model of "private voluntary regulation" is that information collected through factory audits will be used both by labor rights NGOs and consumer groups to exert pressure on global brands to reform their sourcing practices as well as by the brands themselves, who rely on this information to police and pressure their suppliers into improving standards in their factories. Should the factories fail to remedy various workplace problems, brands are expected to switch their orders to supposedly more "ethical" producers.

[1] For a good description of this movement, see Jenkins (2001), Mamic (2004), and Schrage (2004). See also David Vogel, "Private Global Business Regulation," *Annual Review of Political Science* 11 (2008): 261–82; Tim Bartley, "Institutional Emergence in an Era of Globalization: The Rise of Transnational Private Regulation of Labor and Environmental Conditions," *American Journal of Sociology* 113, no. 2 (2007): 297–351.
[2] For more on this, see Baccaro (2001) and Elliot and Freeman (2003). See also ILO, "Strategies and Practice for Labour Inspection (GB.297/ESP/3)" (2006); ILO, *Labour Administration and Labour Inspection* (Geneva: International Labour Conference, 100th Session, 2011).

Given their widespread use, we might expect these private compliance programs to be highly effective, but do these initiatives actually lead to better working conditions and enforced labor rights in global supply chains? If so, under what conditions? This chapter addresses these questions by first reviewing the various debates and controversies surrounding private compliance programs, then assessing the underlying assumptions and key features of this model of corporate self-regulation, and finally illustrating how these programs work in practice by analyzing the compliance efforts of two major global corporations – ABC[3] and Hewlett-Packard – both seen as leaders in corporate social responsibility and pioneers in developing corporate codes of conduct and private monitoring schemes. The following chapter then examines private compliance in greater detail through a case study of Nike, the world's leading athletic footwear brand and a major player in the debates surrounding corporate efforts to regulate labor standards in global supply chains.

Private Compliance: A Review of the Literature

Codes of conduct and efforts aimed at monitoring compliance with these codes have a long history. Whereas initially these efforts focused primarily on corporate compliance with national regulations overseeing various business practices (i.e., preventing corruption), over time, monitoring efforts have become increasingly directed at compliance with private, voluntary codes of conduct, especially as they apply to labor, health and safety, and environmental standards.[4]

Critics of private compliance programs argue that they displace more thorough government and union intervention and are designed *not* to protect labor rights or improve working conditions but rather to limit the legal liability of global brands and prevent damage to their reputations.[5] Others, however,

---

[3] For confidentiality reasons, we use a pseudonym for this company.

[4] For an interesting historical review of corporate codes of conduct and their evolution over time, see Rhys Jenkins, "Corporate Codes of Conduct: Self-Regulation in a Global Economy," United Nations Research Institute for Social Development (UNRISD) at http://www.eldis.org/static/DOC9199.htm. Another interesting historical parallel can be found in Gay W. Seidman, "Monitoring Multinationals: Lessons from the Anti-Apartheid Era," *Politics & Society* 31, no. 3 (2003): 381–406.

[5] For a review of the displacement hypothesis, see Timothy Bartley, "Corporate Accountability and the Privatization of Labor Standards: Struggles over Codes of Conduct in the Apparel Industry," *Research in Political Sociology* 14 (2005): 211–44. The concern for displacement is often alluded to in much of the literature, and more directly in Jill L. Esbenshade, *Monitoring Sweatshops: Workers, Consumers, and the Global Apparel Industry* (Philadelphia: Temple University Press, 2004); "Overview of Global Developments and Office Activities Concerning Codes of Conduct, Social Labeling and Other Private Sector Initiatives Addressing Labour Issues," report GB.273/WP/SDL/1(Rev.1) from the 273rd Session of the Working Party on the Social Dimensions of the Liberalization of International Trade, International Labour Organization Governing Body, Geneva, November 1998, http://www.ilo.org/public/english/bureau/exrel/global/index-wpsdg.htm; Dwight W. Justice, "The Corporate Social Responsibility Concept and Phenomenon: Challenges and Opportunities for Trade Unionists" (paper

argue that private voluntary self-regulation is not an attempt to undermine the state but rather an appropriately flexible response to the reality of global production networks and the low capacity of developing country states to fully enforce labor laws and regulations (Ruggie 2003; Nadvi & Wältring 2004; Vogel 2008). According to this second group, *under certain conditions*, the compliance efforts of brands, multistakeholder initiatives, and NGOs can work to strengthen government enforcement of national laws, particularly when states lack the capacity or the resources to carry out systematic factory inspections (Fung et al. 2001; O'Rourke 2003; Bartley 2005; Rodriguez-Garavito 2005).

A second debate over private compliance programs focuses on whether those conducting the audits can be trusted to make accurate and honest assessments of factory conditions and transparently report their findings. Critics identify a number of important conflicts of interest that exist among the key actors involved in the monitoring process (Esbenshade 2004; National Research Council 2004; Pruett 2005; Rodriguez-Garavito 2005). Given that brands and their suppliers may have an interest in hiding labor violations rather than reporting them, how trustworthy are these internal audits? Might not the moral hazard for these interested parties be too great? Nor does auditing by "third party" organizations escape observers' skeptical regard. If the third parties are NGOs, how competent are they in assessing certain technical issues (for example, air quality)? If, instead, these third-party auditors are private monitoring firms, how forthcoming will they be, given that they most likely hope to please their clients (the brands and their suppliers who pay for these services) and generate future business? In response to these criticisms, various procedures and policies were established to promote greater transparency and oversight by "independent" organizations. Increasingly, external auditors, ranging from for-profit social auditing companies to local NGOs, are being certified by multistakeholder initiatives (MSIs) like the Fair Labor Association (FLA) and the Fair Wear Foundation. These institutional mechanisms are meant to bolster the creditability of monitors. Still, some observers (for example, the Worker Rights Consortium) argue that monitoring must be completely independent of brands and suppliers to be truly effective.

A third debate concerns the growing number and diversity of codes of conduct and auditing protocols as well as the uneven quality[6] of the audits being

---

presented at the ILO Training Seminar: "Trade Union Training for Global Union Federations in Asia/Pacific on Globalization, Workers' Rights and CSR," Kuala Lumpur, November 28–December 3, 2005) http://training.itcilo.org/actrav/courses/2005/A3-50909_web/resources/technical_files/3.2%20CSR_unions.PDF; and Henry J. Frundt, "The Impact of Private Codes and the Union Movement" (paper presented at XXIII International Congress of the Latin American Studies Association, Washington, DC, 2001).

[6] For a critique of existing auditing practices, see Pruett (2005).

performed. A 2003 World Bank study estimated that more than 1,000 corporate codes of conduct existed in that year (Smith & Feldman 2003:2). More recent estimates are difficult to find, but the numbers of firms with their own Code of Conduct must certainly have grown.[7] The diversity of codes and monitoring schemes being applied to global suppliers is well documented (Brown 2005; Jenkins 2001; O'Rourke 2003). Underlying these different codes and implementation systems are very different principles and goals. Whereas some codes emphasize freedom of association and anti-discrimination policies, others instead focus on "living" (as opposed to minimum) wages, excessive working hours, and health and safety issues. Some codes are monitored by internal, company staff, while others are audited by third-party, external consultants or NGOs. Many suppliers have to implement multiple codes of conduct, which causes redundancies and confusion. Some factories complain of "monitoring fatigue," given that they are monitored multiple times a year on behalf of each of the global brands they work for. In addition, suppliers complain of being placed in "compliance limbo" between different and conflicting code requirements.

In short, private compliance programs vary tremendously in terms of the issues being investigated (wages, work hours, working conditions, child labor, freedom of association, health and safety issues, sexual harassment, and so on), methodology employed to collect information (for example, interviews – with or without workers, on-site or away from the factory – documents, observations), length of time spent conducting the audit, level of skill or expe rience or independence of the monitors, and methods of reporting the information collected (Jenkins 2001; O'Rourke 2003). Given this marked diversity in the design and implementation of private compliance programs, the room for controversy over whether these programs are accurate, thorough, let alone effective is enormous.

Yet regardless of the specific points raised or the positions being defended in these debates, almost all the participants share a set of common assumptions about how compliance in global supply chains should or could work. In other words, the various arguments over codes of conduct and private monitoring programs are all framed in the same way,[8] and it is this frame, these shared assumptions, that need to be analyzed in order to assess whether or not private compliance efforts can, in fact, drive improvements in working conditions in today's globally dispersed world of production.

---

[7] Although the exact number of companies with codes of conduct is difficult to accurately assess, one proxy for their diffusion can be the number of firms that signed on to the United Nations' Global Compact. Nearly 5,000 firms have signed onto this parallel voluntary initiative, which seeks to, among other things, promote decent working conditions.

[8] See Donald Schon and Martin Rein, *Frame Reflection: Toward the Resolution of Intractable Policy Controversies* (New York: Basic Books, 1994).

Key Features and Underlying Assumptions of Private Compliance Programs

The traditional compliance model derives its assumptions from three distinct (but related) literatures regarding the governance of global supply chains (sometimes referred to as commodity or value chains), the role of auditing/monitoring in promoting corporate accountability, and alternative models of regulatory enforcement. Because the key insights of each of these literatures have combined to form the theoretical underpinnings of the private compliance model, it is crucial to examine their core assumptions to better understand both the model's promise and its limitations.

The prevalence of *asymmetric power* relations between global buyers and their geographically dispersed suppliers is a central assumption of the private compliance model. Derived from the work of Gary Gereffi and his various collaborators on global commodity/supply/value chains,[9] this assumption holds that the economic leverage that global brands exercise over their suppliers translates into their ability to enforce compliance with codes of conduct. In its original formulation, the global commodity chain literature describes the geographic dispersion of production networks and the role key actors like global buyers and vertically integrated transnational manufacturers play in the governance of these networks. In "buyer-driven" value chains, global brands maintain their authority over their suppliers by controlling key (high-value-added) functions like product development, design, marketing, and brand management while outsourcing to their suppliers only low-value added, labor-intensive manufacturing activities. As such, they not only impose strict conditions regarding cost, quality, and delivery times but also determine whether and to what extent their suppliers (and often the developing countries in which they are located) can upgrade their productive capacities and thereby improve their standing in the international division of labor. Although much of the literature on industrial upgrading focuses primarily on the establishment of product and process standards, this analysis has been extended to include environmental and labor standards.[10] The logic of this argument is as follows: if all-powerful global brands are willing and able to dictate commercial terms and product standards on their "weak" and/or "dependent" suppliers, they must also be capable of forcing these same suppliers to comply with codes of conduct and labor standards, assuming they have genuine interest in doing so.

A related literature on transnational activist networks (sometimes referred to as "global civil society") shares these same assumptions. It is precisely because global brands are so powerful and visible to the public that they have

[9] Gary Gereffi, John Humphrey, and Timothy Sturgeon, "The Governance of Global Value Chains," *Review of International Political Economy* 12, no. 1 (2005): 78–104.

[10] Lizbeth Navas-Alemán and Luiza Bazan, "Local Implementation of Quality, Labour and Environmental Standards: Opportunities for Upgrading in the Footwear Industry," SEED Working Paper No. 45 (Geneva: International Labour Organization, 2003).

become targets for transnational activist groups and other NGOs. The Achilles heel of these powerful global corporations is their reputation (brand value).[11] Thus, transnational activist groups employ consumer boycotts and other "campaigns" to force global corporations to adopt "voluntary" codes of conduct and impose various "independent" monitoring systems on their suppliers.[12] This activist strategy relies on information generated from factory audits, which they employ to "name and shame" companies that mistreat "their" employees (i.e., the employees of their suppliers) and to mobilize other activists and the media.

> Without external monitoring, claims of corporate social responsibility may simply be a new marketing ploy. In order for consumers to be able to hold companies accountable they need accurate information, provided by independent monitors, who are not simply working on behalf of the companies themselves.[13]

The importance and quality of **information** derived from factory audits (preferably independent, third-party audits) constitutes the second key assumption underlying the private compliance model. Information collected through factory audits is central to this model because it is used by both labor rights NGOs and consumer groups to exert pressure on global brands to reform their sourcing practices and by the brands themselves to police and pressure their suppliers to improve standards within their factories. According to Elliott and Freeman,[14] there exists a "market for standards" in which informed consumers respond with their wallets to activist demands that global brands take responsibility for labor conditions in supplier factories. These purchasing decisions will induce global brands to adopt codes of conduct and exercise their leverage over their suppliers to enforce compliance with these codes. According to this line of argument, accurate information about factory working conditions obtained through audits and various verification mechanisms is the best way to create a

---

[11] In a recent study of the Cambodian garment industry, Oka has found that suppliers working for reputation-conscious buyers do, in fact, perform better in terms of labor compliance than suppliers working for less reputation-conscious buyers. See Chikako Oka, "Accounting for the Gaps in Labour Standard Compliance: The Role of Reputation-conscious Buyers in the Cambodian Garment Industry," *European Journal of Development Research* 22, no. 1 (2010): 59–78.

[12] See, for example, Margaret E. Keck and Kathryn Sikkink, *Activists Beyond Borders: Advocacy Networks in International Politics* (Ithaca, NY: Cornell University Press, 1998); Gay Seidman, *Beyond the Boycott: Labor Rights, Human Rights, and Transnational Activism* (New York: American Sociological Association's Rose Series: Russell Sage Foundation Press, 2007).

[13] Seidman, *Beyond the Boycott*, who quotes: Ronen Shamir, "The De-Radicalization of Corporate Social Responsibility," *Critical Sociology* 30 (2004): 669–89.

[14] Kimberly Ann Elliott and Richard B. Freeman, "White Hats or Don Quixotes? Human Rights Vigilantes in the Global Economy" (Cambridge, MA: National Bureau for Economic Research, 2001), and *Can Standards Improve under Globalization?* (Washington, DC: Institute for International Economics, 2003).

"credible commitment" for global buyers, guaranteeing that they enforce their own codes of conduct.

It is precisely because audit-generated information plays such a pivotal role in the traditional compliance model that so much of the debate has focused on various proposals aimed at ensuring its quality, reliability, and transparency. In some proposals, information obtained through monitoring is shared *within* global firms – between compliance officers and other, more business-focused (e.g., purchasing, operations, product) managers – to encourage suppliers to improve the quality and efficiency of their production systems. According to this argument, exchange of information inspires learning, which in turns generates a virtuous cycle of process, product, and workplace improvements.[15] Another proposal suggests that audit information collected by commercial and independent monitors should be exchanged *among* brands and various multistakeholder groups and would serve as the basis for an externally verified, public ranking system aimed at guiding the decision making of concerned consumers and investors. Transparency combined with the constant threat of customer (and investor) sanctions would induce firms to compete for higher rankings, gradually leading to a "ratcheting up" of labor standards.[16] In short, once the proper information system is in place, firm incentives can be structured in a manner that is consistent with consumer preferences. And once this incentive system is operational, global brands will use their superior bargaining power vis-à-vis their suppliers to improve labor standards.

The third assumption, foreshadowed in the earlier discussion on power relations and information, concerns the correct mix of *incentives* required to induce changes in behavior among key actors in these global production networks. Drawing on economic models of regulatory compliance (sometimes referred to as deterrence theory), this assumption portrays compliance with codes of conduct as the product of a simple calculation by utility maximizing actors.[17] The costs of compliance are measured against the probability of being caught out of compliance, the probability of being punished for this "offense," and the severity of the punishment for failing to comply with the codes. Assuming that the costs of achieving or even remaining in compliance are fixed, whether or not a supplier chooses to actually comply with voluntary codes of conduct will depend on the values of the foregoing three variables (the probability of getting caught, size of the penalty, and cost of compliance). This may explain why so many corporate and NGO compliance programs seek to measure or

---

[15] Charles Sabel, "Learning by Monitoring," in Neil Smelser (Ed.), *The Handbook of Economic Sociology* (Princeton, NJ: Princeton University Press, 1994), 137–65.

[16] Archon Fung, Dara O'Rourke, and Charles Sabel, *Can We Put an End to Sweatshops? A New Democracy Forum on Raising Global Labor Standards* (Boston: Beacon Press, 2001).

[17] Gary S. Becker, "Crime and Punishment: An Economic Approach," *The Journal of Political Economy* 76, no. 2 (1968): 169–217.

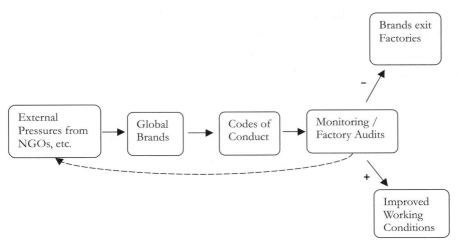

FIGURE 2.1. Traditional model of Code of Conduct/compliance.

grade their suppliers' performance vis-à-vis compliance. In theory at least, well-performing factories will be rewarded with increased or long-term orders (or both), whereas poorly performing plants will suffer the consequences for poor compliance through either a reduction of their orders or even the termination of their business relationship with the global buyers. In sum, the private compliance model is based on a hypothetical self-reinforcing cycle in which high-quality information generated by independent and transparent audits is used by both consumer groups and NGOs to pressure global brands to adopt codes of conducts *and* by these same all-powerful brands to either reward or punish suppliers for their performance (compliance) with these codes. Figure 2.1 depicts the causal linkages assumed in this model.

Assessed separately (and even in combination), the underlying assumptions of the private compliance model might seem reasonable. But when considered more carefully, it becomes clear that they rest on theoretically misguided and empirically weak underpinnings, which could explain why after more than a decade of concerted efforts by global brands and labor rights NGOs alike, private self-regulation has yet to deliver on its promise of sustained improvements in labor rights and working conditions in today's emergent centers of global production. This is not to say that private regulation has not delivered any improvements in working conditions. As we see in the next chapter, certain improvements have, in fact, taken place under this private self-regulating model. The point, however, is that these improvements seem to have reached a plateau: basic improvements have been achieved in some areas (e.g., health and safety) but not in others (e.g., freedom of association, limits on excess overtime). Moreover, these improvements appear to be unstable in that many factories cycle in and out of "compliance" over time. To understand the limitations of the private compliance model, let me now turn to a critical analysis of its core theoretical and empirical assumptions.

Notwithstanding the commonly held idea that large, powerful "Northern" global brands are riding roughshod over their smaller suppliers based in developing countries, power relations within global supply chains are far from asymmetrical.[18] In fact, closer examination of the various levels at which power is assumed to work in the private compliance model (i.e., between global corporations and their suppliers; between compliance officers and the managers of the factories they inspect, and between compliance and other "business" (purchasing, sourcing, product) managers within the same global corporations), reveals much more complex and subtle power relations among the various parties.

In some industries – footwear and electronics, for example – Asian-based suppliers have grown tremendously both in size and sophistication and thus wield a tremendous amount of influence over the global brands they serve.[19] These suppliers have developed core competencies in both manufacturing and product design and development, and thus, over time they have developed a more collaborative "partnership" with global buyers. In other sectors (i.e., apparel), we see the opposite phenomenon. For most apparel suppliers, individual global brands constitute a small fraction of their total business (and thus of dedicated factory capacity), and even this is usually for only part of the year – one or two seasons – with no guarantee that orders will be repeated in the future. In this context, it is not at all clear that global buyers have the ability or leverage (let alone the credibility) to pressure these suppliers to raise wages, reduce working hours, or even invest in costly improvements to their production systems in order to improve working conditions. It is an open secret that few brands ever exit factories, even when they are found not to be in compliance with the codes of conduct and that most compliance officers have less influence than their purchasing or sourcing colleagues when deciding whether to place (or continue) an order with a noncompliant factory. Moreover, when brands do leave a factory, they lose any leverage that they once had if the factory finds other, less demanding clients. If the factory does go out of business, this penalizes both the workers and the management, and as a result, many labor rights groups are now pressuring brands to stay with factories and work to remediate problems rather than exiting. All of this challenges the received wisdom that global brands, if only they were willing, are able to "force" their suppliers to comply with their codes of conduct.

---

[18] For a more sophisticated analysis of buyer-supplier relations in today's global economy, see Suzanne Berger, *How We Compete: What Companies around the World Are Doing to Make It in Today's Global Economy* (New York: Doubleday, 2006).

[19] Gereffi, Humphrey, and Sturgeon, "The Governance of Global Value Chains." In *Review of International Political Economy* 12, no. 1 (2005): 78–104.

Yet even if power relations were as straightforward as the private compliance model assumes, it is not at all clear that global brands and their suppliers would really know what to do to improve working conditions because the root causes of many of these problems are not often identifiable through standard audit processes. The fundamental limitations of audits, in a variety of settings, have already been documented.[20] In most workplaces, compliance would require constant vigilance by monitors trained in a variety of fields (i.e., health and safety, human rights, operations management, labor relations, etc.), and the costs (in terms of people, resources, time) of such a system are much too high for most global buyers, let alone their suppliers. But even if such a system could be installed, it is not clear that it would ever fully work. Writing about occupational health and safety regulations in the 1970s, Steven Kelman describes a remarkably familiar scenario:

A number of regulations involve conditions that are frequently changing. Slippery or cluttered floors may be clean today but messy tomorrow. A rope used as a hoist may have been sound when inspected last week but developed a defect this week. . . . These are some of the things that can go wrong when an employer is willing to comply with regulations voluntarily. How much more difficult, then, is achieving compliance where an employer would be unwilling to comply with some enforcement effort.[21]

In other words, even if one could afford to design and implement a rigorous monitoring system, it is not at all clear that a factory "audit" would be the most appropriate method of collecting, let alone communicating, up-to-date information about factory conditions.[22] This might explain why information gathering through factory inspections cannot, in and of itself, bring about the kinds of changes in working conditions, employment relations, and managerial behavior required to improve labor standards in most supply chain plants. This is especially true of many suppliers whose own operations are often impacted by unreliable power grids, late arrivals of key inputs and materials, and even delayed (and changed) orders from their buyers. All of these extra-factory variables can have an impact on working hours and working conditions within the factories, but none would appear in a traditional factory audit, no matter how rigorous it is designed or implemented.

[20] Steven Kelman, *Regulating America, Regulating Sweden: A Comparative Study of Occupational Safety and Health Policy* (Cambridge, MA: MIT Press, 1981); Marilyn Strathern, *Audit Cultures* (London: Routledge, 2000); Michael Power, *The Audit Society: Rituals of Verification* (New York: Oxford University Press, 1997).

[21] Kelman, *Regulating America, Regulating Sweden*, A Comparative Study of Occupational Safety and Health Policy (Cambridge, MA: MIT Press), 178–9.

[22] For a fascinating description of the limits of traditional monitoring systems, see T. A. Frank, "Confessions of a Sweatshop Inspector," *Washington Monthly* 40, no. 4 (April 2008): 34–7. For another fascinating account of the limits of monitoring approaches, even by well-financed, well-trained, committed auditors, see Gay W. Seidman, "Constructing a Culture of Compliance," in *Beyond the Boycott*, 102–31.

Finally, there now exists an extensive body of literature on regulatory effectiveness (or lack thereof) in an array of arenas that indicates that companies comply with laws, regulations, and standards *not* simply because these "amoral calculators" have been compelled to do so by the threat of sanctions (deterrence model), but instead because many of them have been assisted and/or educated to comply with regulations and standards by high-performing compliance officers and auditors.[23] For example, in their study of regulatory effectiveness in diverse workplaces (i.e., nursing homes, chemical plants, manufacturing establishments, etc.), Bardach and Kagan argue convincingly that more aggressive, rule-based, "legalistic" enforcement practices sometimes discourage rather than encourage responsible behavior among corporations:[24]

The beneficial effects of legalistic regulation, however, should not blind us to the fact that the unreasonableness and unresponsiveness associated with those regulations can keep the full potential of regulations from ever being realized. From the sum contributions to regulatory effectiveness brought about by threat we must subtract the unnecessary costs and lost opportunities for progress that can result from legalistic narrow mindedness, from its tendency to destroy cooperation, and from its stimulation of legal and political resistance.[25]

Although the deterrence approach led to greater enforcement of rules and regulations in some settings, in many others, it generated unintended consequences and unnecessary costs that resulted in less compliance overall.

This literature documents how the "deterrence" approach to compliance has rendered the factory inspection process overly bureaucratic. Auditors arrive with lengthy, detailed checklists aimed at exposing record-keeping lapses and easy-to-detect code violations rather than discovering the sources or root causes of these various workplace problems. Suppliers, in turn, "learn" to be inspected by preparing and sometimes doctoring their records and doing the absolute minimum to remain "within compliance" of the buyers' codes of conduct. Rather than dedicating the time and resources to redress serious problems, these factory managers engage in a "ritual" of compliance while growing cynical and resentful of it, and sometimes outright resistant to the audit process as a whole.

---

[23] For an interesting description of such compliance officers, see Susan Silbey, Ruthanne Huising, and Salo Vinocur Coslovsky, "The 'Sociological Citizen': Related Interdependence in Law and Organizations," *L'Annee Sociologique*, 59, no. 1 (2009): 201–29. For a compilation of how high-performing compliance officers behave in an array of different countries and industries, see the special issues edited by Susan Silbey of *Regulation and Governance* 5, no. 1 (Spring 2011).

[24] Eugene Bardach and Robert A. Kagan, *Going by the Book: The Problem of Regulatory Unreasonableness* (Philadelphia: Temple University Press, 1982).

[25] Ibid., 93.

In sum, more careful examination of the assumptions underlying the private compliance model reveals its serious theoretical and empirical limitations. Power relations among the key actors in the supply chains are far from unidirectional or unambiguous, and thus render simple responses (e.g., comply or else) unrealistic. Given the complex and interdependent nature of relations among the different actors in the supply chain, it is not clear whose behavior (i.e., the brands, the purchasing agents, the auditors, the suppliers, etc.) should be induced to change. Likewise, the incentives underlying this model of private regulation are far from clear and thus provoke mixed, often contradictory behaviors. Suppliers are asked to invest in improved labor and environmental conditions but are pressured to (and rewarded for) producing ever-cheaper goods with shorter lead times. Even when some suppliers do invest in new systems or training programs aimed at improving labor and environmental standards, they are not always rewarded for these investments, since price-sensitive and fashion-conscious buyers may shift next season's orders to less expensive or more responsive suppliers elsewhere. Finally, the information on which this entire system rests is by its very nature incomplete, biased, and often inaccurate and cannot serve as a reliable base for well-informed and reasoned strategies aimed at remediating poor working conditions in the suppliers' factories.

In short, regardless of how well-financed, well-staffed, committed, or even transparent these private compliance systems are, they will always suffer shortcomings because of the faulty assumptions underlying and shaping their core practices. This explains why global corporations have continued to struggle with various labor issues within their supply chains notwithstanding their significant investment in resources, personnel, and time. Because of their inherent shortcomings, private compliance programs simply cannot tackle these problems in and of themselves. To illustrate these difficulties, the following section presents a series of vignettes from our field research on suppliers producing for different brands, competing in different industries, and located in different countries, but all struggling to improve labor standards and working conditions through private compliance initiatives.

Notes from the Field: How Private Compliance Programs "Work" in Practice

Reliable Information? A Closer Look at the Audit Process
Across the different companies, industries and regions analyzed for this project, my field research consistently observed the enormous difficulties auditors faced as they sought to collect accurate, objective, and comprehensive information about working conditions and labor standards in the factories they inspected. These difficulties did not result solely from the nature of the audit process itself, which as described earlier, is ill-suited at observing, let alone measuring, various components of labor standards, (i.e., unimpeded expression of freedoms and

rights), but also to resource constraints and the inadequate training of many of the auditors themselves. These factors combine to make the information generated by the factory audits often inaccurate, biased, and incomplete.

The factory audit is modeled on the financial audit in that it is based on a long checklist of items to be "inspected" and "verified." That approach privileges documentary records such as pay stubs, birth certificates, and attendance records rather than careful and time-intensive examination of the factory work processes or interviews with workers.[26] Most auditors working for (or with) global brands typically spend one or two working days on a factory audit, and more than half of this time is consumed by reviewing documents, while the physical inspection of the factory or interviews with workers (when these take place) may take only a few hours. Thus, the audit is based primarily on factory records, which the auditors themselves claim to be unreliable and often inaccurate. With limited time, auditors cannot verify all factory records, making it difficult to find noncompliance in factories that falsify records. For example, a senior auditor my students and I interviewed explained, "Mandatory overtime, a double set of payrolls, you might find it, you might not find it. Failure to pay the Christmas bonus is not possible to find if you don't find the double set of books, because if you only base it on the official set of payrolls, everything matches perfectly."

In all the regions that my students and I visited during the course of the fieldwork for this project, auditors cited lack of transparency and poor record keeping as two major problems impeding the accurate collection of information on factory conditions. In China, auditors described the typical interaction with factory management as a "cat and mouse" game in which auditors uncover fabricated documents on wages and overtime hours, and managers promise to come clean and produce real figures but instead only present a new set of fabricated books and develop yet another way to hide violations in follow-up audits. Auditors have become highly skilled at "catching" such hidden violations by developing "tricks," such as examining the pattern of wrinkles on the identification cards of suspected underaged workers or asking them their Chinese zodiac signs rather than their ages, or checking the "broken needle record" for evidence of unauthorized overtime. Although such tactics attest to the creativity and determination of the auditors, they also reveal how easily the auditors can become engrossed in this "game" spending already scarce time trying to "trap" management and workers in lies, rather than uncovering the root causes of many labor compliance issues.

---

[26] This monitoring process is common among leading multinationals, multistakeholder groups such as the Fair Labor Association, and even the International Labor Organization's (ILO's) Better Factories Cambodia program. See ILO, "Monitoring Process Brochure" (2007) at http://www.betterfactories.org/content/documents/1/Monitoring%20Process%20Brochure%20(en).pdf.

The lack of transparency and cooperation by factory management is exacerbated by the extremely challenging task of auditing all of the suppliers with sufficient frequency and rigor to accurately assess their compliance to the company's Code of Conduct. Auditors are stretched thin, and given the amount of time that they dedicate to each factory audit, doing a thorough job is nearly impossible. For example, in China, the three auditors employed by ABC, a major global apparel brand, conducted 138 audits in 128 factories in one year, meaning that each auditor visited 3 or 4 factories per week. Because the team leader must also review all audit reports and attend to other administrative work, the brunt of the audits fell on two junior auditors who spent Monday through Thursday visiting factories dispersed throughout the country and Friday in the regional office writing up their reports. To cope with this lack of time, auditors "satisfice" by moving quickly through a factory until they have uncovered a set number of violations. An auditor in Latin America acknowledged that he regularly misses code violations in the factories he inspects and could easily "find more problems with more time" but that after he discovers forty noncompliance items during his visit, he calls it a day and moves on to the next factory. A review of hundreds of audit reports of the different global brands that we studied for this research project revealed that they were filled out neither completely nor consistently across all regions and among all auditors. Whole sections were left blank, violations were undocumented, and corrective action plans varied tremendously. Clearly, the auditors largely decide for themselves what items should receive most of their limited time and attention.

The academic and professional background of most compliance officers further distorts their ability to collect accurate and comprehensive information through the audit process. Most of the auditors that my graduate students and I interviewed were hired for their training and experience in either operations or human resources management.[27] As a result, they are more likely to notice and report on blocked aisles, uncharged fire extinguishers, and irregular personnel records rather than worker or union harassment, illegal firings, or failure to pay severance. The pattern of noncompliance items discovered through the audit process at the factories we visited bears out this set of biases, as health and safety and wages and overtime violations were uncovered much more commonly than violations related to freedom of association, worker-management relations, or illegal or improper dismissals.

---

[27] A few of the auditors we interviewed were neither industrial engineers nor human resources managers but rather were trained in foreign languages, and this, plus their commitment to human rights, seems to be their principle qualification. As a result of this mixed background, many global brands organize training workshops for their compliance staff to better prepare them for their jobs. But this training, as helpful as it is, cannot fully compensate for the other structural problems inherent in the traditional compliance model.

Flawed Incentives? Whose Behavior Do We Want to Change, Anyway?

Yet even if all of the auditors we interviewed across the various supply chains we studied had been trained in a variety of different disciplines (i.e., human resources management, operations management, health and safety, human rights, etc.), and even if all the audits conducted by compliance staff were accurate and comprehensive, it is not at all clear that this information would succeed in changing factory workplace conditions. Consider how audit information is translated into purchasing decisions: fieldwork at suppliers working for global brands competing in different industries and located in different countries revealed that orders are often in the pipeline well before audits have been scheduled and that these global companies continue to place orders in many factories that have serious compliance issues. This reality does little to create the "right" incentives needed to shift the "calculus of compliance" by raising the cost of code violation above the cost of compliance and motivating steady improvements in factory conditions. While sourcing departments continue to squeeze factories on price, compress lead times, and demand high-quality standards, compliance officers visit the factories and document the problems but do little to change the root causes underlying poor working conditions. One auditor we interviewed reported that "if [the sourcing department] has already sold the sample before I set foot in the factory, I know that we will give them business no matter what."

Conversely, "good" factories are seldom rewarded by a sourcing strategy that is designed to seek out the cheapest sources of production rather than factories with the best working conditions. An executive at ABC's headquarters made it clear to us that in her division, pulling out of a factory or an entire region can be a matter of twenty cents per garment because the average price amounts to only $6.75.[28]

In summary, whereas the private compliance model assumes that working conditions in supplier factories can improve through a combination of audits and threats, our field research at the suppliers of several major global brands, competing in different industries and operating across the globe, illustrates the empirical weaknesses of these assumptions. In the private compliance model, accurate information collected through independent auditors informs global brands where to place their orders, and how best to reward (or punish) their suppliers for their compliance with the Code of Conduct. In reality, the information collected through the audits is biased, incomplete, and often inaccurate. As for using incentives to promote compliance, the threat of sanctions in the form of reduced orders for noncompliant suppliers is rarely enforced, and factories that systematically improve their working conditions are not always

---

[28] This price reflects the Free on Board, or FOB price, which denotes the price of the good minus its shipping to market. Companies vary on who (manufacturer or buyer) is responsible for the cost of shipping.

rewarded (again, in the form of increased orders). Even if this threat were enforced, it could create perverse outcomes by punishing workers along with management and removing any continued incentive for factories to improve working conditions.

To better illustrate the limitations of the private compliance model, we now turn to an examination of the compliance programs of two global corporations – ABC and Hewlett-Packard (HP) – competing in two very different industries (apparel vs. electronics) but both seen as leaders in corporate social responsibility. Given the visibility, reputation, and commitment expressed by both of these companies, we would expect that their compliance programs would be especially effective. In many ways, these two global corporations serve as "most likely" cases[29] for effective private compliance programs. However, as the brief case vignettes that follow illustrate, notwithstanding years spent by both corporations developing ever more comprehensive codes, monitoring tools, remediation plans; hiring growing numbers of internal compliance specialists; conducting hundreds of factory audits; and working with external consultants, NGOs, and industry groups, both companies' own data suggest that working conditions among their suppliers continue to face serious problems.

Private Compliance Efforts at ABC and HP

ABC

ABC is a major global apparel company that produces dress shirts, sportswear, outerwear, and other garments that are marketed under a variety of major brand names and private labels, ranging from low-cost goods to high-end fashion. The company began producing dress shirts as a small family firm in the late nineteenth century and gradually became a global leader by acquiring several well-known brands with their own product lines and retail operations. In response to increased, low-cost, foreign competition, ABC (like most of its competitors) initially shifted its manufacturing activities to lower cost countries in Latin America and Asia and eventually began outsourcing production to independent suppliers. In 2010, ABC's total revenue amounted to $4.6 billion, and the company sourced its products from more than 350 factories in 55 countries in the Americas, Asia, Europe, and Africa.

Like other global corporations, ABC's moves to cut labor costs and offshore production generated financial benefits for the company but also exposed it to the risks associated with sourcing production from low-cost factories with poor working conditions. In the early 1990s, one of ABC's factories in Central America became the target of a major six-year international labor-organizing

[handwritten margin note: "What are Risks"]

---

[29] For more on different approaches to selecting case studies, see Harry Eckstein, "Case Study and Theory in Political Science," in Harry Eckstein (Ed.), *Regarding Politics: Essays in Political Theory, Stability and Change* (Berkeley: University of California Press, 1991): 117–76.

campaign that brought together US and local labor, religious, and human rights advocacy groups.[30] These activists accused the company of paying wages that were below the poverty level and of repressing union-organizing drives through intimidation, bribery, excessive disciplinary actions, and threats of violence. The scandal hit ABC hard, because it cast doubt on the veracity of the company's efforts to promote itself as socially responsible. Along with the Levi-Strauss Company, ABC was in 1991 one of the first global corporations to develop a voluntary Code of Conduct for its suppliers. ABC was also a founding member of the Apparel Industry Partnership, a multistakeholder organization that included NGOs, apparel brands, and unions formed under the Clinton administration to regulate labor conditions in offshore factories.[31]

During the 1990s, ABC expanded its human rights program, developed an elaborate monitoring system to uncover violations of its code, hired a senior vice president for human rights, and built up its human rights group. This group now includes twenty-one full-time and twelve part-time staff to monitor suppliers for compliance with the company's Code of Conduct. Over time and through various efforts, ABC has established itself among the most socially responsible companies in the industry. Official company policy states that no orders will be placed with supplier factories that have not passed the company's human rights (Code of Conduct) audit. As a member of the FLA, ABC must submit to annual, external, independent audits of its suppliers to verify the robustness of ABC's monitoring, training, and auditing standards. The results of these external audits led to ABC's accreditation by the FLA, which stated: "the Board not only found them to be in compliance [with FLA requirements] but noted an exemplary display of leadership in the spirit of corporate responsibility." In short, all indications suggest that ABC takes its compliance program seriously, and other groups (e.g., the FLA) have held up ABC's compliance program as one of the best in the industry.[32]

Notwithstanding the significant public pressure on ABC to improve working conditions in its suppliers' factories and the efforts and resources ABC has dedicated to promoting compliance with its Code of Conduct, over the course of this research project, in which my students and I examined both ABC's

[30] See Ralph Armbruster-Sandoval, "Globalization and Transnational Labor Organizing: The Honduran Maquiladora Industry and the Kimi Campaign," *Social Science History* 27, no. 4 (2003): 551–76; Ralph Armbruster-Sandoval, *Globalization and Cross-Border Labor Solidarity in the Americas: The Anti-Sweatshop Movement and the Struggle for Social Justice* (New York: Routledge, 2005); Henry J. Frundt, "Central American Unions in the Era of Globalization," *Latin American Research Review* 37, no. 3 (2002): 7–53.

[31] The Apparel Industry Partnership subsequently became the Fair Labor Association (FLA), which remains active.

[32] ABC is at the forefront of private firms engaged in trying to govern labor standards. Although absolute levels of compliance may appear low, ABC maintains relatively high levels of compliance compared with other firms. Moreover, ABC's compliance program remains open to external monitoring and evaluation.

TABLE 2.1. *Compliance Status for ABC Active Suppliers as of May 2006*

	USA and Canada	Latin America and Caribbean	Europe, Middle East, Africa	South Asia	East Asia	Total
Approved	100%	74%	50%	14%	12%	24%
Requires follow-up	0%	22%	0%	27%	7%	14%
In progress	0%	4%	50%	3%	9%	8%
Not approved	0%	0%	0%	56%	72%	53%
Total number	100%	100%	100%	100%	100%	100%

factory audit reports and visited suppliers located in China, India, Bangladesh, the Dominican Republic, and Honduras, we found significant compliance issues among many of ABC's suppliers. For example, we analyzed the results of ABC's own audit data for the 210 factories that ABC reported to the FLA and were actively producing for ABC in May 2006.[33] Out of these 210 factories, only 51 (24 percent) were in full compliance with the company's Code of Conduct. Another 53 percent of these suppliers were explicitly "not approved," and 22 percent were categorized as either "in progress" or "requiring follow-up," meaning that some combination of "terminal," "significant," and/or "minor flaws," as described by the company's auditing protocol, were found during the audit, and thus, the factory should be placed on hold – not allowed to produce for ABC – until these issues were rectified. In East Asia, 72 percent of the factories actively supplying ABC were technically not approved to produce for the company. In South Asia, 56 percent of the active suppliers had not been approved by the Human Rights audit (see Table 2.1).

Violations of the code's health and safety, overtime, and work hours, as well as freedom of association provisions, were widespread not only in Asia but also across Latin America, Europe, and the Middle East. In 2009, of the

[33] This list of factories was developed by crossing ABC's internal factory database with the list of factories that ABC submits to FLA to be included in FLA's external auditing program. We were unable to directly use ABC's complete internal database, which includes data on 1,311 factories because many factories no longer producing for ABC were not correctly coded as inactive, thus distorting the analysis by including many factories that are in fact out of the compliance system. By using the FLA list, we were able to correct for this data problem in ABC's internal data and make a more conservative estimate of the factories that are indeed in ABC's compliance program. If anything, these data likely overstate the degree of compliance in ABC's factories because they do not include "licensee" factories that are not submitted to FLA. However, by making a conservative estimate noncompliance, these data show that there is a large mismatch between ABC's policy and its own estimates of factory compliance.

306 "active" factories supplying ABC, only 70 were "in compliance," with the remaining 236 requiring some form of follow-up, remediation, or warning. Our field research at ABC's suppliers in both Asia and Latin America revealed that ABC's compliance program faced many of the challenges described earlier in this chapter – incomplete information generated by faulty factory audits, flawed incentives in terms of not always rewarding suppliers that demonstrate improvements in their working conditions while continuing to work with other factories that had persistent problems in terms of wages, working conditions, excess working hours, and so on – and this from a company that is held up as a leader in social responsibility by multistakeholder initiatives like the FLA. Our field research on HP, a high-tech company competing in a completely different market than ABC, also uncovered remarkably similar patterns of noncompliance.

Hewlett-Packard

HP is a leading electronics firm with a globally dispersed supply base and a strong commitment to social and environmental responsibility. In fiscal year 2010, HP shipped in excess of 64 million personal computers and employed approximately 325,000 individuals in 170 countries. It has four operating divisions: Imaging and Printing, Personal Systems Group, Enterprise Business, and Financial Services. During fiscal year 2010, HP operated in more than 170 countries, contracting with approximately 1,000 suppliers in more than 1,200 locations. These suppliers provide product materials and components, in addition to manufacturing and distribution services. Most suppliers for HP are located in developing countries in four main geographical regions: Asia Pacific, Central and Eastern Europe, Greater China, and Latin America.

Established in 1939, HP has been committed to social and environmental issues throughout its history. The "HP Way" refers to a management philosophy that emphasizes integrity, respect for individuals, teamwork, innovation, and contribution to customers and the community (Packard 2006). Although HP has a history of union avoidance at its facilities, it has exhibited a strong and longstanding commitment to social and environmental responsibility.[34] Consistent with this culture, HP became an early advocate of global labor standards. For instance, in the late 1990s HP relocated printer-manufacturing activities that were previously based in Vancouver, Washington, to outsourced production locations overseas; as HP engineers supervised this transition, they became aware of the consistently poor working conditions and absence of labor

---

[34] Although HP has avoided unionization of its own facilities, the firm mandates that its suppliers respect local laws pertaining to freedom of association and collective bargaining. HP's 2009 Code of Conduct (version 3.01) reads: "Participants are to respect the rights of workers as established by local law to associate freely on a voluntary basis, seek representation, join or be represented by Works Councils, and join or not join labor unions and bargain collectively as they choose" (HP 2009: 3).

standards within select supply chain partners. During one supplier visit, these engineers took multiple photographs surreptitiously, which they then assembled into an album and distributed internally within the company. In 2002, the company developed its first supplier Code of Conduct in response to both this internal mobilization and to external pressures from NGOs and other civil society groups concerned about labor conditions in the industry. This was the first Code of Conduct in the electronics industry and provided an important foundation for the industry-wide standards that were later established through the Electronics Industry Citizenship Coalition (EICC).

The EICC was established in 2004 when eight leading electronics firms, including HP, sought to improve the working conditions and environmental impacts of their suppliers through the development of an industry-wide Code of Conduct. By 2008, EICC membership had grown to include forty-five firms with a collective 1.2 trillion in revenue, employing 3.4 million workers (EICC 2009a). EICC-affiliated firms require their suppliers (and in some cases, their own facilities) to comply with the EICC code. The first EICC code was developed in 2004, and has since been revised three times, the most recent revision occurring in 2011. Although the code was initially implemented more or less independently by each member of the EICC, firms affiliated with the EICC have made significant progress over time to coordinate their efforts by moving toward a common pool of auditors and sharing audit results in an effort to reduce audit fatigue among suppliers and eliminate conflicting standards, two issues that often hamper private monitoring efforts (O'Rourke 2002; Nadvi and Wältring 2004).

The code is divided into seven sections, the first covers broad Code of Conduct compliance issues and is followed by six more specific sections addressing labor, health, the environment, labor management, environmental health and safety management, and ethics. Audits across suppliers and national settings are based on an evaluation of fifty-three EICC items that are independently assessed for compliance outcomes, and first-time audits usually take two days to complete. Depending on severity, issues may be flagged as a "major violation," "minor violation," or "observation." A major violation (also referred to as "nonconformance") refers to the inability of a supplier's management system to comply with a core EICC standard. Select major nonconformances can also be denoted as zero-tolerance items. Such issues include the utilization of underage workers, forced labor, health and safety issues posing immediate danger or serious injury, and violation of environmental laws posing serious and immediate harm to the community. Minor violations refer to more isolated concerns such as a temporarily blocked emergency exit or missing safety equipment. Finally, observations are generally a recognition that a superior means of documenting or monitoring a process or procedure may exist. Audit items flagged as observations are not considered a code violation.

As part of this research project, HP shared their internal audit data containing both quantitative compliance data and qualitative evaluations, gleaned

TABLE 2.2. *Hewlett-Packard – Fully Compliant Facilities by Region and Issue*

	Asia Pacific		CE Europe		Greater China		Latin America	
	Total	% of Total	Total	% of Total	Total	% of Total	Total	% of Total
All sections (full compliance)	4	6.1%	1	4%	1	0.7%	1	2.8%
All sections (no major violation)	21	31.8%	9	36%	2	1.3%	13	36.1%
Labor (full compliance)	34	51.5%	22	88%	8	5.4%	9	25%
Labor (no major violation)	42	63.6%	23	92%	16	10.7%	26	72.2%
Health and safety (full)	20	30.3%	5	20%	4	2.7%	11	30.6%
Health and safety (no major violation)	46	69.7%	17	68%	36	24.2%	18	50%
Environment (full compliance)	26	39.4%	12	48%	14	9.4%	14	38.9%
Environment (no major violations)	47	71.2%	21	84%	62	41.6%	22	61.1%
Labor management system (full compliance)	26	39.4%	14	56%	17	11.4%	5	13.9%
Labor mgm system (no major violations)	57	86.4%	23	92%	110	73.8%	26	72.2%
H&S management system (full compliance)	22	33.3%	8	32%	36	24.2%	12	33.3%
H&S mgm system (no major violations)	55	83.3%	23	92%	119	79.9%	30	83.3%
Total	66	100%	25	100%	149	100%	36	100%

from on-site evaluations of 276 globally dispersed suppliers from 2003 through 2009. An analysis of HP's internal audit reports show that most of HP's suppliers have several nonconformances with the code, even after several years of engagement by HP's internal corporate responsibility program. In fact, only seven of HP's almost 300 suppliers were in complete compliance with the EICC code. Moreover, the audits suggest a significant variation in the frequency, magnitude, and type of code violations across geographic regions (see Table 2.2).

Thus, ABC is not the only company that has experienced difficulties in promoting improved working conditions and labor rights among its suppliers through private compliance programs; other major global corporations with different histories and cultures and competing in very different industries have had trouble as well. How can companies as diverse as ABC and HP – both of which have clearly invested significant resources and time in developing their compliance programs – continue to struggle with labor rights violations within their respective supply chains?[35] What, if anything, can be done to improve this situation? The next chapter addresses these questions through an in-depth case study of Nike, the world's largest branded athletic footwear and apparel company and a central player in the controversies surrounding labor standards and private compliance programs in global supply chains. Chapter 3 documents Nike's difficulties in promoting improved working conditions and labor standards among its suppliers through its own sophisticated compliance program – difficulties that are remarkably similar to those described in this chapter. Yet, the case study of Nike will also illustrate the conditions under which private compliance programs, when combined with other capability-building initiatives and supported by strong public institutions and laws, can actually drive sustained improvements in employment practices and labor standards among its suppliers.

---

[35] The limitations of private compliance programs are by no means unique to ABC or HP but rather characterize the experiences of other leading firms competing in an array of different industries. See Xiaomin Yu, "Impact of Corporate Code of Conduct on Labor Standards: A Case Study of Reebok's Athletic Footwear Supplier Factory in China," *Journal of Business Ethics* 81 (2008): 513–29; Niklas Egels-Zandén, "Suppliers' Compliance with MNC's Codes of Conduct: Behind the Scenes at Chinese Toy Suppliers," *Journal of Business Ethics* 78 (2007): 45–62; Tanya Korovkin and Olga Sanmiguel-Valderrama, "Labour Standards, Global Markets, and Non-State Initiatives: Colombia's and Ecuador's Flower Industries in comparative perspective," *Third World Quarterly* 28, no. 1 (2007): 117–35; and Stephanie Barrientos and Sally Smith, "Do Workers Benefit from Ethical Trade? Assessing Codes of Labour Practice in Global Production Systems." *Third World Quarterly*, 28, no. 4 (2007): 713–29.

3

Does Private Compliance Improve Labor Standards?

Lessons from Nike

What role can corporate codes of conduct and private compliance programs play in improving working conditions in global supply chains? How does this system of private voluntary regulation relate to other strategies and regulatory approaches aimed at enforcing labor standards? This chapter builds on the more general overview presented in Chapter 2 and addresses these questions through a detailed case study of Nike, the world's largest athletic footwear and apparel company. Given the central and highly controversial place Nike occupies in debates over globalization and labor standards, it serves in many ways as a "crucial case" through which to explore the effect of private compliance initiatives on labor standards in global supply chains.[1] Using a unique data set based on factory audits of working conditions in more than 900 of Nike's suppliers located across fifty countries, plus field research at Nike suppliers in China, Turkey, Mexico, and the United States, this chapter illustrates both the potential and limitations of this model of private voluntary regulation.

The core empirical analysis presented in this chapter addresses three basic questions. First, how bad (or good) are working conditions at Nike's various suppliers? Second, what determines variation in working conditions among these suppliers? (In other words, what accounts for the greatly differing working conditions across factories producing more or less the same products for the same brand?) We need to understand the baseline working conditions (and the determinants of these conditions) at these factories to assess whether private compliance initiatives have any effect on improvements in labor standards. And third, are working conditions improving over time at these factories, and if so, what role does private compliance play in these improvements? The case study of Nike will shed light on the limits of traditional private compliance programs and also elucidate how under certain conditions – long-term

---

[1] For more on "crucial" case methodology, see Eckstein (1991).

relationships, frequent interactions, and strategic partnerships between global buyers like Nike and their suppliers – these private initiatives can promote significant improvements in labor standards. Moreover, the analysis presented in this chapter shows how strong public institutions and laws support and enhance the effectiveness of these private voluntary programs. The chapter concludes by pondering the broader implications of these findings for efforts aimed at improving working conditions and enforcing labor through private voluntary programs.

Nike and the Athletic Footwear Industry

The athletic footwear industry has experienced explosive growth over the past two decades. In 1985, consumers in the United States alone spent $5 billion and purchased 250 million pairs of shoes (Korzeniewicz 1994). In 2009, they spent more than $17 billion on athletic footwear (National Sporting Goods Association 2010). Although the industry is highly segmented – by different sports, models, and price – the branded shoe market is dominated by a few large companies: Nike and Adidas alone account for almost 60 percent of the global athletic footwear market (Channel News Asia 2008). Since displacing Adidas and Reebok in the 1980s, Nike has become the largest and most important athletic shoe company in the world. Even after the merger between Reebok and Adidas, Nike still controls more than 36 percent of the global athletic footwear market (Channel News Asia 2008).

Founded as Blue Ribbon Sports (BRS) in 1964 by Phil Knight and Bill Bowerman, each of whom invested $500 in the start-up, the company has evolved from an importer and distributor of Japanese specialty running shoes to the world leader in the design, distribution, and marketing of athletic footwear. According to company legend, Nike's business model was developed by Knight while he attended Stanford Business School in the early 1960s. Knight realized that while lower-cost Japanese producers were beginning to take over the US consumer appliance and electronics markets, most leading footwear companies (for example, Reebok and Converse) were still manufacturing their own shoes in higher-cost countries like the United States. By designing and marketing high-performance athletic shoes in the United States but outsourcing production to lower-cost Japanese producers, Knight believed that Blue Ribbon Sports could undersell its competitors and break into this market. As a result, Blue Ribbon Sports began to import high-tech sports shoes from Onitsuka Tiger of Japan. As sales increased to almost $2 million in the early 1970s, BRS parted ways with Onitsuka. The Nike brand was launched in 1972, and the company officially changed its name to Nike, Inc. in 1978.

Nike developed a strong working relationship with two Japanese shoe manufacturers, Nippon Rubber and Nihon-Koyo, but as costs increased in Japan during the 1970s (due to a combination of a tighter labor market, the impact of the first oil crisis on Japan's economy, and a shift in the dollar/yen exchange rate as a result of the so-called Nixon shock),[2] Nike began to search for alternative, lower-cost producers. During the same period, Nike opened up its own shoe factories in Maine and New Hampshire, hoping to develop a reliable local source to supply its growing domestic market, but also began to cultivate suppliers in Korea, Thailand, China, and Taiwan. By the mid-1980s, as costs continued to increase in both Japan and the United States and as the Korean and Taiwanese governments created a number of incentives to develop their footwear industries,[3] Nike closed its US factories and sourced almost all of its production from Asia. By 1982, 86 percent of Nike's athletic footwear came from Korea and Taiwan.[4]

Over time, as Korea and Taiwan also began to develop, costs began to rise in these countries as well, and Nike urged its suppliers to relocate their operations to other, lower-cost countries. The company worked with its lead suppliers to open up manufacturing plants in Indonesia, China, and Vietnam. By guaranteeing abundant orders and placing Nike employees at these new factories to help monitor product quality and production processes, Nike was able to help its lead vendors establish an extensive network of footwear factories throughout Southeast Asia. By 2011, Nike's products were manufactured in 930 factories in fifty countries, employing more than one million workers (Nike 2012: 50). Nike itself employs about 38,000 direct employees, the vast majority of which work in the United States (Nike 2012: 8). In 2010, the company made about US$19 billion in revenues, of which $10.3 billion came from footwear sales and $5 billion from apparel (Nike 2010b: 92).

Although it is still primarily known as a footwear company, Nike competes in other, very different sectors. Only 73 of its 930 suppliers are producing shoes, and most of these suppliers are located in Asia. In contrast, Nike apparel products are manufactured in 529 factories distributed throughout the world (Nike 2012: 31). These differences are due both to the rules governing international trade in the two industries and to the underlying nature of these industries: footwear factories are usually large, capital-intensive facilities, whereas garment factories are usually smaller, easy-to-establish, and extremely labor-intensive operations. Whereas footwear quotas were eliminated by the mid- to late 1980s (leading to a consolidation of the industry), until January 2005, the garment trade was very much shaped by quotas (the Multi-Fiber Arrangement). Even today various tariffs and "voluntary" export restrictions between China and both the European Union and the United States have prevented the formation of a truly "free market" in garments.

[2] For more on these years, see Murukami (1987).
[3] These and other government incentive programs are nicely described in Amsden (1989). See also Brian Levy, "Transaction Costs, the Size of Firms and Industrial Policy: Lessons from a Comparative Case Study of the Footwear Industry in Korea and Taiwan," *Journal of Development Economics* (November 1991): 151–78.
[4] For more on the evolution of Nike's strategy, see Christensen and Rikert (1984), Rosenzweig (1994), and Strasser and Becklund (1991).

These industry differences strongly conditioned the kinds of relationships that Nike developed with its various suppliers. For example, in footwear, Nike was able to develop long-term relations with several large Korean and Taiwanese firms. When Nike designers create new footwear designs and styles for upcoming seasons, this information is relayed to some of these partnering suppliers, who, in turn, develop the prototypes. Once these prototypes are approved, these lead suppliers send the product specifications to their various plants throughout Southeast Asia, where production can take place almost immediately. This level of trust and coordination facilitates both production and (presumably) compliance activities for Nike. In apparel, given short product cycles and volatile fashion trends, the situation is completely different. Nike works with numerous suppliers, most of which are also producing apparel in the same factories for other (often, competitor) companies. Because of the tendency of different apparel suppliers to specialize in particular products or market segments, together with the rapidity of shifts in consumer preferences or fashion trends, Nike sometimes enters into very short-term contracts with these companies, and may place limited orders. The result is diminished influence over these suppliers and, in particular, diminished ability to regularly monitor the production processes and working conditions at the suppliers' factories.

The same strategies that permitted Nike to grow at an impressive rate over the past several decades – taking advantage of global sourcing opportunities to produce lower-cost products and investing these savings in innovative designs and marketing campaigns – have also created serious problems for the company. As early as the 1980s, Nike was criticized for sourcing its products in factories and countries where low wages, poor working conditions, and human rights problems were rampant. Then, over the course of the 1990s, a series of public relations nightmares – involving underpaid workers in Indonesia, child labor in Cambodia and Pakistan, and poor working conditions in China and Vietnam – tarnished Nike's image. As Phil Knight lamented in a May 1998 speech to the National Press Club, "The Nike product has become synonymous with slave wages, forced overtime, and arbitrary abuse."[5]

At first, Nike managers took a defensive position when confronted with the various labor, environmental, and occupational health problems found at their suppliers' plants: workers at these factories were not Nike employees, and thus Nike felt no responsibility toward them. By 1992, this hands-off approach changed as Nike formulated its Code of Conduct, requiring its suppliers to observe some basic labor, environmental, and health and safety standards. (See Appendix 3.1 for the most recent version of Nike's Code of Conduct.) All suppliers – current and potential – are obligated to sign this Code of Conduct and post it within their factories. Over time, Nike adjusted its Code of Conduct as a result of its own experiences with monitoring and its evolving understanding

---

[5] Detail about these events can be found in Locke (2003).

of how best to strengthen its compliance program, and in response to external critics who argued that Nike was not doing enough to address workplace issues among its suppliers. For example, in 1998, Nike increased the minimum age for footwear factory workers to eighteen and for apparel workers to sixteen. It has also insisted that all footwear suppliers adopt US Occupational Safety and Health Administration standards for indoor air quality.

To enforce compliance with its Code of Conduct, Nike conducted numerous training sessions with its suppliers, and by 2005, it assembled a team of ninety compliance staff based in twenty-one countries to monitor these suppliers.[6] By 2009, Nike employed 120 people who dedicated a substantial amount of their time on compliance.[7] In recent years, Nike has reorganized its compliance program and integrated it with its sustainability group. In addition to these compliance specialists, Nike also employed about 1,000 production specialists working at or with its various global suppliers. All Nike personnel responsible for either production or compliance received training in Nike's Code of Conduct, Labor Practices, and Cross-Cultural Awareness policy, as well as in its Safety, Health, Attitudes of Management, People Investment and Environment (SHAPE) program.[8]

In addition to the initial, new source approval process that all potential suppliers of Nike must undergo,[9] all factories were, until recently, subjected to three different types of audit: a basic environmental, safety and health (SHAPE) audit, a more in-depth management and working conditions audit (M-Audit), and periodic inspections by the Fair Labor Association (FLA). The SHAPE inspection was rolled out in 1997 and was typically performed by Nike's field-based production and sourcing staff. The goal of this audit was to provide a general picture of the factory's compliance with labor, environment, and safety and health standards.

Launched in the summer of 2002, the M-Audit was the most rigorous of Nike's audits and was seen as the core of its compliance program. The M-Audit, always conducted by Nike's in-house compliance specialists, provided in-depth assessment of the labor-management practices and working conditions at the factories. A typical M-Audit took forty-eight hours to complete, was spread out over several days, and was announced beforehand. Each M-Audit reported a numeric score (0–100), where a score of 100 meant that the factory was in full compliance with Nike's Code of Conduct. The M-Audit covered more than eighty items, focused on hiring practices, worker treatment, worker-management communications, and compensation. Each item accounted for a specific weighting with respect to the overall score. As a result

---

[6] See Chapter 4 of Nike (2005).

[7] Nike (2010a): 24.

[8] The evolution of Nike's corporate responsibility practices is nicely described in Zadek (2004).

[9] In 2004, only 57 percent of factories that underwent this process were approved. See Nike (2005: 18) for more on this process.

of this scoring system, factories with different types of problems or mixes of compliance issues could receive similar overall scores.[10]

Independent monitoring by the FLA, of which Nike is a member, was also conducted on a sample (5 percent) of Nike suppliers every year. The FLA is a multistakeholder initiative that brings together companies, universities, and NGOs and supervises independent monitors' unannounced inspections of supplier factories. All FLA reports, with the individual factory identities masked, are made public on the organization's website (www.fairlabor.org).

As part of this research project, Nike provided data from all three of the above audits, as well as from its Compliance Rating program. Most of the data presented in this chapter focuses on the late 1990s through 2005, the period when traditional compliance efforts at Nike and other major corporations were at their heyday. However, several of these programs have evolved over time, and whenever possible, we have updated our analyses with more recent compliance data obtained from Nike. Because of the mixed quality of the SHAPE audits and the limited numbers of the FLA audits, this chapter focuses on data derived from the M-Audits and the Compliance Rating program. In addition, Nike provided access to its sourcing database, which includes descriptive information (age of facility, total number of employees working at the facility, nationality of the owners of the facilities, and so on) for each factory producing goods for the company.

Does Private Compliance Work? A Look at the Data

Using data from Nike's M-Audits and the Compliance Rating program, this section addresses three questions raised in the previous chapter concerning private compliance programs and their impact on workplace conditions in global supply chain factories.[11] First, using systematic data collected by Nike's compliance staff, what can we learn about the actual conditions in these factories? Second, if the data reveal variation in working conditions among Nike's suppliers, what accounts for this variation? Why do factories producing more or less the same goods for the same brand treat their workers so differently? And third, are working conditions improving over time in these factories? Given Nike's large investments in its various compliance efforts since the late 1990s, how successful have these remediation efforts been?

---

[10] For more on the M-Audit and its scoring system, see Nike (2005): 35–6.

[11] This section draws on a previous article, "Does Monitoring Improve Labor Standards? Lessons from Nike," that I published with two graduate students, Fei Qin and Alberto Brause (Locke, Qin, Brause, 2007). As a result, when discussing the analyses, I often use the pronoun "we" to give fair credit to my collaborators. One possible limitation of our analysis is that it is based on internal company audits and thus may be biased in favor of the company. However, as the following analyses will illustrate, these data nonetheless reveal serious issues with working conditions and labor rights among Nike's suppliers. Thus, although we cannot completely rule out the lack of bias in our data, we can also show that these audit reports were not completely "cleaned up" for external audiences.

TABLE 3.1. *Summary Statistics of M-Audit Scores, 2002–2005*

	Mean	SD	Number of Observations
Apparel	0.66 (.008)	0.15	357
Footwear	0.68 (.02)	0.17	64
Equipment	0.64 (.015)	0.16	109
Total	0.65 (.007)	0.16	575[12]

$F(2,572) = 1.35$ Prob $> F = 0.26$.
Bartlett's test for equal variances: $\chi 2(2) = 3.3183$ Prob $> \chi 2 = 0.190$.
Note: Standard errors are in parentheses.

How Good or Bad Are Working Conditions?

To begin to address the question of what actual working conditions are like, we first turn to some descriptive data on Nike's supply base, derived from the M-Audit database. As described earlier, each M-Audit reports a numeric score (0–100) that represents a percentage against a perfect compliance score. A score of 100 indicates that the individual factory is in full compliance with Nike's Code of Conduct. Table 3.1 presents the mean scores and standard deviations for all factories (575) that underwent M-Audits in Nike's three major lines of business (footwear, apparel, and equipment) between 2002 and 2005. Because this program was launched in the summer of 2002 and because audits are time-consuming, not all Nike suppliers had undergone an M-Audit at the time the company shared its data. The data presented here indicate that the performance of Nike's suppliers, although not perfect (a score of 100), was also not horrible (a score of 0). This suggests that although not all Nike suppliers are perfect workplaces, neither are most of them "sweatshops."

In fact, as illustrated in Figure 3.1, there was considerable variation in performance on the M-Audit across Nike's supply base. Factories' scores ranged from 20 percent to a near-perfect (90 percent) score. Figure 3.2 reveals that this pattern of variation cuts across the major product lines of Nike.

In other words, regardless of what the factory was producing, whether garments or footwear or even some types of sports equipment, compliance scores varied from near-perfect compliance to very poor performance.

Noncompliance among Nike suppliers persists through many years of auditing. More recent compliance rating data, which uses letter grades as opposed to numerical scores to measure factory compliance, shows that over the 2009–12 period the proportion of A-grade facilities has fallen over time, with most

---

[12] Forty-five additional factories received an M-Audit but we were unable to classify them by industry. Thus, they are included in the total but not in the industry columns.

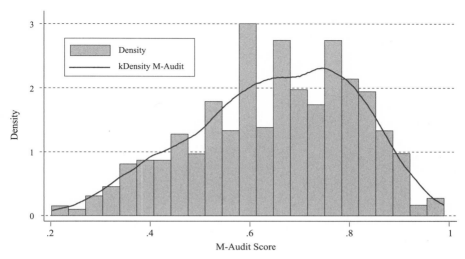

FIGURE 3.1. Distribution of M-Audit scores, 2002–5.

facilities clustering around grades of B and C.[13] In short, after a decade of auditing, many problems remain in Nike's supply chain.

When analyzing these data along geographic lines to see how factory performance on the M-Audit may have been shaped by the region in which the factories are located, we found more pronounced variation. Factories located in the Americas and the Europe/Middle East/Africa (EMEA) region almost always performed above 50 percent on the M-Audit and often closer to 100 percent. However, in the North Asian (which includes China and Vietnam) and South Asian (which includes Indonesia and India) regions, the M-Audit scores were much more dispersed.[14] Figure 3.4 illustrate this regional variation for the period 2002–5.

Thus, we observe that working conditions at Nike's suppliers (as expressed through their compliance scores) exhibited a large degree of variation across factories in the world. These regional patterns in compliance have also persisted over time. Compliance data from 2011 shows higher compliance in the

[13] In this new scoring system, an A grade indicates that the factory is "fully compliant" with Nike's Code of Conduct, and a B grade indicates that the factory is "mostly compliant" with only isolated violations of M-Audit standards. A grade of C, however, indicates that the factory is "noncompliant" and has serious system failures (e.g., not providing employees with formal employment contracts, occasionally using underage workers, violating local laws governing the use of migrant workers). A D grade indicates that the factory is not only "noncompliant" but is unable or unwilling to redress its compliance issues and demonstrates a general disregard for Nike's codes and standards. For more on this updated scoring of Nike's audits, see Nike 2010a: 44.

[14] We examine the Americas, the EMEA, North Asia, and South Asia because these are the four macroregions Nike employs (and denotes) to organize its operations.

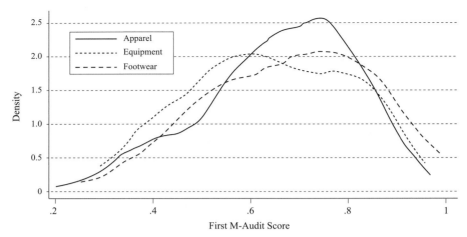

FIGURE 3.2. First M-Audit score by product type.

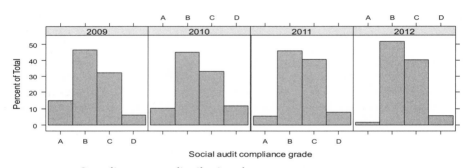

FIGURE 3.3. Compliance score distributions by year, 2009–12.

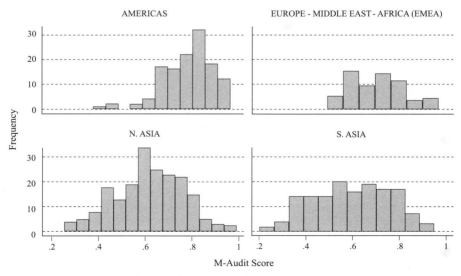

FIGURE 3.4. First M-Audit score by region (2002–5).

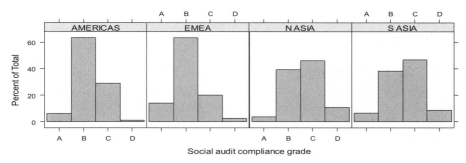

FIGURE 3.5. Compliance score distributions by region, 2011.

Americas and EMEA. Asian facilities continue to lag behind, with mean compliance scores closer to C than B.

In short, based on an analysis of Nike's own factory audit data of more than 900 factories located in fifty countries for the years 2002–12, we see that some of their suppliers' factories are in or close to full compliance with the company's Code of Conduct, while others suffer from endemic problems including low wages, unsafe working conditions, excessive work hours, harassment, and so on. Even within regions – within individual countries, in fact – labor standards, as captured by both the earlier M-Audit scores and later compliance grades, varied tremendously. How do we explain this variation? In other words, why did factories that made more or less the same products for the same brand treat their workers so differently?

Explaining the Variation in M-Audit Scores

To explain variation in working conditions and labor standards indicated by the M-Audit scores, we employed a two-step model. To isolate actual workplace conditions (as measured by the compliance score) from the potential impact of the monitoring process, we first examined the variation of the *initial* M-Audit[15] scores across factories, using an ordinary least squares model. In this model, we considered two principal groups of independent variables: factory characteristics and the supplier factory's relationship with Nike.

Factory characteristics. The literature on private compliance suggests that a variety of factors – ownership, size of plant, and the type, complexity, and price of the product being manufactured – may all affect labor conditions

---

[15] We analyze initial scores rather than panel data here so that we can isolate actual workplace conditions (as indicated by compliance score) from the potential impact of the monitoring process. A factory's second M-Audit score may be influenced by its having been audited once already. It would thus be difficult to include the second M-Audit score in the study of the cross-sectional variation of the actual workplace conditions without explicitly modeling the impact of the monitoring process on the second M-Audit outcome.

in the factories. Some have speculated that factories owned and managed by foreigners treat their workers worse (for a variety of linguistic and cultural reasons) than do factories whose owners and managers share the workers' nationality.[16] Others have claimed that larger, more bureaucratic, "modern" factories, are in a better position to treat their workers well than smaller, less formally managed plants, because they can introduce modern management and personnel systems (Moran 2002:16). Finally, much has been written about the importance of skill and tacit knowledge in the production of differentiated, high-value added products. From this, we speculate that perhaps factories producing more complex (and expensive) products, which require more skilled labor, will treat their workers as valuable assets (Piore and Sabel 1984; Kochan et al. 1986). We investigated whether factory ownership (foreign-owned as opposed to domestic-owned), factory size, and product type (footwear, apparel, or equipment) may all affect compliance.

Relationship with Nike. The second major dimension we investigated was the relationship between the supplier factory and Nike. Frenkel and Scott (2002) have argued that brands develop two distinct types of compliance relationships with their suppliers: a hands-on, cooperative relationship with some suppliers, and an arms-length, more distrustful "compliance" relationship with others. These differences, according to Frenkel and Scott, can shape not only the style but also the substance of compliance programs within the factories. Gereffi, Humphrey, and Sturgeon (2005) have described different relations of power between suppliers and global buyers in different types of global value chains. When transactions take place through competitive markets or suppliers depend on a few customers, buyers have more power over their suppliers and thus can dictate the terms of the contracts. On the other hand, when suppliers have unique capabilities that cannot be easily transferred to competitors, they retain some power with respect to their buyers. Applying this framework to private monitoring schemes, we would expect higher levels of compliance among suppliers that are more dependent on Nike for their business or produce more commoditized goods. Conversely, if suppliers possess unique skills or produce specialized products that cannot be easily found in the market, we would expect that they have more power to resist Nike's compliance pressures. To evaluate whether these patterns exist, we investigated both the *length of time* Nike has been contracting with the supplier (on the assumption that the longer the business relationship, the greater the "trust" between Nike and the individual supplier) and whether the supplier was designated by Nike as a *strategic partner*. Strategic partners for Nike either possess unique capabilities and are involved in collaborative design and product development processes (in footwear) or are permitted to source their own materials and are seen

---

[16] A variation of this argument is advanced by Mosley (2010), who argues that labor rights at plants owned by multinational corporations are better protected and respected than at outsourced, contractor factories.

as long-term partners (in apparel). Mixed labor compliance among strategic partners might be expected, because some of them have more power to resist Nike's demands for low-cost, high-quality products made under sweat-free conditions.[17]

To further assess the relationship between Nike and its suppliers, we investigated the *amount of capacity the factory dedicates to Nike* (as opposed to other brands) and the *number of visits Nike personnel (compliance and production) make to the factories in any one year.* We hypothesized that if a factory dedicates more capacity to Nike, it would be more vulnerable to Nike's demands, and thus its labor compliance (M-Audit) score should be higher. In addition, given the importance information collected through audits plays in the private compliance model and that some scholars have reported that increased frequency of labor inspections led to improved workplace conditions and code compliance (Esbenshade 2004, Chapter 3), we hypothesized that the more frequently a factory was audited, the better its record of compliance (as expressed by a higher M-Audit score).

Country and Industry Effects

Earlier, we saw tremendous variation in M-Audit scores by region. To seek to understand what might be driving this pattern, we investigate the "country effect" on compliance scores by employing the Rule of Law Index from the World Bank's World Wide Governance Indicators[18] as a proxy for a country's legal and regulatory environment. The Rule of Law Index[19] measures the extent to which agents have confidence in and abide by the rules of a given country (Kaufmann et al. 2004). The measures include perceptions of crime incidence, the effectiveness and predictability of the judiciary, and the enforceability of contracts. The index is measured in units ranging from -2.5 to 2.5, where higher values correspond to better governance outcomes. To control for the industry effect, we first looked at all Nike suppliers and then inserted industry dummy variables for footwear, apparel, and equipment. We also looked at within-industry variation. Table 3.2 presents the summary statistics of these different independent variables.

---

[17] Of course, an alternative to the global value chain (view of power relations within supply chains) is Charles Sabel's work on how buyer–supplier collaboration in manufacturing and design can lead to innovation and the development of trustlike relations; see Sabel (1994).

[18] The World Bank's Worldwide Governance Indicators project defines governance as the set of traditions and institutions through which authority in a country is exercised. The political, economic, and institutional dimensions of governance are captured by six aggregate indicators: voice and accountability, political stability and absence of violence, government effectiveness, regulatory quality, rule of law, and control of corruption. For detailed construction, see Kaufmann, Kraay, and Mastruzzi (2006).

[19] We also considered other governance indices in the Worldwide Governance Indicators and other country-level indicators. We get similar qualitative results. In Appendix 3.3, we present the regression values that result when we replace the rule of law index by the Economic Freedom index compiled by the Heritage Foundation.

TABLE 3.2. *Summary Statistics of Selected Independent Variables*

	Mean	SD
Total number of employees	1095	1952
Ownership (1 = foreign, 0 = local)	0.37	0.48
Strategic partner (1 = yes, 0 = no)	0.19	0.39
Number of SHAPE visits	5.52	4.49
Months with Nike	60.4	58.0
Percentage for Nike	47.3%	33.6%
Apparel	0.67	0.47
Footwear	0.12	0.33
Equipment	0.21	0.40
Index of rule of law of factory country	0.11	0.74

The different variables were combined in the following OLS model: (1.1)

M-Audit = a_0 + a_1 Log total employees + a_2.(ownership)
a_3.(number of visits by Nike) + a_4.(strategic partnership)
a_5.(duration of relationship with Nike) + a_6.(percentage for Nike)
   + a_7.(rule of law) + a_8.(apparel) + a_9.(footwear) + ¡.

Using OLS regressions, we next sought to determine whether composite M-Audit scores are correlated with dimensions of factory characteristics and/or with the closeness of the relationship between the supplier and Nike. Consistent with the conceptual model, we focused on the initial M-Audit scores of the individual factories. The results are reported in Table 3.3. We also examined the relationship between individual components of the M-Audit (such as wages and work hours) and different dimensions of factory characteristics and different levels of the relationship with Nike, and found consistent results. These are reported in Appendix 3.5.

The regression analyses suggest the following:

1. *At the country level*, the strength of a country's regulations and institutions (using the Rule of Law Index as a proxy) has a positive relationship with M-Audit scores. The first column in Table 3.3 shows that the Rule of Law Index itself explains 11 percent of the variation in first M-Audit score. Even when the analysis controls for regional effects (the Americas vs. South Asia), the coefficient on the Rule of Law result, although reduced by about one-third, remains statistically significant. This suggests that factories located in countries with better legal or regulatory environments did better, on average, in labor compliance. I return to the potentially important implications of this finding for the efficacy of private voluntary regulation later in this chapter.

2. Controlling for country and industry variables, *at the factory level*, there exists a statistically significant negative relationship between factory

TABLE 3.3. *Ordinary Least Squares models of M-Audit Scores, 2002–4*

	(1)	(2)	(3)	(4)	(5)
Rule of Law	.074***	.04***	.045***	.047***	.027*
Index	(.0086)	(.0084)	(.013)	(.013)	(.011)
Log no. of			−.025***	−.022**	−.0133*
employees			(.007)	(.007)	(.0068)
Foreign owned			−.03†	−.025	−.019
			(.017)	(.017)	(.016)
No. of SHAPE			.002	.002	.0038†
visits			(.002)	(.002)	(.002)
Strategic			.047*	.05*	.002
partner			(.021)	(.02)	(.020)
Months with			−.00034†	−.00034†	−.000014
Nike			(.0002)	(.0002)	(.0002)
Percentage for			−.071**	−.066**	−.031
Nike			(.026)	(.027)	(.025)
Apparel			−.008	.014	−.0035
			(.019)	(.019)	(.018)
Footwear			.12***	.12***	.088**
			(.035)	(.035)	(.03)
Region: EMEA		−.061**			−.081***
		(.022)			(.024)
Region: North		−.14***			−.16***
Asia		(.016)			(.021)
Region: South		−.17***			−.18***
Asia		(.017)			(.022)
Year 2003				.046*	
				(.023)	
Year 2004				.071**	
				(.028)	
Constant	.64***	.75***	.82***	.75***	.85***
	(.064)	(.013)	(.045)	(.054)	(.04)
Observations	568	568	355	355	355
R^2	0.11	0.27	0.21	0.23	0.36

EMEA = Europe/Middle East/Africa.
Significance levels: †$p < .1$, *$p < .05$, **$p < .01$, ***$p < .001$.

size, measured by total number of employees, and M-Audit performance. This suggests that working conditions in smaller factories were better than in larger factories.[20] One possible explanation for this somewhat counterintuitive

[20] To analyze the impact of factory size on M-Audit scores, we ran two tests. First, we compared individual factories against the average size of plants in their respective industries to see if the individual plants were either above or below the industry average. Second, we sorted our sample into 10 subgroups, according to their size (number of employees), with the first subgroup

finding could be that relatively smaller factories (which have on average more than 1,000 employees) are easier to control and monitor than larger facilities, some of which employ tens of thousands of workers.

3. After controlling for two other variables – factory location and industry – the analyses suggest that who owns a factory (foreign vs. national) has a statistically significant relationship with M-Audit scores. In other words, it appears that workers received worse treatment in factories owned by their compatriots than in foreign-owned factories. This is consistent with Mosley's (2010) findings concerning the impact of different modalities of global production on labor standards as well as with Oka's (2010a, 2010b) work on reputation-conscious buyers in the Cambodian garment sector.

4. Within the category of Nike-related variables, the number of visits by Nike personnel and whether the factory is a strategic partner were found to be positively associated with M-Audit scores. On the other hand, the duration of the relationship with Nike and the percentage of capacity dedicated to Nike are negatively related to the M-Audit scores. All four coefficients are statistically significant. Some of these results contradict the expectations derived from the private compliance model, where we would expect that factories that are more dependent on Nike for their business would be more amenable to its compliance demands and where we would imagine that suppliers with unique skills and capabilities (strategic partners) would be most able to resist Nike's compliance demands. Our results suggest that the relationship between Nike and its strategic partners are more aligned with Sabel's (1994), or Frenkel and Scott's (2002) portrayal of buyer–supplier relations than the impression advanced by the global value chains literature.

When analyzing how frequently Nike staff visited individual factories, we were able to separate out different types of Nike personnel (for example, compliance auditors as opposed to quality specialists or sourcing directors). When we removed compliance staff from the analyses, we still obtained the same positive, statistically significant results. This suggests that this positive relationship *is not* the result of more frequent factory inspections (policing) or information gathering (auditing). Instead, something besides auditing must have an effect on compliance. One possibility is that factories that had a closer relationship with Nike were also those with more face-to-face contact with the Nike sourcing and production teams and, as such, engaged in various initiatives aimed at improving their operations (i.e., lean manufacturing systems, total quality improvement programs). These, in turn, may have produced positive spillover effects on labor conditions. Another possible explanation is that frequent visits by production and sourcing staff (but not compliance managers) led to greater

containing the smallest 10 percent of factories and the tenth subgroup containing the largest 10 percent. We then ran regressions using these subgroup dummies. In both tests, the larger factories had significantly lower M-Audit scores.

trust and a better working relationship between the brand and its suppliers. This explanation is also consistent with Frenkel and Scott's (2002) comparative case study of two Adidas suppliers and Sabel's (1994) work on trust and collaborative manufacturing practices. These relationships are explored in greater detail in subsequent chapters. Interestingly enough, frequency of visits is not a function of whether a supplier is a strategic partner. The interaction effect of these two variables is not statistically significant.

5. The negative relationship between M-Audit scores and the duration of Nike's relationship with its suppliers could be explained in two ways: perhaps those factories with a longer working relationship with Nike were also older factories (that is, possessed older plant and equipment), with resultantly poorer working conditions, or perhaps Nike has become increasingly demanding in terms of labor compliance and thus more recent suppliers, having achieved or surpassed more stringent selection criteria, are better equipped to comply with Nike's Code of Conduct. Indeed, interviews with Nike compliance staff indicate that the company has, in fact, stepped up demands for compliance by its suppliers, and newer suppliers may also possess more modern technologies and factory structures.

The negative relationship observed between the percentage of capacity dedicated to Nike and the M-Audit score suggests that power relations, as manifest in the supplier's level of dependence on Nike for business, do not seem to be driving compliance within Nike's supply chain. In other words, the supposedly greater power Nike exercises over suppliers that dedicate a greater fraction of their productive capacity to the company does not automatically translate into better performance on the M-Audit. If anything, the opposite is true, suggesting that there may be something else going on between Nike and those of its suppliers that are more dependent on it for their business. Perhaps some of these compliance issues have to do with Nike's own upstream business practices and not simply the willingness or ability of its suppliers to comply with Nike's Code of Conduct. This suboptimal relationship between Nike's upstream business practices and compliance issues downstream among its suppliers has been acknowledged by Nike and other global brands and is the focus of Chapter 6.

6. Contrary to arguments that suppliers suffer from "audit fatigue," multiple brands with different monitoring programs may be promoting improvements and learning within the factory. These different brands may also engage in informal cooperation with one another, thus presenting a more united front to the suppliers, who, in turn, respond to these common pressures. Interviews with compliance managers at Nike and other brands confirmed that informal information sharing and coordination does in fact take place among brands sourcing from the same factories. This is consistent with more recent work in the Cambodian garment sector that found that suppliers working with reputation-conscious buyers reported better labor compliance than suppliers working with non–reputation-conscious buyers and that this performance improved with the

TABLE 3.4. *Initial and Subsequent M-Audits*

	Mean	SD	Observations
First M-Audit score	0.65	0.16	575
Second M-Audit score	0.70	0.16	117
Third M-Audit score	0.82	0.07	5

increase in numbers of reputation-conscious buyers working with the same supplier (Oka 2010a).

The Change in Labor Compliance over Time

Since the late 1990s, Nike has substantially expanded its compliance staff, invested heavily in the training of its own staff and that of its suppliers, developed more and more rigorous audit protocols, internalized much of the auditing process, worked with third-party social auditing companies and NGOs to double check its own internal audits, and spent millions of dollars to improve working conditions at its supplier factories. Interviews conducted during field research for this project with Nike auditors and compliance staff suggested that these people are serious, hardworking, and moved by genuine concern for workers and their rights. Given all that Nike has invested in staff, time, and resources since the late 1990s, have conditions at their suppliers' factories improved? In other words, did private compliance lead to improvement of working conditions? I seek to evaluate this third question by analyzing historical data provided by Nike on both the M-Audits and the Compliance Rating scores.

Changes in M-Audit Scores

Table 3.4 summarizes the means and standard deviations of the first, second, and third M-Audit scores that were included in the data we received from Nike. By 2005, 117 factories had undergone two M-Audits, and 5 factories were audited a third time. The descriptive statistics show an improvement, and Table 3.5, presenting initial M-Audit scores year by year, shows that in general the performance on the audits improved from 2002 to 2004 (we ignored the 2005 number because the data we received included only a few observations for that year).

Thus, on average and over time, both for factories undergoing their first audit and for factories that have been monitored more than once, working conditions (as expressed in their M-Audit scores) appear to be improving. This would suggest that Nike's private compliance program works.[21] Moreover, as

---

[21] We conducted several tests to investigate whether there was a systematic upward or downward bias in the selection of factories audited a second or third time. First, we compared the initial

TABLE 3.5. *Time Trend for M-Audit Score*
(First M-Audit Only)

Year	Mean	SD	Observations
2002	0.638	0.130	61
2003	0.643	0.167	351
2004	0.673	0.155	159
2005	0.44	0.081	4

stated previously, Nike has become more stringent in its initial screening of factories, weeding out factories with poor compliance records.[22]

The Change in Compliance Ratings

To assess more thoroughly whether factory conditions have been improving over time, we also examined the Compliance Ratings (CRs) that all Nike suppliers were assigned. Because these ratings are easier to understand than are M-Audit scores, they are used more often by Nike managers to guide production and sourcing decisions. The goal of the Compliance Rating program is

M-Audit scores of factories that did not receive subsequent audits with the scores of those that did, to see whether Nike chose to reaudit those factories that did better the first time around. The comparison of the distribution of the M-Audit scores of the single-audited factories against the distribution of the initial scores of the multiple-audited factories is shown in Figure A1. The T-test results are presented in Table A1. We see from Table A1 that there is no statistically significant difference between the two groups. Figure A1 also shows that two waves of M-Audits have very similar probability densities. We then explored whether the sample of factories that received second M-Audits was biased in any way toward certain factory characteristics (size, age, location). We conducted probit models with "whether a factory received a second M-Audit" as the dependent variable. The results are shown in Table A2. The probit models show that there does appear to have been some bias in the sample of factories that received a second audit. Strategic partners and factories that dedicated a larger proportion of their capacity to Nike were more likely to receive a second M-Audit. In fact, strategic partnership itself explains a big proportion (15 percent) of the variation in the likelihood of a second M-Audit. Moreover, factories located in countries with a lower rule of law index, or with weaker legal and regulatory systems, were also more likely to be reaudited. This suggests that the biases go in two different directions and, thus, more or less cancel each other out. We know from our analyses of the first round of M-Audits that strategic partners usually performed better (had higher scores) than nonstrategic partners. However, we also learned from the analyses of the first round of M-Audits that performance in these audits tended to be worse for factories located in countries with weaker regulatory systems and factories with a greater percentage of capacity dedicated to Nike. Interviews with senior compliance managers at Nike indicate that the company chose to concentrate its resources on both high-risk factories and suppliers with which it hopes to develop more long-lasting relationships.

[22] For more on this, see Nike, Inc., "Innovate for a Better World: FY05–06 Corporate Responsibility Report," May 31, 2007: 39–42.

TABLE 3.6. *Summary of Compliance Rating by Score*

Score	A	B	C	D	Total
Count	571	1,945	699	471	3,686
Percentage	16%	53%	18%	13%	100%

TABLE 3.7. *Summary of Compliance Rating by Year*[23]

Year	2001	2002	2003	2004
Mean score	2.99	2.95	2.56	2.58
Observations	220	1,132	1,004	1,323

to develop a tool that integrates compliance and sourcing decisions. A grade (A–D) is given by the local compliance managers and is based on all audits and factory visits by Nike staff as well as by the FLA. (See Appendix 3.2 for an explanation of the grading system.) At the time Nike shared its initial audit data with us for this project, the Compliance Rating Database contained more than 700 factories with more than one CR rating, enabling us to examine the change in workplace conditions as measured by the CR grade given to the factory over time. To assess change over time in the CR, we first describe the overall ratings of all Nike suppliers and how they have evolved over time and then examine individual factories, comparing their first grade with their last to evaluate how conditions have evolved.

Tables 3.6 and 3.7 present summary statistics for the CR grades assigned to Nike's suppliers. There are 3,686 observations of CR ratings in total, with half of the factories receiving a B grade. From 2001 to 2004, the average CR score declined, most obviously in 2003 and 2004. Figure 3.6 illustrates the shift in the distribution of grades over time. In 2003 and 2004, the number of factories that received an A grade dropped dramatically, and the number of factories receiving a C or D grade increased.

However, it is important to note that the pools of factories that received the CR scores differed from year to year. Thus, based on these aggregate data, we do not know whether the overall CR performance of Nike's supply base worsened over time or if Nike has paid increasing attention to poor-performing factories. However, when we look at the *same factories* over time, comparing their very first CR grade with their last, a more negative picture emerges. Between 2001 and 2005, almost half of the factories experienced no change in their rating, and more than 36 percent experienced a decrease in their CR

---

[23] To translate the letter grades into numerical scores, we assigned values to each letter: A = 4, B = 3, C = 2, D = 1.

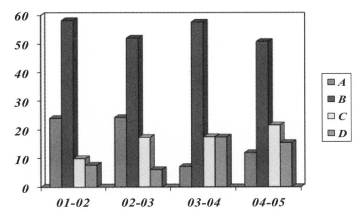

FIGURE 3.6. The distribution of Compliance Rating (percentage) from 2001 to 2004.

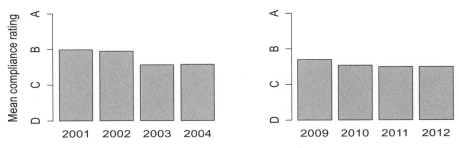

FIGURE 3.7. Mean Compliance Ratings over 2001–4 and 2009–12.[24]

grade. In other words, according to Nike's own CR data, workplace conditions in almost 80 percent of its suppliers either remained the same or worsened over time (see Table 3.8).

In more recent years, the mean CR of Nike suppliers has remained largely stable. Figure 3.7 shows the mean CR over two periods of four years. In aggregate, we see little change in compliance over time in either period.

Thus, according to one measure, the M-Audit score, factory workplace conditions appear to have been improving (slightly) between 2002 and 2005, whereas on another measure (also generated internally by Nike's own staff and with scores covering a longer time period a longer time), workplace conditions were either stagnant or getting worse. This apparent contradiction can in some

[24] Nike changed its auditing standards between the two periods, such that 2001–4 and 2009–12 compliance ratings are not directly comparable. However, in both periods, we see similarly stagnant or declining compliance. These means are based on 3,679 audits conducted between 2001 and 2004 and 10,511 audits conducted between 2009 and 2012.

TABLE 3.8. *Changes in Compliance Rating Grades of Individual Factories over Time (2001–4)*[25]

Change in CR Rating	Frequency	Percent
−3 (Down by 3 degrees)	20	2.62
−2 (Down by 2 degrees)	74	9.70
−1 (Down by 1 degree)	181	23.72
0 (No change)	323	42.33
1 (Up by 1 degree)	116	15.20
2 (Up by 2 degrees)	42	5.50
3 (Up by 3 degrees)	7	0.92
Total	763	100

part be explained by noting that the two tools are measuring different things: the M-Audit privileges documentary evidence and company records, whereas the CR program is a more subjective appraisal of factory management's attitudes toward these issues. Interviews with Nike compliance staff suggest that these ratings are, in fact, picking up different facets of the factory reality. Another possible explanation for the divergence in results between these two compliance scoring systems is that suppliers are learning how to perform on the M-Audit by better preparing their documents and perhaps even coaching their workers but that Nike's local compliance staff are not fooled and are grading suppliers on what is actually happening on the factory floor. This latter explanation is supported by our interviews with compliance managers in the field and at Nike headquarters.

The data and analyses presented in this section show that working conditions at Nike's suppliers (as indicated by each factory's score on the M-Audit) were quite mixed. Some factories appear to have been substantially or fully compliant with Nike's Code of Conduct, but others have been suffering from persistent problems with wages, work hours, and health and safety. This variation in working conditions appears to be the result of *country effects* (the labor inspectorate's ability or willingness to enforce labor laws and standards in the country in which the factory is located), *factory characteristics* (the age and size of the factory), and the *relationship between Nike and the particular supplier* (whether the supplier is a strategic partner, how often Nike (noncompliance) staff visit and interact with the factory, and who else is sourcing product from the same factory). These findings suggest that notwithstanding Nike's very real interests in improving its image vis-à-vis these issues and the company's considerable efforts and investments since the late 1990s to improve working conditions among its suppliers, the results produced by its private compliance

---

[25] The change in CR is calculated as the score from the most recent audit minus the score from the earliest audit.

programs have been limited, and perhaps mixed. As we saw in the previous chapter, these findings are by no means unique to Nike but characterize the compliance program of other global corporations operating in very different industries.

Recognizing these limitations, in more recent years, Nike has modified its compliance program to supplement factory auditing with more collaborative initiatives aimed at uncovering "root causes" of workplace problems and diffusing human resource management "best practices" among its suppliers. It has also updated its various audit tools and grading systems to make them more accurate and transparent to suppliers and to its own business units. In addition to these efforts to improve and supplement its monitoring systems, Nike has begun an extensive review of the company's own upstream business processes – such as product development, design, and commercialization – to identify potential drivers of excessive overtime among suppliers.

Yet, the analyses of Nike's internal audit data also generate insights into the conditions underlying more effective private compliance programs. Recall that when Nike enters into more collaborative, mutually beneficial, and long-term relations with some of its suppliers – as it does, for example, with its strategic partners – working conditions and labor standards at these particular factories improve. The same is true when Nike managers (product quality and operations staff, not compliance officers) visit the suppliers with greater frequency. This suggests that under certain conditions – long-term relations, frequent interactions, mutually beneficial collaborations between Nike and its suppliers – its private compliance program can work. This finding is consistent with other research on collaborative buyer–supplier relations in the automobile, footwear, furniture, metalworking, and steel industries that shows that when global corporations are able to establish more collaborative relations with some of their suppliers, these same suppliers are able to upgrade their production and employment relations systems in ways that benefitted the buyers, their suppliers, and even the workers employed at their suppliers' factories (Sabel 1994; Helper, MacDuffie and Sako 1998; Frenkel and Scott 2002; Herrigel 2010; Ivarson and Alvstam 2010a). Understanding how these more collaborative buyer–supplier relations translate (at times, not always) into improved working conditions and labor standards is the focus of the next two chapters.

Another important insight arising from this case study of Nike concerns the role of public institutions and laws. Recall that the strength of a country's laws and institutions has a strong and positive relationship to the compliance scores of Nike's suppliers, accounting for 11 percent of the variation in the M-Audit scores. Deciphering precisely the relationship between national laws and institutions and private compliance programs is difficult. In our interviews with managers, auditors, NGO representatives, and even local government officials, my graduate students and I learned that this could entail everything from more active government labor inspectors inspecting the supply chain factories with greater frequency and rigor and thus enforcing national labor and employment regulations (thus driving up the private compliance scores) to more efficient local bureaucrats who expeditiously granted various permits to local factories (thus certifying their compliance with various environmental, zoning, and health and safety codes). There exists tremendous variation in the efficacy of local permitting agencies and given the importance of up-to-date records for traditional compliance programs, this factor also seemed to shape compliance scores. In still other cases, we witnessed a creative division of labor between state labor inspectors and private auditors, where each actor – more often implicitly than explicitly – supported the others' regulatory work by inspecting the same workplaces but focusing on different issues or even covering different geographic territories and thus extending the reach of overall compliance through this spatial division of labor (for a detailed description of this process, see Amengual 2010).

Regardless of the specific mechanism, it is clear from both Nike's audit data and our own field research, that the effectiveness of private regulatory programs is very much tied to the strength of public authoritative rule-making institutions. This suggests that even as manufacturing stretches across national borders, folding the work of many workers employed in myriad factories into a single product, the fate of these workers remains tied to the domestic institutional endowments of their home countries. We return to this issue in subsequent chapters.

Because of the various flaws associated with the private compliance model and in an effort to capitalize on the compliance benefits generated by more collaborative buyer–supplier relations, many global corporations, lead suppliers, and multistakeholder initiatives have begun to shift their compliance efforts away from policing and punishment, toward capability-building and technical assistance. According to proponents of this alternative model, when auditors possess the technical, personal, and behavioral skills to engage in joint problem solving, information sharing, and reciprocity with the factory managers, more effective enforcement of regulations and standards follows. In the alternative capability-building model, auditors become involved not simply in inspecting factories but rather in providing suppliers with the technical know-how and "management systems" they need to run both more efficient and ethical factories. As such, the "good inspector" behaves much like the "good cop": tough but sensitive to particularistic situations, using his or her discretion to promote problem solving and rehabilitation rather than coercion and punishment.[26] The following chapter evaluates whether this alternative,

---

[26] Robert Kagan and John Scholz, "The Criminology of the Corporation and Regulatory Enforcement Strategies," in Keith Hawkins and John M. Thomas (Eds.), *Enforcing Regulation* (Boston: Kluwer-Nijhoff Publishing, 1984); James Q. Wilson, *Varieties of Police Behavior: The Management of Law and Order in Eight Communities* (Cambridge, MA: Harvard University Press, 1968).

capability-building approach is more effective at improving working conditions and labor standards for the millions of people working in global supply chains today.

Appendix 3.1. Nike Code of Conduct

At Nike, we believe that although there is no finish line, there is a clear starting line.

Understanding that our work with contract factories is always evolving, this Code of Conduct clarifies and elevates the expectations we have of our factory suppliers and lays out the minimum standards we expect each factory to meet.

TABLE A1. *Comparison of the First M-Audit Score between Factories Monitored Once and Factories Monitored Multiple Times*

	First M-Audit Score		
	Mean	SD	No. of Observations
Factories with only one M-Audit	0.65	0.16	458
Factories with more than one M-Audit	0.64	0.16	117
Test	difference = mean (first m-Audit score of single m-Audit factories) – mean (first m-Audit score of multiple m-Audit factories) Ho: diff = 0. $T = 0.7643$, degrees of freedom = 573.		

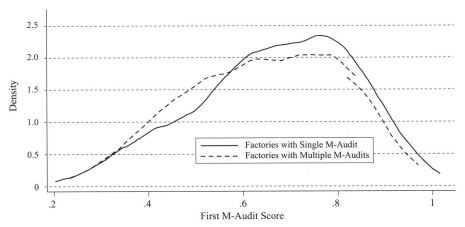

FIGURE A1. First M-Audit score of factories with only one M-audit vs. multiple M-Audit. *Note:* the vertical axis denotes the probability density function.

TABLE A2. *Probit Regression of the Likelihood of Subsequent M-Audits*

	Coefficient (SD)		
First M-Audit score	−.2802		−1.89***
	(.6384)		(.66)
Strategic partner		1.3152***	1.07****
(1 = yes 0 = no)		(.1436)	(.22)
Log no. of employees			.11
			(.10)
Ownership			.34*
(1 = foreign, 0 = local)			(.19)
No. of visits			.0001
			(.026)
Months with Nike			−.0002
			(.0026)
Nike percentage			0.92***
			(.31)
Rule of Law			−.25*
			(.14)
Apparel			.82***
			(.26)
Footwear			.79**
			(.39)
Region EMEA			−.97***
			(.34)
Region North Asia			−.97****
			(.27)
Region S. Asia			−.98***
			(0.32)
Constant	−.6481**	−1.1594***	−.98
			(.76)
No. of observations	575	575	355
R^2		.15	.28
LR $\chi 2(1)$ / LR $\chi 2(13)$		85.97***	117.8****

EMEA = Europe/Middle East/Africa.
Significance level: $*p < .1$, $**p < .05$, $***p < .01$, $****p < .001$.

It is our intention to use these standards as an integral component to how we approach NIKE, Inc. sourcing strategies, how we evaluate factory performance, and how we determine with which factories Nike will continue to engage and grow our business.

As we evolve our business model in sourcing and manufacturing, we intend to work with factories who understand that meeting these minimum standards is a critical baseline from which manufacturing leadership, continuous improvement and self-governance must evolve.

Beyond the Code, Nike is committed to collaborating with our contract factories to help build a *leaner, greener, more empowered and equitable supply chain*. And we will continue to engage with civil society, governments, and the private sector to affect systemic change to labor and environmental conditions in countries where we operate.

We expect our contract factories to share Nike's commitment to the goals of reducing waste, using resources responsibly, supporting workers' rights, and advancing the welfare of workers and communities. We believe that partnerships based on transparency, collaboration and mutual respect are integral to making this happen.

Our Code of Conduct binds our contract factories to the following specific minimum standards that we believe are essential to meeting these goals.

Employment Is Voluntary
The contractor does not use forced labor, including prison labor, indentured labor, bonded labor or other forms of forced labor. The contractor is responsible for employment eligibility fees of foreign workers, including recruitment fees.

Employees Are Age 16 or Older
Contractor's employees are at least age 16 or over the age for completion of compulsory education or country legal working age, whichever is higher. Employees under 18 are not employed in hazardous conditions.

Contractor Does Not Discriminate
Contractor's employees are not subject to discrimination in employment, including hiring, compensation, promotion or discipline, on the basis of gender, race, religion, age, disability, sexual orientation, pregnancy, marital status, nationality, political opinion, trade union affiliation, social or ethnic origin or any other status protected by country law.

Freedom of Association and Collective Bargaining Are Respected
To the extent permitted by the laws of the manufacturing country, the contractor respects the right of its employees to freedom of association and collective bargaining. This includes the right to form and join trade unions and other worker organizations of their own choosing without harassment, interference or retaliation.

Compensation Is Timely Paid
Contractor's employees are timely paid at least the minimum wage required by country law and provided legally mandated benefits, including holidays and leaves, and statutory severance when employment ends. There are no disciplinary deductions from pay.

Harassment and Abuse Are Not Tolerated

Contractor's employees are treated with respect and dignity. Employees are not subject to physical, sexual, psychological or verbal harassment or abuse.

Working Hours Are Not Excessive

Contractor's employees do not work in excess of 60 hours per week, or the regular and overtime hours allowed by the laws of the manufacturing country, whichever is less. Any overtime hours are consensual and compensated at a premium rate. Employees are allowed at least 24 consecutive hours rest in every seven-day period.

Regular Employment Is Provided

Work is performed on the basis of a recognized employment relationship established through country law and practice. The contractor does not use any form of home working arrangement for the production of Nike-branded or affiliate product.

The Workplace Is Healthy and Safe

The contractor provides a safe, hygienic and healthy workplace setting and takes necessary steps to prevent accidents and injury arising out of, linked with or occurring in the course of work or as a result of the operation of contractor's facilities. The contractor has systems to detect, avoid and respond to potential risks to the safety and health of all employees.

Environmental Impact Is Minimized

The contractor protects human health and the environment by meeting applicable regulatory requirements including air emissions, solid/hazardous waste and water discharge. The contractor adopts reasonable measures to mitigate negative operational impacts on the environmental and strives to continuously improve environmental performance.

The Code Is Fully Implemented

As a condition of doing business with Nike, the contractor shall implement and integrate this Code and accompanying Code Leadership Standards and applicable laws into its business and submit to verification and monitoring. The contractor shall post this Code, in the language(s) of its employees, in all major workspaces, train employees on their rights and obligations as defined by this Code and applicable country law; and ensure the compliance of any subcontractors producing Nike branded or affiliate products.

Last updated August 2010. http://nikeinc.com/pages/compliance (accessed July 26, 2012).

Appendix 3.2. Nike's Compliance Rating System

Grade	Compliance Rating Criteria	Description
A	No more than five minor issues outstanding on the Master Action Plan (MAP) *and* no more than 20 percent of MAP items past due.	Noncompliance issues that do not reach levels defined as C or D issues (see below).
B	More than five minor issues, but no serious or critical issues outstanding on the MAP *and* no more than 30 percent of MAP items past due.	Noncompliance issues that do not reach levels defined as C or D issues (see below).
C	One or more C-level issues, but *no* D-level issues, outstanding on the MAP or more than 30 percent of MAP items past due.	• Lack of basic terms of employment (contracts, documented training on terms, equal pay, discriminatory screening) • Noncompliance to local laws on treatment of migrant workers • Less-than-legal benefits not related to income security (e.g., leave) • Excessive hours of work: greater than 60 hours/week but less than 72 hours/week • Exceeding legal annual overtime work hour limit for 10 percent or more of the workforce • Not providing one day off in seven • Verbal or psychological harassment or abuse • Conditions likely to lead to moderate injury or illness to workers • Conditions likely to lead to moderate harm to the environment or community
D	One or more D-level issues outstanding on MAP *or* Serious issues past due; or more than 40 percent of open MAP items past due.	• Unwillingness to comply with Code standards • Denial of access to authorized Nike compliance inspectors • Falsification of records and coaching of workers to falsify information • Homework, or unauthorized sub-contracting • Underage workers • Forced labor: bonded, indentured, prison

(conitnued)

(conitnued)

Grade	Compliance Rating Criteria	Description
		• Denial of worker rights to Freedom of Association where legal
		• Pregnancy testing
		• Confirmed physical or sexual abuse
		• Paying below legal wage
		• Denial of benefits tied to income security
		• No verifiable timekeeping system
		• Exceeding legal daily work hour limit or work in excess of 72 hours/week for 10 percent or more of the workforce
		• Not providing one day off in 14 days
		• Conditions that can lead to death or serious injury
		• Conditions that can lead to serious harm to the environment

Source: Nike Corporate Responsibility Report: Part II. FY 2004, p. 25. http://www.nike.com/nikebiz/gc/r/fyo4/docs/FYo4_Nike_CR_report_pt2.pdf (accessed June 21, 2006).

Appendix 3.3. Explaining the Variation of First M-Audit Score: Alternative Country Level Indices

In this appendix, we present the regression results for First M-Audit scores on selected variables using a different country-level index than the World Bank's Rule of Law Index used in the text (Table 3.4). Here, we use instead the Economic Freedom Index compiled by the Heritage Foundation.[27] The Index of Economic Freedom measures 161 countries against a list of fifty independent variables divided into ten broad factors of economic freedom. Scores ranges from 1 to 5. Low scores are more desirable. The higher the score on a factor, the greater the level of government interference in the economy and the less economic freedom a country enjoys. The Index of Economic Freedom includes the broadest array of institutional factors determining economic freedom.[28]

[27] For details on the index of Economic Freedom, see Kane T. and R. Holmes and M. A O'Grady. 2007 *Index of Economic Freedom: The Link Between Economic Opportunity and Prosperity.* Or, visit the following website: http://www.heritage.org/index.

[28] These are corruption; nontariff barriers to trade; the fiscal burden of government; the rule of law; regulatory burdens on business; restrictions on banks; labor market regulations; and informal market activities.

TABLE A3. *Regression Result of First M-audit Score on Selected Variables: Using Economic Freedom Index*

	Coefficient (SD)				
Economic Freedom Index	−0.12****	−0.065****	−0.083****	−0.089****	−0.041***
	(0.001)	(0.0011)	(0.016)	(0.016)	(0.016)
Log no. of employees			−0.016**	−0.012*	−.012*
			(0.007)	(0.007)	(0.007)
Ownership			−0.03*	−0.022	−0.019
			(0.017)	(0.017)	(0.016)
No. of SHAPE visits			0.002	0.002	0.0037*
			(0.002)	(0.002)	(0.002)
Strategic partner			0.038*	0.04*	0.004
			(0.021)	(0.02)	(0.020)
Months with Nike			−0.00038*	−0.00037*	−.000014
			(0.0002)	(0.0002)	(0.0002)
Nike percentage			−0.049*	−0.042	−0.026
			(0.026)	(0.027)	(0.025)
Apparel			−0.0067	0.013	−0.0017
			(0.019)	(0.0192)	(0.018)
Footwear			0.11***	0.11***	.0085***
			(0.035)	(0.035)	(0.03)
Region EMEA		−0.040*			−0.069***
		(0.022)			(0.025)
Region North Asia		−0.12****			−0.15****
		(0.017)			(0.021)
Region South Asia		−0.14****			−0.17****
		(0.018)			(0.023)
Year 2003				0.048**	.
				(0.023)	
Year 2004				0.080***	.
				(0.028)	
Constant	0.99****	0.94****	1.01****	00.94****	0.96****
	(0.031)	(0.03)	(0.04)	(0.047)	(0.04)
No. of observations	568	568	355	355	355
R^2	0.18	0.28	0.24	0.26	0.36

EMEA = Europe/Middle East/Africa; SHAPE = Safety, Health, Attitudes of Management, People Investment and Environment.
Significance level: $*p < .1$, $**p < .05$, $***p < .01$, $****p < .001$.

Table A3 presents the regression results. The results are similar to what we reported in Table 3.4. (The sign of the economics index is negative here. Note that low Economic Freedom Index is better, whereas a high Rule of Law Index is more desirable.)

TABLE A4. *Two-Level Hierarchical Model of First M-Audit Score on Selected Variables (Level One: Factories; Level Two: Regions)*

	Coefficient (SD)			
Rule of Law Index	0.038****	0.04****	0.029***	0.032***
	(0.01)	(0.009)	(0.011)	(0.011)
No. of Shape Visit			0.0036*	0.0036*
			(0.0018)	(0.002)
Ownership	−0.027**	−0.019	−0.028*	−0.020
	(0.013)	(0.014)	(0.015)	(0.016)
Log (No. of Employees)			−0.011*	−0.012*
			(0.0064)	(0.007)
Strategic partner	0.048***			0.004
	(0.15)			(0.019)
Month with Nike			0.0001	−0.0003
			(0.0001)	(0.0002)
Nike percentage		0.041**		−0.027
		(0.019)		(0.016)
Apparel			0.021	0.012
			(0.017)	(0.018)
Footwear			0.073***	0.102****
			(0.032)	(0.032)
Year 2003	0.029	0.031		0.046**
	(0.018)	(0.02)		(0.021)
Year 2004	0.046**	0.056***		0.066***
	(0.02)	(0.023)		(0.025)
Constant	0.63****	0.616****	0.72****	0.69****
	(0.041)	(0.042)	(0.057)	(0.064)
Region random effect:				
SD (constant)	0.074	0.07	0.083	0.080
SD (residual)	0.14	0.13	0.13	0.13
No. of observations	568	463	355	355
No. of groups	4	4	4	4
χ^2	37.72****	33.14****	53.12****	57.74****
Log-restricted likelihood	301.1	245.4	201.7	181.5

Significance level: *$p < .1$, **$p < .05$, ***$p < .01$, ****$p < .001$.

Appendix 3.4. Explaining the Variation of First M-Audit Score: Hierarchical Models

In this appendix, we present the regression results for First M-Audit scores in hierarchical settings. We use two-level hierarchical models: factory as the first level and region the second level. The regression results are similar to that of Table A4.

TABLE A5. *Regress Results of M-Audit Subscores on Selected Variables*

	Wage Standard	Hours Standard
Index of Economic Freedom	−0.0722***	−0.09***
	(0.025)	(0.03)
(log) No. of employees	−0.013	−0.061****
	(0.01)	(0.01)
Ownership	−0.002	0.004
	(0.026)	(0.03)
SHAPE visit	−0.00079	−0.000002
	(0.003)	(0.004)
Strategic	0.028	0.09**
	(0.03)	(0.04)
Month with Nike	−0.00012	0.00055
	(0.0003)	(0.0004)
Nike percentage	−0.105***	−0.146***
	(0.041)	(0.05)
Apparel	0.032	0.0006
	(0.029)	(0.04)
Footwear	0.15***	0.254****
	(0.05)	(0.068)
Year 2003	0.003	0.035
	(0.036)	(0.045)
Year 2004	0.04	0.02
	(0.04)	(0.05)
Constant	1.02****	1.17****
	(0.07)	(0.09)
No. of Observations	355	355
R^2	0.11	0.21

SHAPE = Safety, Health, Attitudes of Management, People Investment and Environment.

Appendix 3.5. Explaining Variation in Specific M-Audit Items: Wages and Work Hours

In this appendix, we present the regressions of two M-Audit items – wages and work hours – on selected variables to examine whether there are differences between our analyses using the composite M-Audit with its constituent items. Overall, the results are similar qualitatively to the results reported in Table 3.4: the country-level macro variable is still significantly positively correlated with M-Audit subscores. Factory size is still negatively related to subscores. Strategic partners is significant, but not so robust. Nike percentage is negatively related to sub-M-Audit scores. There is one interesting contrast between wage and work hours in their relations with the number of employees. The log number of employees has a significant negative relationship with hour but does not associate with wage.

4

Capability Building and Its Limitations

As the shortcomings of the traditional compliance model became increasingly apparent, scholars and practitioners alike began to embrace an alternative approach to combating poor labor standards in global supply chains, built around the concept of capability building (sometimes referred to as capacity building). The capability-building model starts with the observation that factories throughout the developing world often lack the resources, technical expertise, and management systems necessary to address the root causes of compliance failures. Whereas the traditional compliance model sought to deter violations by policing and penalizing factories, capability building aims to *prevent* violations by providing the skills, technology and organizational capabilities that enable factories to enforce labor standards on their own. By providing suppliers with the technical know-how and management systems required to run more efficient businesses, this approach aims to improve these firms' financial situations, thus allowing them to invest in higher wages and better working conditions. At the same time, for these factories to run more "lean" and/or "high-performance" operations, management must not only reorganize work but also up-skill and perhaps even empower shop-floor workers (e.g., to stop the line when identifying persistent quality problems). Capability-building programs envision a mutually reinforcing cycle in which more efficient plants invest in their workers and that these more skilled and empowered employees, in turn, promote continuous improvement processes throughout the factory, rendering these facilities more and more efficient and therefore more capable of producing high-quality goods on time, at cost, in the quantities desired by ever-more demanding customers, while at the same time respecting corporate codes of conduct.[1]

---

[1] This is not the first time that organizations have sought to improve working conditions and labor standards through technical assistance programs. For an interesting historical example of

In fact, the promise of this supposed win-win scenario has motivated many global companies (including Nike, Hewlett-Packard, and ABC), lead suppliers, multistakeholder initiatives, and international organizations to embrace this approach in recent years. Nike, for instance, launched its "Generation 3" compliance program a few years ago in an effort to promote "sustainable manufacturing" among its suppliers. This new compliance strategy blends together traditional factory monitoring with capacity-building efforts and root-cause analysis (Nike 2010a: 35). Several multistakeholder initiatives have also shifted away from traditional compliance and toward capability building in their efforts to promote labor standards in global supply chains. The Fair Labor Association's "sustainable compliance program" (known as FLA 3.0) was developed in response to the apparent weaknesses of traditional compliance programs. The FLA found that factory audits not only generated poor-quality information but also undermined trust between global brands and their suppliers. To address these concerns, the FLA launched its sustainable compliance program in 2008. FLA 3.0 promotes a more collaborative approach toward compliance by engaging the suppliers in the audit process and by creating mechanisms (e.g., root-cause analysis) aimed at tackling persistent problems such as excess overtime.[2] Social Accountability International (SAI) launched its certification process (SAI 8000), which verifies not only factory compliance with SAI's Code of Conduct but also factory-level management systems that promote both ongoing compliance and productivity and quality gains. Even international organizations like the International Labor Organization (ILO) have embraced capability building as a way to promote "decent work" through its Factory Improvement and Better Work programs.

In this chapter, I consider whether and to what extent capability-building initiatives actually improve working conditions and labor rights in global supply chains. This chapter begins by tracing the concept of capability building back to its intellectual foundations. Although global corporations and multistakeholder initiatives have only recently adopted capability-building practices, the concept can be traced back to earlier debates around foreign aid and institution building, industrial upgrading in developing countries, and, finally, normative theories of development. After briefly examining the theoretical literature underlying this recent shift toward capability building, I turn to a series of empirical cases of capability-building initiatives that cover a range of strategies across multiple industries and socioeconomic contexts. These cases were chosen to illustrate both the potential and the limitations of capability building

such programs in the US garment industry, see Steven Fraser, *Labor Will Rule: Sidney Hillman and the Rise of American Labor* (Ithaca, NY: Cornell University Press, 1991).
[2] Fair Labor Association, "FLA 3.0 – Toward Sustainable Compliance http://www.fairlabor .org/fla/go.asp?u=/pub/mp&Page=FLA3. For an overview of the methodology behind the Sustainable Compliance Initiative, see http://tp.fairlabor.org/en/introductions/the-sustainable-compliance-initiative-sci.

efforts by showing how they actually work in supply chain factories producing very different products (hence subject to different market pressures and supply chain dynamics) and operating in countries with highly varied regulatory frameworks. As such, these cases serve as plausibility probes aimed at exploring the viability of this alternative approach to improving labor conditions in global supply chains.

Notwithstanding significant improvements over traditional compliance approaches, this chapter shows that the capability-building enterprise faces its own serious drawbacks, based on its underlying assumptions concerning the root causes of suppliers' labor problems and how best to address them. Because of these assumptions, most capability-building initiatives embrace a highly technocratic approach to supply chain factory "upgrading" that may help address certain problems at factories engaged in these programs but eschews both more distributive issues and concerns with enabling rights, that are core to labor standards enforcement.

Capability Building – Theoretical Roots and Mechanisms

The Movement Away from Traditional Compliance

Whereas traditional compliance appears to have failed at improving working conditions in a consistent and sustainable manner, an alternative approach based upon "pedagogy," "commitment," and technical assistance has been advanced as a more effective means to enforce labor standards. In an earlier study of export factories in the global apparel industry, Locke, Amengual, and Mangla (2009) argued that a commitment-based model – one that promotes information sharing and trust between auditors and suppliers – can overcome some of the weaknesses of more traditional, strictly audit-based compliance approaches. Instead of punishing factories for poor performance, we documented various cases in which auditors went beyond their traditional roles by consulting factory management about problem areas and jointly identifying solutions. Similarly, an initiative promoted by the International Labor Organization (ILO) in Cambodia's apparel export sector found that workplace conditions improved significantly when ILO monitors made repeat factory visits and provided detailed feedback to management on how to correct deficiencies in the production process (Polaski 2006). These mechanisms extend beyond private governance initiatives. In the context of state enforcement, Piore and Schrank (2008) highlight the comparative advantages of the "Latin model" of labor regulation, which involves repeated interactions between labor inspectors and factories, and promotes joint consultation and problem solving.

Although some aspects of the traditional compliance approach (e.g., information gathering through factory audits, threat of sanctions) coexist with and serve as background conditions for this more pedagogical approach (Locke et al. 2009; Pires 2008), capability-building initiatives are quite distinct from the standard approach to compliance that we saw in the previous chapters.

Efforts to promote transparency through greater information exchange and trust building between auditors and factory management departs significantly from the prevailing mechanisms of "inspection" and "deterrence." Rather than treating suppliers as calculating agents motivated by a desire to cheat their way through inspections, the capability-building approach conceives of them as willing partners who simply lack certain organizational skills necessary for effective enforcement. Such skills include the ability to collect and process relevant information regarding labor violations, technical skills to analyze the root causes of those violations, and finally, the organizational capacity to effectively monitor and implement requisite changes over time. Where did these ideas come from? How is it that developing country suppliers, once viewed as both uncommitted and untrustworthy when it came to promoting labor standards within their facilities, came to be thought of as willing but somewhat needy partners, requiring support from global brands, multistakeholder initiatives, and even the ILO? To understand how this model has become a tool for enforcing labor standards in global supply chains, the following section traces the intellectual foundations of capability building more generally.

Capability-building initiatives aimed at improving labor standards in global supply chains build on three distinct but interrelated literatures concerning international aid, industrial upgrading, and normative theories of development.

International Aid and Capacity Building

Capability building first gained favor in planning and development circles as a response to (and rejection of) more centralized and technocratic approaches to development. Leading scholars like Robert Chambers (1983, 1994) argued for a participatory approach to rural development, one that enabled communities to cultivate local knowledge as an instrument for more effective planning by both state and nonstate agencies. For these scholars, development came to be understood as a process of reducing vulnerabilities and building the capacities of individuals and organizations to respond to adverse events and unforeseeable circumstances. As policymakers began to embrace civil society as a partner in the development process, capacity building became a key instrument to strengthen the organizational capabilities of nongovernmental organizations (NGOs) and other groups in civil society so that they could act more effectively on behalf of the poor (Eade 1997).

This push toward capability building gained momentum among international aid agencies in the 1990s, as neoliberal-inspired policies lost favor. These policies and their associated structural adjustment/deregulation efforts were blamed for the widening income disparities and environmental degradation that took place within the developing countries that embraced (or were forced to embrace) these policies. In light of these persistent problems, capability building was seen within international aid circles as a means to improve the quality of governance, build local institutions on behalf of the poor, and achieve environmental sustainability.[3] Among aid agencies, the United Nations Development Program (UNDP) was a forerunner in embracing a capability-building framework for its aid programs: its "capacity development" model focused on helping governments, civil society groups, and other stakeholders gain the requisite skills, knowledge, and experience needed to improve the quality of life for the poor. The UNDP's model included programs to improve the implementation capacity of agencies to deliver public goods and services as well as sectorial programs aimed at enhancing the organizational capabilities and technical expertise of local firms. Along with the UNDP, the World Bank also embraced capacity building in its efforts to promote development; its 2003 World Development Report, *Sustainable Development in a Dynamic World*, focused on combatting poverty through greater economic productivity. Unlike previous reports, the 2003 World Development Report highlighted several persistent problems afflicting developing countries – environmental degradation, income inequality, and social upheaval – and proposed capacity building as the solution to these problems. Capacity building was understood by the report as (1) building institutions to disseminate new technologies, (2) investing in human capital, and (3) improving coordination between state and nonstate agencies at the local, national, and global levels.

Capability Building in Global Value Chains

Alongside this shift among international aid and development programs, capability building also gained prominence through the research on global value chains. As we saw in the previous chapters, the global value chain (GVC) framework developed by Gary Gerreffi and his associates focuses on the economic, technological, and organizational processes through which producers become integrated into the global economy, and consequently, the opportunities and constraints these processes create for developing countries (Gereffi and Korzeniewicz 1994; Gereffi 2005). According to this school of thought, the distribution of power between global buyers and their suppliers (and also between developed and developing countries) determines who sets the rules of exchange and how the economic "gains" from these exchanges get distributed across various actors in the supply chain.

Employing this framework, Kaplinksy (2000, 2005) argued that despite new economic opportunities presented by globalization, producers in developing countries often lack the ability to negotiate and compete with lead firms and are therefore relegated to low-value-added segments of the supply chain. To break out of these low-value-added traps, other studies employing the GVC model have focused on the opportunities for firms in developing countries to achieve

---

[3] For an interesting review and critique of this approach to development assistance, see Judith Tendler, *Good Government in the Tropics* (Baltimore: Johns Hopkins University Press, 1997).

greater economic gains by upgrading their activities and entering more value-added segments of the supply chain. Gereffi (1999), for example, documents how organizational learning can occur in the apparel supply chain, enabling producers to upgrade from garment assembly to full-package networks. Ivarson and Alvstam (2010a, 2010b) document how IKEA's furniture suppliers in China and Southeast Asia upgraded their capabilities through technical assistance and organizational learning provided by IKEA. Humphrey and Schmitz (2002) underscore the significance of interfirm cooperation and supportive local institutions and argue that the manner in which industrial clusters are inserted into GVCs can either enable or disable producers' attempts to upgrade. Commonly cited mechanisms for industrial upgrading include organizational learning, technology and skill transfer, and investment in capabilities like human resources. Capability building is understood within this stream of research as an iterative process of learning and innovation (Morrison, Pietrobelli et al. 2008). Yet economic upgrading is not always accompanied by "social" upgrading. In their study of quality, labor, and environmental standards in Brazil's footwear industry, Navas-Alemán and Bazan (2005) found that capacity building and social upgrading do not always go hand in hand. Depending on the governance structure of the supply chain and the role played by local government, some standards (e.g., technical standards) get implemented more effectively than others (e.g., labor and environmental standards).[4]

Capability Building as a Normative Ideal

Alongside these more academic and policy-oriented debates surrounding the possible role of capability building in promoting industrial upgrading and economic development, political philosophers developed normative theories regarding the role of capability building in the development process. Noteworthy within this literature is Amartya Sen's (1999) capabilities approach to development. Whereas many prominent theories of development have tended to treat the poor and otherwise disadvantaged as mere recipients of economic policy, Sen conceptualizes them as active agents and participants in the process of development. By taking their role in development seriously, he asks us to look beyond narrow metrics such as growth of per capita GDP and consider other mechanisms through which development can empower the poor, enhance their quality of life, and expand the freedoms they enjoy. Freedom, which is central to his theory of development, is understood as the capabilities that an individual possesses to lead the kind of life he or she values. Exclusive

[4] In an effort to further understand how best to combine economic and social upgrading in global value chains, various scholars working within the GVC framework have launched a new project focused specifically focused on these issues. For an overview, see Stephanie Barrientos, Gary Gereffi, and Arianna Rossi, "Economic and Social Upgrading in Global Production Networks: Developing a Framework for Analysis," Working Paper 2010/03, Capturing the Gains Project, University of Manchester, 2010.

emphasis on policies that generate income growth ignores other sources of deprivation that the poor face, such as lack of basic health care and literacy, the absence of workers' rights, and restrictive gender norms. For Sen, capability building is understood as not just a fiscal investment in education and health or a technical process of improving the quality of public service delivery, but also as a *political* process of enhancing the quality of representative institutions within the state to empower citizens to participate in that same process.

Although each of these literatures conceptualizes "capability building" in a slightly different way and embraces this strategy for somewhat different purposes, together they make a strong case for promoting technical assistance, skill development, and organizational learning as a way of combating poverty and promoting development. Thus, it should come as no surprise that global brands, lead suppliers, multistakeholder initiatives, and even international organizations would embrace this approach as a way to improve working conditions and labor rights in global supply chains. In the wake of the limited success with (but significant controversy surrounding) the traditional compliance model, an alternative approach that rested on more "technical" (and supposedly less politicized) mechanisms like the diffusion of best practices, structured problem solving, continuous improvement, and so forth naturally appealed to various actors in global supply chains. Because global corporations and their suppliers had already deployed some of these same tools and processes successfully to tackle other issues (product quality, for example),[5] capability building seemed like a clear improvement over the traditional compliance model. But is it?

The following section reviews several empirical cases that sought to improve working conditions and labor standards in global supply chains through capability-building initiatives. These programs represent a wide range of capability-building strategies across a variety of country, industry, and socioeconomic contexts. Notwithstanding the differences across these cases, a few common themes emerge. First, most (but not all) capability-building efforts did generate improvements, particularly in areas such as physical plant upgrading, enhanced productivity and quality, and even the reduction of certain code violations, especially in the area of health and safety. Second, despite these improvements, other significant issues persisted, especially concerning wages, work hours, and the ability of workers to organize collectively and form independent unions. These findings highlight a significant gap between the theoretical mechanisms proposed by the literature and the practical processes by which capability-building programs are implemented. Part of the gap, I argue,

---

[5] This approach was popular not just among global buyers but also some of their lead suppliers. For an interesting study of capability-building efforts in the Indian textile industry, see Nicholas Bloom et al., "Does Management Matter? Evidence from India," Stanford GSB Research Paper No. 2074 (December 2010).

lies in the underlying assumptions of most capability-building programs. I discuss these assumptions and their implications at the end of this chapter. The next chapter examines this process in greater detail through a structured comparison of two of Nike's Mexican apparel suppliers. This matched pair analysis illustrates the conditions that enable capability-building efforts to fulfill their promise of improving not just productivity and quality but also working conditions and labor standards at global supply chain factories.

Capability Building in Practice

Upgrading through Factory Inspections: Vignettes from ABC's Supply Chain

During our field research on ABC and its global suppliers, my graduate students and I visited numerous factories throughout the world that sought to improve labor standards by enhancing their organizational and managerial capabilities. At these factories, we observed auditors collecting information and using this information to redress various violations in the Code of Conduct. But instead of simply employing factory audits and the threat of sanctions (in the form of reduced or terminated orders) to drive better compliance, information gathering (as imperfect as it is), and the tracking of workplace conditions over time were employed to engage factory managers in various capability-building exercises that would allow them to tackle workplace problems in a cost-effective and sustainable manner. The frequent presence of auditors in these factories, and the fact that they had been visiting these same factories for several years, meant that these auditors had developed a different kind of relationship with the factory managers. Rather than act as "inspectors" whose job focused primarily on uncovering Code of Conduct violations and punishing management for these infractions, these auditors acted more like consultants by engaging in joint problem solving, information sharing, and the diffusion of best practices that were in the mutual self-interest of the suppliers, the auditors, and the global corporations for which they work. As such, the incentives of the various actors appeared to be better aligned. Factory managers gained valuable advice, sometimes even technical assistance, that allowed them to improve their operations and hence their competitiveness. At the same time, these improvements in "management systems" were often accompanied by (and at times relied on) improvements in working conditions and thus benefited the workers employed at these factories as well. Finally, by embracing the role of consultants or advisors and layering this on top of their traditional role as compliance officers, the auditors were able to enrich their own jobs and gain legitimacy both in the eyes of the firms they audited (by giving them valuable advice) as well with ABC's headquarters, because their work was clearly leading to sustained improvements in working conditions and labor standards among a select group of ABC's suppliers. And although the threat of sanctions was still present in these settings, it served less to "force" the suppliers to comply with

ABC's Code of Conduct than as a background condition or fallback mechanism, aimed at "fostering" the joint problem-solving initiatives underway at these factories.[6] If anything, through these various activities, auditors and factory managers alike came to recognize their mutual dependence and thus their continued need to cooperate and communicate openly with each another.[7]

To illustrate this capability-building approach, the following section will describe how instances of information sharing and joint-problem solving between factory managers and ABC auditors led to the resolution of critical labor problems at suppliers operating in very different countries and regions throughout the world.

Improving Competitiveness and Compliance at Sula Shirts

One factory that we studied in Honduras, Sula Shirts,[8] illustrates how competitiveness and labor conditions can improve in tandem, and how ABC's capability-building efforts were key to this transformation.[9] Sula, located near the Port of Cortez, employed at the time of our research more than 1,400 workers that cut and assembled dress shirts for ABC (which accounted for 90 percent of their production) and other major brands. The Honduran owners of this factory began producing clothing in the 1920s, originally for the local market and for the banana companies that had large operations at that time. As the company grew, it began exporting to the United States, and by the 1970s, Sula began working with ABC through a licensing agreement to produce ABC brands for the local market. In 1989, Sula started to assemble ABC branded shirts for export to North America. By 2001, Sula had switched from assembling precut materials to full-package production. With full package, Sula receives design specifications from ABC and is responsible for purchasing the material inputs, cutting the fabric, assembling the garments, and packaging the garments so they are ready (down to the price tag) to be sold in North American retail stores.

China's entry into the World Trade Organization and the recession in late 2001 provoked global brands to exit Central America and move toward Asia

---

[6] See Richard E. Walton, Joel E. Cutcher-Gershenfeld, and Robert B. McKersie, *Strategic Negotiations: A Theory of Change in Labor-Management Relations* (Ithaca, NY: Cornell University Press, 2000) for more on the differences and synergies between the forcing and fostering approaches to labor-management relations.

[7] For more on how situations of pervasive uncertainty can complicate power relations among otherwise unequal actors, hence leading them to cooperate and communicate more openly with one another, see Joshua Cohen and Joel Rogers, "Power and Reason," in Archon Fung and Erik Olin Wright (Eds.), *Deepening Democracy: Institutional Innovations in Empowered Participatory Governance* (London: Verso, 2003): 237–55.

[8] This is a false name to protect the identity of the factory.

[9] This section draws heavily on Richard M. Locke, Mathew Amengual, and Akshay Mangla, "Virtue out of Necessity?: Compliance, Commitment, and the Improvement of Labor Conditions in Global Supply Chains," *Politics and Society* 37, no. 3 (September 2009): 319–51.

in search of lower production costs. Over the past several years, hundreds of Central American factories have closed down. This trend was accelerated in 2005 with the end of the Multi-Fiber Arrangement (MFA), which had regulated global garment trade through quotas, and thus created a place for Central American producers in the global textile-apparel industry. Following the demise of the MFA, the only way many Central American producers believed they could compete with producers from South and East Asia was through cutting wages, sweating workers, and succumbing to a classic "race to the bottom."

Notwithstanding their long relationship with Sula, ABC made it clear that the factory was no longer competitive with its East Asian rivals and that if the factory did not alter its strategy, ABC would cease to source from Sula. Interestingly, ABC helped Sula develop a new, more viable strategy based on rapid replenishment: quickly producing small batches of goods in response to changing market demands. With "quick turnaround," Sula would take advantage of its proximity to North American markets, making speed and responsiveness the crux of its competitive strategy; ABC could count on rapid replenishment of styles that had proven popular in the market place but that could not be sourced from their lower-cost but more distant suppliers in East Asia.[10]

ABC invested a tremendous amount of time and resources to help Sula make this transition. For example, ABC sent several full-time staff with experience in running quick turnaround operations to the Sula factory to help factory management through "test runs" of quick turnaround orders, to minimize time-consuming errors, and to maintain high levels of quality. In addition, ABC took Sula staff to other production facilities (including what was, at the time, its only remaining shirt factory in the United States), to observe replenishment in action and learn through experience.

ABC and Sula came to a new agreement on financing the fabric used for rapid replenishment orders through which ABC would continue to own the fabric that was stored at Sula's warehouses until the fabric was pulled off the shelf, which signaled Sula's "purchase" of this input. By freeing up the working capital that Sula would normally need to invest in its fabric inventory for quick turnaround, ABC mitigated the tremendous costs (and risks) faced by Sula in this transition, and this shift in financial burden allowed Sula to stock a variety of fabrics necessary to react quickly to changing consumer demands. Describing an earlier switch from assembly to full-package production, the factory's general manager said that mismanagement of fabric inventory could

---

[10] It takes two days to ship garments by sea from Honduras to the United States, whereas for China it takes between twelve and eighteen days, and for India forty-five to sixty days, see Robert Devlin, Antoni Estevadeordal, Andrés Rodríguez-Clare (Eds.), *The Emergence of China: Opportunities and Challenges for Latin America and the Caribbean* (Washington, DC: Inter-American Development Bank, Cambridge, MA: David Rockefeller Center for Latin American Studies, Harvard University, Harvard University Press, 2006): 188.

bankrupt a factory in two months, because inventoried fabric at Sula is worth in excess of $1 million.

The move to rapid replenishment, although providing a new basis for competitiveness, was not a panacea for compliance, because quick turnaround can put pressure on labor standards, especially overtime.[11] Under normal production, Sula would receive orders from ABC two and a half months before the date that the shirts have to be shipped. For their production lines dedicated to rapid replenishment, Sula has only one week to ship the finished product after receiving the order. Common delays in production (e.g., late inputs, inaccuracies in order specifications, quality issues) can only be made up by overtime, particularly in the finishing and packing departments, which execute the last stage of the production process before shipment. Moreover, the rapid changes in style demanded by a replenishment strategy provoked a large drop in efficiency because of time-consuming adjustments to machinery and loss of efficiency from workers.[12] Initially, the lines dedicated to quick turnaround experienced 20 percent drops in efficiency because of the constant switching of styles, exacerbating pressures for long overtime hours to complete orders.

Soon after Sula began its rapid replenishment operations, the factory began to encounter problems complying with ABC's Code of Conduct. Working-hours violations were uncovered during a routine audit by ABC in which auditors found that a portion of the workers had exceeded the maximum overtime limits and that workers were not given one day of rest per week. To redress these issues, Sula at first added an additional night shift from 6:30 PM to 4:00 AM, and the auditors from ABC returned and verified that excessive working hours were reduced with this new system in place. However, this strategy to reduce overtime did not last long because paying night wages increased costs significantly. At this point, having encountered increased costs in their effort to comply with the code, Sula could have gone back to its previous practices but ABC continued to monitor working time at the factory and to pressure Sula to comply with its Code of Conduct. Crucially, ABC combined elements of the traditional compliance model (monitoring and the threat of sanctions) with technical assistance to find a solution that reconciled competitiveness with compliance. As a result, and with the assistance of ABC, Sula introduced a more flexible shift structure, improved the efficiency of the operations dedicated to rapid replenishment, and relocated machines so that replenishment production took place in a dedicated area of the factory. The factory also placed red tags on the replenishment bundles so that workers knew they were a priority,

---

[11] See Verité, "Excessive Overtime in Chinese Supplier Factories: Causes, Impacts, and Recommendations for Action," http://www.verite.org/news/Excessiveovertime; Clean Clothes Campaign (2008); and Raworth and Kidder (2009).

[12] The complexity of dress-shirt production, involving more than seventy operations, rules out modular or lean production and lends the process toward a progressive bundle system, in which shirts move through islands of thirty-year-old machines, originally created for use in factories in Alabama, which have been shipped by ABC to Sula's factory.

assigned quick turnaround status to a select group of workers who were skilled at making rapid adjustments, and solicited their input about how to streamline the process. Workers' suggestions included sorting the replenishment orders by style, color, and size so that switching between styles would require fewer machine adjustments. Whereas previous production methods made it inefficient to run a style for less than a day, consolidating and sorting by style, color, and size allowed workers to streamline thread changes and machine calibration, thereby minimizing lost time. These changes made quick turnaround production economically viable, practically eliminating the initial 20-percent drop in efficiency. The changes were possible because of the consistent pressure on Sula to comply, the technical assistance from ABC giving Sula the means to comply, and the commitment by ABC to keep sourcing from Sula as it made the costly transition. Months later when we visited the factory, there were no signs of excess overtime, and Sula was filling quick turnaround orders, which they saw as the one path to remain competitive.[13]

Tackling Excess Overtime: The Case of Ambar Designs

Ambar Designs was established in the late 1990s in the fast-growing city of Bangalore, India. It is one of thirteen factories owned by a major garment export house in South India. At the time of our field research, the factory employed more than 1,000 workers who cut, sewed, finished, and packed woven tops and bottoms for several leading brands. ABC has been sourcing woven tops and bottoms at Ambar for nearly eight years, although at the time of our fieldwork, it accounted for just 10 percent of production in the factory. Excess overtime had always been a major problem at Ambar, where workers routinely clocked well beyond the state-mandated sixty hours per week and many worked more than seven consecutive days without a day of rest, in violation of Indian labor law. But over the past few years, the factory has reduced overtime significantly. ABC's ability to facilitate positive changes at Ambar, even though it takes up only a small share of the plant's production capacity, reveals how auditors can help improve labor conditions in India not merely through threats and sanctions but by building relationships with company managers and providing them with the technical assistance they need to run more efficient and ethical operations.

To better situate the case of Ambar, we must first take into account the institutional and cultural context underlying India's integration into the global apparel market.[14] Since independence, the Indian state used a range of

---

[13] We confirmed the improved working conditions with local labor rights NGOs that support the workers at Sula Shirts, government officials who field complaints, and four days of interviews and observations in the factory.

[14] This discussion relies heavily on Henrietta Lake, "Production and Principles: A Study of Work Organization in the South Indian Apparel Industry" (Ph.D. dissertation, Tufts University, 2006).

regulatory mechanisms and policies that encouraged small-scale production in the apparel sector. Only recently have firms shifted to mass production for export markets, which brings a new set of organizational challenges, from sourcing fabric to maintaining productivity.[15] Perhaps the greatest challenge is learning how to manage a newly formed industrial workforce, where worker absenteeism and turnover tend to be high. The majority of workers, particularly in South India, are young women who commute to urban apparel factories from the city outskirts and rural villages nearby. Having a predominantly female, rural workforce carries another set of labor-related issues, as stricter regulations are placed on the hours that women can work, factories are required to provide crèches for their children, and, given widespread undernourishment and high rates of anemia, subsidized food and health facilities are necessary.

These were the conditions faced by Ambar Designs, which in 2005 and 2006 was among the 80 percent (24 out of 30) of active South Indian suppliers producing for ABC that faced significant problems of excess overtime. Interviews conducted during our field research revealed that seventy-five-hour workweeks had been common at Ambar. The most commonly cited reason for this overtime concerned production delays and supply chain problems, such as late arrival of materials, problems with the color and quality of fabrics, and other inputs. These delays can have a cascading effect because factory managers often compensate for them by having machine operators work longer hours and/or reducing their weekend breaks. The crunch to get orders out on time is exacerbated by the fact that customers increasingly demand shorter lead times and higher-quality products. Excess overtime at Ambar was also exacerbated by high rates of absenteeism and turnover of workers; typically, 4 to 5 percent of workers at Ambar (mostly sewing machine operators) were absent on a given day, and the factory experienced between 5 and 8 percent monthly turnover of its workforce. Rather than address these problems directly or plan around them, factory managers had workers take up the extra work, many of whom welcomed the opportunity to earn additional income.

An ABC auditor identified the problem of excess overtime at Ambar after several audits and worked with the corporate human resources manager to develop a plan to address it. This manager was willing to work with the ABC auditor because, unlike other auditors, she believed the ABC auditor was far more "sensitized" to the local conditions of the factory. In her experience, the compliance programs of most brands lead to "fire fighting" in preparation for auditor visits, but she found the ABC compliance program to be "far more sensitive to the economic and social conditions in which the factory is working." To tackle excess overtime at Ambar, the ABC auditor worked with Ambar's management to uncover the "root causes" of this persistent problem. A combination of poor supply chain planning and lack of coordination among the

---

[15] For more on these challenges, see Nicholas Bloom et al., "Does Management Matter? Evidence from India," Stanford GSB Research Paper No. 2074 (December 2010).

company's operations managers, supply chain managers and human resources managers led to consistent shortages of workers capable of handling volatile fluctuations in orders. Through a series of information exchanges, training sessions, and the sharing of best practices from other factories in the industry, the ABC auditor was able to help Ambar coordinate more effectively among its functional areas, smooth out its production processes, and thus eliminate the need for excess overtime at the factory.

Health and Safety Improvements in the Dominican Republic

Heat is a constant problem in factories in the Dominican Republic, especially in factories that have large areas dedicated to ironing and laundering garments. One ABC auditor showed factory managers how to enhance their existing ventilation systems (fans) and reduce heat in the factory by opening up additional holes in the roof above the ironing area. Four months later, when we visited the factory, new fans and vents had been installed, and the temperature had been reduced. This same auditor also instructed the management of another factory on how best to install new water fountains, enhance access to the emergency exit, develop a new ventilation system, and better identify shop-floor workers responsible for first aid. None of these changes were costly; it was simply that the factories' management did not know how to create a safer and healthier work environment. Through simple capability-building initiatives and the sharing of best practices, the auditors were able to help factory managers improve working conditions in their plants.

Promoting these kinds of low-cost solutions helped move factories toward compliance. For example, workers often use noxious chemicals to remove stains on garments, and thus chemical exposure is often a serious problem in factories that cannot afford modern ventilation systems. Because of the high costs of purchasing and installing these modern ventilation systems, many factories in the Dominican Republic have resisted correcting this very real health and safety hazard in their plants. ABC's auditors searched for a solution that would not incur high costs for their suppliers. The solution they found was to move the chemical-intensive processes to the edge of the factory, which is open to the outside and to install a series of powerful fans to push the fumes outward. This generated a much cheaper solution than what the auditors would have insisted on had they stuck to their traditional roles as "compliance officers," and as a result, the solution was actually implemented and not resisted by factory management.

ABC's auditors in the Dominican Republic spend a lot of time visiting many different factories, and as such, often act as agents of change, diffusing innovative ideas from factory to factory. For example, an endemic problem in many factories is the lack of protective guards on the sewing machines that are designed to prevent workers from being injured by needles. In many factories this becomes an especially serious problem because highly pressured workers remove the guards to work faster, and inevitably, there are numerous injuries without them. The auditors say they can tell if needle guards are missing simply by checking the factory's infirmary records for extensive needle puncture wounds. Managers often resist requests from the auditors to install needle guards because they say that workers will just continue to take them off, and to constantly replace them is costly. One ABC auditor discovered a solution to this problem while visiting a factory where she noticed that the needle guards were welded on to the sewing machines, thus making them difficult to remove. Leveraging her frequent presence (and ongoing relationship with managers) at many local factories, she quickly diffused this practice among them by taking photographs of the original welded needle guard and showing them to all factory managers she met. Instead of threatening the factories with sanctions unless they repaired the problems, she instructed the managers on how to find solutions.

All the auditors of these vignettes went beyond their traditional compliance role; in addition to "inspecting" factories and documenting workplace problems, these same auditors also worked with the factories to develop innovative solutions to an array of different workplace problems. In some instances, this entailed enlisting ABC's operational managers to help instruct the factory on how best to implement rapid replenishment; in others, it was to help promote coordination among the suppliers' functional staff so that production schedules could be better planned and excess overtime avoided. In still other cases, the auditors acted as agents of innovation, sharing low-cost solutions to an array of health and safety problems. In our discussions with ABC auditors throughout the globe, they told us how "coaching," "mentoring," and engaging in joint problem solving became a central part of their jobs.

After years of working within the traditional compliance system, many of these auditors realized that even when they approved a factory, there was a good chance that the factory would backslide and the problems would return in subsequent audits. As one auditor noted: "finding the problems is not a problem for me, the problem is making them comply and getting them to comply sustainably." To improve the sustainability of compliance, another ABC compliance manager said that he came to the conclusion that "if we can explain to [factory managers] why [they] have to do this stuff and the benefits, they are going to be more apt to sustain it and do it."

As a result, many of the auditors we interviewed began to see a large part of their job as helping to bring factories into compliance (auditors as consultants), rather than threatening factory managers who do not comply (auditors as police).[16] They see themselves, in their own words, as "teachers," "psychologists," or "salesmen," trying to convince factory management that compliance

---

[16] See Kagan and Scholz, "The Criminology of the Corporation and Regulatory Enforcement Strategies," in Keith Hawkins and John Thomas (Eds.), *Enforcing Regulation* (Boston: Kluwer/Nijoff, 1984): 69–74.

is in their own interest and show them how to comply. At times, they find ways to improve productivity and compliance and "kill two birds with one stone." For example, one manager from ABC's compliance team said that by creating "a voluntary program [for overtime] . . . you require the management to go through an exercise of evaluating their planning techniques." Forced overtime is reduced, and production is improved through better planning. Not all issues or factories are amenable to this capability-building approach – some factory managers simply do not "get it" and for some issues, such as freedom of association, these citizenship rights need to be enforced not one factory at a time but throughout the territory, and this entails a more active role by the state rather than by a small group of activist auditors. Notwithstanding these limitations, the capability-building approach to supply chain compliance is becoming an important part of the auditors' practice in some (but by no means all) of the factories we studied, leading to sustained improvements in working conditions.

Whereas these vignettes from ABC's suppliers in South Asia and Central America illustrate the potential advantages of capability-building efforts (especially when compared with the more traditional compliance approach), the following two sections, also drawn from our field research, shed light on some of the limitations of this model.

The Mixed Results of Capability-Building: Lessons from the ILO's Factory Improvement Program

Another capability-building initiative that my graduate students and I studied for this research project is the ILO's Factory Improvement Program (FIP). Launched in 2002 with support from the Swiss State Secretariat for Economic Cooperation and the US Department of Labor, the FIP involved intensive capacity-building efforts at the factory level, with the goal of raising compliance with international labor standards while improving overall competitiveness. The FIP was originally implemented in Sri Lanka's garment export sector but soon expanded to Vietnam and India, where it was implemented in medium-large factories across a number of industries.

The FIP consists of seven modules that combine off-site training with in-factory consultancy over a period of ten months. The modules include (1) Workplace Cooperation, (2) Quality, (3) Productivity, (4) Cleaner Production, (5) Human Resources, (6) Health and Safety, and (7) Workplace Relations. A professional expert is hired to lead each module and share relevant knowledge, skills, and experiences with factory managers, primarily through off-site training sessions and factory visits. In addition to these external experts, locally based service providers are hired to train factory managers in each of the program modules. These local service providers conduct factory visits to provide on-site assessments and advice to factory managers and engage in routine monitoring of each factory, reporting the findings to the ILO. A central goal of the FIP is to increase worker involvement, primarily through the creation of

Factory Improvement Teams (FITs), which are given training along with dedicated responsibilities for each program module. By developing these teams and linking them to factory improvement goals, the FIP seeks to enhance dialogue and build mutual understanding between workers and management.

During the summer of 2007, my graduate students and I conducted field research on the ILO's Factory Improvement Programs in Vietnam and India to assess the impact of this ambitious capability-building initiative on working conditions and labor standards. What we discovered was that this program was especially effective at promoting productivity and quality gains for participating factories. Factories across the board introduced significant changes around production planning, the work environment, and worker incentive schemes. Changes that appeared small on the surface – neater factory layout, the use of containers to store materials, and improved bundle labeling – helped enhance factory productivity and reduce costs. Quality standards also improved significantly as factories began to track defect rates systematically and using this information to conduct root cause analyses. In some factories, productivity and quality gains emerged through increased worker involvement and cooperation with management. Yet, the most challenging task for most participating factories was enhancing social dialogue between management and workers, because in most of them the very idea of social dialogue was a completely new concept. Communication was usually one-way, with management telling workers what to do in a paternalistic manner. Formal grievance procedures were rarely implemented and even in larger factories with consultation committees in place, workers were underrepresented. Understanding these mixed results sheds light on the relative strengths and weaknesses not just of the ILO's FIP, but also on many other capability-building initiatives aimed at improving labor standards through enhanced factory competitiveness.

FIP Vietnam

In 2007, the ILO launched the FIP in the garment sector of southern Vietnam, partnering with the Vietnam Chamber of Commerce and Industry (VCCI) to deliver and monitor the program. The seven FIP modules were implemented by local experts and combined offsite training with in-plant consultancy in twelve garment export factories: ten in Ho Chi Minh City and two in Binh Duong province. Several of the participating factories had previously invested in various quality and process improvement initiatives like ISO 9000, but the impact of these past programs on overall performance was limited. In contrast to these prior initiatives, the FIP was seen as both more comprehensive in that it focused not just on one issue – quality versus productivity – but on several key challenges facing local factories, and participatory, as it engaged shop floor workers in the actual improvement processes. The limited success of past productivity and quality improvement efforts was blamed on lack of worker commitment and poor communication between managers and workers. The FIP, with its FITs, would correct these past shortcomings.

During the summer of 2007, I visited six of the twelve participating factories and collected data on wages, accidents, worker grievances, turnover, defects, productivity, and even energy consumption for all twelve participating FIP factories. Both these data and our field research revealed that significant improvements had indeed taken place in just about all of the plants engaged in the FIP. In one factory with a history of poor communication between managers and workers, the FIT instituted a number of new initiatives, including a regular feedback mechanism (i.e., interviews and surveys) for workers, and also organized periodic social events to foster a more cooperative organizational culture within the plant.

Enhanced dialogue between management and workers helped produce positive changes in areas such as quality control and productivity. Most factories showed a decline in defect rates, and in some cases, the improvements were dramatic. In one factory, for example, in-line defects went down from 50 percent in January of 2007 to 10 percent by October of 2007. Significant improvements also took place in the area of occupational health and safety. Capacity-building efforts focused on creating or strengthening health and safety committees within each factory. These committees encouraged dialogue between workers and management and led to the adoption of new practices like the collection of quantitative data on injuries and identification of potential occupational hazards. In some cases, health and safety committees initially did not have worker representatives, but by the end of the module, worker participation was strengthened: a worker survey conducted in one factory at the end of FIP found that nearly 92 percent of workers experienced better working conditions after the program had been implemented (VCCI 2008).

Notwithstanding these positive changes, some workplace issues (supposedly addressed by several modules) and certain factories did not exhibit sustained improvements over the course of the FIP intervention. Employee turnover, wages, and labor accidents fluctuated in many factories over the course of the program, showing little steady improvement. Although some of this fluctuation can be partially explained by the seasonality of production in the garment sector, some of it seemed to be related to the way the FIP was implemented in different factories.

Figures 4.1 and 4.2, based on original data we obtained directly from the FIP's local partner, the VCCI, summarize month-by-month performance of several key performance indicators for all twelve garment factories that participated in the ILO's FIP. Figure 4.1 shows both a dramatic improvement in quality and in the plants' ability to meet production targets over the course of the program. However, as Figure 4.2 shows, similar improvements did not occur in the areas of workplace safety (accidents) or labor turnover rates. When examining the data for individual factories,[17] we discovered that the situation was more nuanced, in which some factories appeared to consistently improve

---

[17] For confidentiality reasons, we cannot share individual factory data or descriptive statistics.

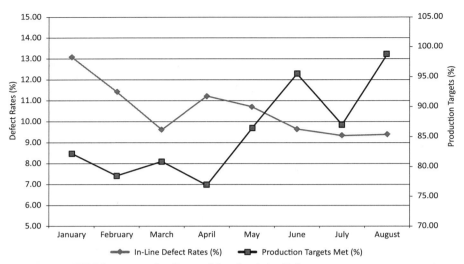

FIGURE 4.1. FIP Vietnam – Quality and Productivity Enhancements

both their business-related and labor-related performance, whereas other plants appeared to focus on and improve only their business-related processes (quality and productivity) but not their labor practices.

During our field research, we observed that factories that possessed either a strong union fighting for worker rights (which in Vietnam means a functionally independent union) or global buyers who continued to pressure factories

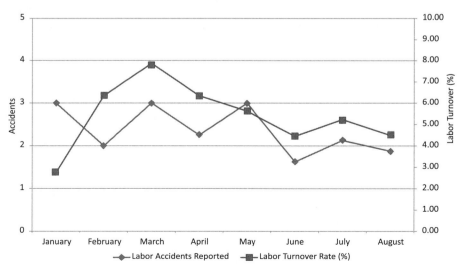

FIGURE 4.2. FIP Vietnam – Monthly Labor Turnover and Accidents

to respect their codes of conduct notwithstanding their participation in the FIP process seemed to experience sustained improvements in both working conditions and productivity/quality, whereas factories lacking strong independent unions and vigilant buyers showed consistent improvements only for business-related outcomes.[18] These findings support the observations made in the Vietnam FIP Final Report, which acknowledged the mixed results of its otherwise very successful program and the fact that workers were underrepresented in many of the FITs (VCCI 2008).

FIP India

The FIP in India was piloted in Faridabad in 2007. Twenty-three factories producing auto components participated in the pilot. Participating factories consisted primarily of small and medium-sized enterprises that lacked managerial capacity and experienced high turnover among workers, many of whom are seasonal migrants from poor, rural states such as Uttar Pradesh and Bihar. Given this high turnover coupled with the prevalence of informal work, the level of cooperation between workers and management in these factories is quite low. Moreover, many of these plants rely on rudimentary technologies and often lack protective gear and safety equipment, posing considerable health hazards for workers.

In response to these and related concerns, the ILO FIP program was initiated with support from the Faridabad Small Industries Association (FSIA). Like FIP in Vietnam, local service providers were hired to train factory management in each of the program modules and to provide on-site assessments and advice to factory managers. They also routinely monitored each factory and reported the findings both to the ILO and to FSIA. In addition, the program hired outside experts to deliver training sessions off-site and to make one factory visit per training module to provide capacity-enhancing expertise. To raise worker involvement, FITs were created in each factory and given dedicated responsibilities associated with each program module.

Notwithstanding the initial poor factory conditions and several implementation challenges, the FIP in Faridabad promoted significant improvements among participating factories, most notably in the areas of factory layout and industrial hygiene. Worker safety was increased by improving the handling and storage of raw materials, work-in-progress, finished products, and even scrap. In addition, some investments were made to improve working conditions more

---

[18] These findings are consistent with recent research on the ILO's Better Work Cambodia Program, which found that suppliers working for reputation-conscious buyers performed consistently better on labor compliance issues than suppliers working for less visible brands or working through intermediaries. See Chikako Oka, "Accounting for the Gaps in Labour Standard Compliance: The Role of Reputation-Conscious Buyers in the Cambodian Garment Industry," *European Journal of Development Research* 22 (2010): 59–78, and Chikako Oka, "Channels of Buyer Influence and Labor Standard Compliance: The Case of Cambodia's Garment Sector," *Advances in Industrial and Labor Relations* 17 (2010): 153–83.

directly, like providing clean drinking water and bathrooms at the factories. In addition, several pilot factories installed new ventilation systems and machine safety guards after they learned that these investments enhanced worker health and safety and lowered production costs. Finally, there was a marked improvement in management-worker relations; many of the physical changes observed in the factories were initiated by teams of workers, who communicated their grievances and suggestions – for the very first time in many cases – directly to factory management.

Still, the FIP program faced serious difficulties in sustaining worker participation, for a variety of reasons. First, FIP service providers relied primarily on factory management to institute changes and program modules were tailored to a managerial audience. As a result, expert training and service provider visits tended to focus on the needs of management, with little worker interaction and training. Even the FIT teams, designed to promote worker-management collaboration, were dominated by managers. One factory director we interviewed expressed a genuine interest in getting his workers more involved in FIP but claimed that he felt uncomfortable inviting his workers to participate in expert training sessions because the external consultants uniformly expressed pro-management views.

Consistent with the FIP's approach in other countries, its program in India depended heavily on the commitment of factory management. In the better-performing factories, managers were motivated to improve their factories. As one factory manager put it, "To become what we intend to as an organization requires us to change. We felt that FIP offered the right platform to figure out what we were missing." Yet, the sustainability of the FIP-inspired improvements was threatened by their inability to fully engage the workers. For example, the high degree of turnover among workers threatened the stability of Factory Improvement Teams. As one factory director put it, "There are some improvements in water, toilets, storage, and definitely some quality and productivity improvements. All of these changes will only last depending on the stability of the FIT management. If the composition of the FIT keeps changing, then the improvements will not stay." Yet, most FIT members (often, supervisors) and factory directors saw little value in training and investing in workers. As in Vietnam, the FIP capability-building approach in India suffered from dramatic differences in power and status between management and workers, which were reinforced by the social hierarchy and organizational culture that prevail in India. Structural problems, such as the lack of basic education for workers, posed an additional challenge that is well outside the remit of a factory-based program, because neither FIP experts nor service providers were trained in enhancing capabilities to a relatively uneducated audience. As a result, worker awareness and involvement in FIP was much lower than that of management: even in the best-performing factories, none of the worker team members interviewed knew which FIP module was being put into effect at the time, and many were not even aware that an ILO program related to working conditions was being implemented in their factory. These findings raise questions regarding the extent to which the capability-building approach, meant primarily as technical assistance and skill-training exercise, can advance, by itself, the rights of workers in contexts like India, where entrenched social inequalities structure employment relations.

Do Capability-Building Programs Really Make a Difference? Evidence from HP's Focused Improvement Supplier Initiative China

As discussed in Chapter 2, HP was a pioneer in promoting private compliance initiatives in the global electronics industry. Yet, HP's approach to regulating workplace practices among its suppliers went beyond auditing their facilities: in addition to these periodic social and environmental audits, the company also promoted various capability-building initiatives among its suppliers in an effort to enhance their managerial skills and systems. Recognizing that managerial and organizational weaknesses are often major drivers of code violations, HP has engaged over one hundred of its suppliers, located in China, Thailand, Hungary, Poland, Mexico, and the Czech Republic, in various capability-building programs (Hewlett-Packard 2009). One such program was the Focused Improvement Supplier Initiative (FISI) in China. This program trained hundreds of participants from diverse suppliers in two regions of concentrated electronics production in China. The issues addressed in these management-focused training workshops included overtime reduction, worker-management communication channels, energy conservation, and the implementation of the new Chinese labor regulations. By working with managers of its key suppliers, this program sought to develop management systems to support compliance with HP's (and Electronic Industry Citizenship Coalition's) standards. The first round of this program began in June 2006.

Using audit data provided to us by HP for this research project, my graduate students and I looked for FISI's impact on program participants by examining audits conducted before and after the program. We selected facilities that participated in the program whose first audit occurred before the start of the program but whose final audit occurred after the training workshops ended one year later. We then identified a "control" group of every Chinese facility working with HP that did not take part in the program, choosing only those with audits both before and after the FISI program, to assess the possible impact of FISI on various workplace issues. Improvements in labor, health and safety, and environmental compliance for both capability building and "control" groups are illustrated in Figure 4.3.

The audit data suggest that participants in the FISI capability-building program improved their compliance in the labor (from 51 to 56 percent) and health (from 33 to 51 percent) sections of the audit, but experienced a small decline (4 percent) in compliance in their environmental practices. This would suggest that the FISI program, on balance, had a positive impact on

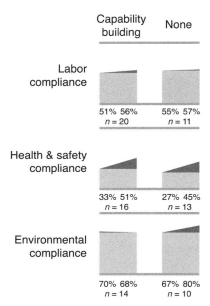

FIGURE 4.3. Capability building and improvement in Chinese suppliers (2006–8). *Note:* Compared suppliers that participated in the Focused Supplier Improvement Initiative 2006–7 against non-participants. Only compared if first audit happened before June 1, 2006, and final audit took place after June 1, 2007, and both had full scores for the relevant audit section. The control group did not participate in subsequent capability-building programs.

participating suppliers. However, audit data analysis of our control group shows that facilities that did not participate in these training workshops also improved compliance in these three areas between their first and final audits in roughly equal measure. It may still be true that the FISI capability-building program did lead to some modest improvements in the participating suppliers' ability to comply with labor, health, and environmental standards, because we do not have counterfactual evidence to assess what would have happened if these particular plants had not participated in this program. Moreover, facilities targeted for the pilot program could have been selected specifically because of their compliance problems, and thus, any improvement (even vis-à-vis plants not participating in the pilot program) could be interpreted as positive. Yet, our analysis of HP's audit data found little evidence that this mechanism alone drove changes in compliance. If anything, these data question the program's efficacy.[19]

---

[19] The capability-building program participants also had, on average, more time between their initial and final audits to address violations. The average time between first and final audits was 2 years, 8 months in the capability-building group and 2 years, 2 months for the control group.

During our field research in the summer and fall of 2009, interviews with managers at factories that had participated in FISI suggested that the capability-building programs did not leave a deep impression upon facility managers. In fact, many of these managers did not have a strong recollection of the content, let alone the key takeaways of their training workshops. In other interviews with HP suppliers, located not just in China but in other Southeast Asian countries, we learned that some suppliers resisted investing in "capability-building" initiatives because they felt that whatever gains generated by these programs were captured by HP and the other global brands they worked for. In other words, innovations in work organization or production systems that generated either greater efficiencies or better quality did not translate into higher margins for these suppliers. The same was true for workers employed in these factories: whereas capability-building initiatives did lead to improved compliance on certain issues, especially health and safety issues, other important concerns like wages and working hours were not remedied by capability-building initiatives alone.

Concluding Considerations: The Politics of Capability Building

The cases featured in this chapter shed light on both the potential and limitations of the capability-building approach to enforce labor standards in global supply chains. In each of the programs examined, marked improvements took place in some factories (in terms of increased productivity and quality) and for some workers (providing cleaner workplaces, better health and safety conditions). By investing in the capabilities of suppliers to address the root causes of labor violations, these initiatives currently represent some of the most innovative practices taking place in the arena of private governance. Yet, we also saw how some of these programs produced mixed or only limited improvements for workers. These mixed results raise serious questions about the extent to which the capability-building approach can lead to sustained and broadly diffuse improvements of working conditions and labor rights in global supply chains. Do the limitations of these programs stem from some inherent defects in the capability-building enterprise? If so, what are these defects?

Some of the differences we observed in our field research can be explained simply by the way different capability-building programs were being implemented. For some – like the initiatives being promoted by ABC's auditors – implementation involved frequent and multiple interactions between the buyers and the suppliers, as well as a commitment by the buyers that they were investing in long-term, mutually beneficial relations with the suppliers. As such, the suppliers, over time and through trial and error, began to "trust" the buyers and eventually embrace the capability-building programs being promoted. However, for some of the other programs we studied, capability building often entailed limited interactions with the buyers, one-shot training sessions, and no sense among the suppliers that participation in these programs or investments in new capabilities would result in long-term contracts or improved buyer–supplier relations. And as we saw in the previous chapters, repeated interactions and long-term, mutually beneficial relations between buyers and suppliers are key to enhanced labor compliance. But aside from these differences in implementation, some of the limitations we observed had to do with more deeply rooted assumptions of the model itself. A closer look at the underlying logic of the capability-building approach reveals that it, like the traditional compliance model, rests on flawed theoretical and empirical assumptions that shape both the design and implementation of many of these programs.

As we saw at the beginning of this chapter, one of the key assumptions underlying capability-building initiatives concerns *industrial and technical upgrading* and its relationship to *social upgrading*. Essentially, the model assumes technical upgrading automatically leads to better working conditions. This assumption is derived from the global value chains literature, which has sought to identify the mechanisms through which supplier factories can improve their economic position within the value chain. Industrial upgrading can take place through a variety of channels, including process improvements that allow for greater efficiency, a shift to higher value-added activities, or the introduction of more technologically advanced forms of production. Although a number of studies have examined how these upgrading strategies affect firms, little attention has been devoted to assessing their impact on workers. Perhaps because industrial upgrading can lead (at times) to skill development, it is often believed (implicitly) also to yield better wages and working conditions for factory workers (Barrientos, Gereffi et al. 2010).

Yet, there are two fundamental problems with this assumption. First, there is little evidence to show that industrial upgrading automatically yields better wages or working conditions. Case studies reveal a mixed picture at best.[20] For example, in their study of global production networks in India, Posthuma and Nathan (2010) find that economic upgrading has not helped to improve conditions for lower tier workers and may have even contributed to the rise of vulnerable jobs. How the economic gains from upgrading is distributed among suppliers, between suppliers and workers, or even among different kinds of workers, cannot be assumed a priori. Although increased profits may be passed on to (some) workers in the form of better wages or working conditions, this will not happen automatically but rather will depend on the power dynamics among different supply chain actors (buyers, suppliers, different categories of workers). Second, this assumption overlooks the fact that the enforcement of some labor standards (particularly enabling rights) may have little to do with

---

[20] That evidence is lacking to back that assumption is perhaps unsurprising. Theoretically, it is unclear why social upgrading has to follow economic upgrading at the factory level, for much the same reason that social development need not follow economic development at the country level. Indeed, the most generic path for upgrading a factory, substituting capital for labor, may well bring with it a decline in wages and downgrading of working conditions.

the profitability or technical sophistication of suppliers but instead hinge on other social and political factors. For instance, standards regarding freedom of association have more to do with the realization of political rights for workers and cannot be enforced effectively one factory at a time, no matter how well managed or technically sophisticated these factories are.

A second, related assumption underlying the capability-building model has to do with its rather simplistic notion of *actor interests*. Essentially, many capability-building initiatives fail to register the divergent (and at times competing) interests of the various actors (i.e., brands, suppliers, workers) involved in global supply chains. As such, they simply assume a win-win scenario in which improvements in some part of the supply chain – say, increased efficiencies at supplier factories – will translate into gains for all actors involved. But as we saw in this chapter, these gains are often not evenly distributed but often accumulate to whichever actors have greater power in particular supply chains. As such, various actors, be they suppliers or even workers, who see little to gain from investing in these efforts resist capability-building programs at times.

A third and final assumption underlying many capability-building programs concerns the universality of the technical and managerial systems and organizational changes being introduced. In other words, the model assumes that regardless of the local context, new management techniques, be they lean manufacturing or quality control systems or even worker-management consultation committees will work more or less in the same way, resulting in more or less the same results. But as we saw in this chapter's anecdotes, the actual implementation of many of these initiatives is shaped by various social, historical, and cultural legacies that can either enhance or hinder the desired effects of any one of these programs.[21]

Together, these three assumptions concerning the commonality of interests among supply chain actors, the universal, context-free nature of the technical systems being promoted, and the somewhat mechanistic relationship between industrial and social upgrading have led to the development and implementation (in many but not all cases) of an overly technocratic approach to capability building and it is this overly technocratic approach that has produced the mixed results we observed in our field research.

As we saw from the ABC supply chain vignettes, when suppliers believed that capability-building programs would lead to greater economic returns in terms of enhanced productivity, improved quality, and perhaps increased orders, they invested in these efforts. In most cases, these investments in production systems, work organization, and management systems translated into at least

---

[21] A similar point was made by Anne Swidler in her analysis of various programs in Africa. Anne Swidler, "African Chiefdoms and Institutional Resilience: Public Goods and Private Strategies." Presented at Center for European Studies, Harvard University, November 2, 2009, and "Return of the Sacred: What African Chiefs Teach Us about Secularization," *Sociology of Religion* 71, no. 2 (2010): 5.

some improvements in working conditions in their factories. But as HP's FISI program illustrated, when suppliers were not convinced that investments in capability-building programs would deliver concrete gains (in terms of higher margins or greater orders from global buyers), their commitment to these programs was limited. In some cases, these suppliers could not even recall the content of their training workshops, and in others cases, the FIP in Vietnam for example, suppliers simply cherry picked between components of the trainings they were interested in (namely, productivity and quality) and ones they chose to ignore (i.e., workplace relations). Thus, understanding how capability-building efforts fit within the broader dynamics and relationships among key actors in global value chains is key to ensuring their efficacy.

In addition to understanding how capability-building initiatives affect different actors within global value chains and clarifying how their costs or gains are distributed among these actors, we must also ask which capabilities are most in need of development. Political philosophers like Amartya Sen have argued convincingly that a broad array of human capabilities are necessary for advancing human well-being. These include not only basic literacy and health but also political rights such as freedom of association. Yet, the programs we analyzed in this chapter for the most part neglect this more capacious definition of capability building and instead take a much narrower view centered on the provision of knowledge and other technical inputs, which are insufficient for protecting the rights of workers. To fully understand the impact of these different approaches to capability building, the next chapter analyzes two of Nike's Mexican apparel suppliers, which pursued distinctly different approaches toward upgrading their production systems. In both cases, the suppliers invested in new technologies and organizational capabilities. But only in one factory, where technical upgrading was linked to enhanced worker voice and empowerment, did the full potential of capability building become realized. Understanding the conditions that shaped these divergent outcomes is key to our understanding of what role capability building can actually play in promoting worker rights and labor standards in today's global supply chains.

5

Alternative Approaches to Capability Building

A Tale of Two Nike Suppliers

What role can capability-building programs play in improving working conditions in global supply chains? Why do capability-building initiatives produce such mixed results among supply chain factories that implement them? How does this approach relate to other strategies and regulatory approaches aimed at promoting just working conditions in global supply chains? This chapter addresses these questions and explores both the potential and limitations of the capability-building model through a detailed matched pair case study of two factories supplying Nike, the world's largest athletic footwear and apparel company. These two factories have many similarities – both are in Mexico, both are in the apparel industry, both produce more or less the same products for Nike (and other brands), and both are subject to the same Code of Conduct. On the surface, both factories appear to have similar employment (i.e., recruitment, training, remuneration) practices, and they received comparable scores when audited by Nike's compliance staff. However, underlying (and somewhat obscured by) these apparent similarities, significant differences in actual labor conditions exist between these two factories. What drives these differences in working conditions? How do they relate to the different approaches to capability building deployed in these two factories? Field research conducted at these two factories reveals that beyond the introduction of new management systems and production techniques, workplace conditions, and labor standards are shaped by very different patterns of work organization and human resource management policies. Consistent with alternative approaches to capability building, some of these policies seek to give voice to and empower shop floor workers, whereas other policies aim to reduce worker voice and discretion. The consequences of these different approaches to capability building for workers and labor standards is significant and explains the variation we observed in the previous chapter.

The matched pair case study presented in this chapter is based on field research conducted over the spring and summer of 2005.[1] More than 90 interviews were conducted with factory owners, managers, workers, nongovernmental organization representatives, union leaders, and various Nike managers both in the United States and in Mexico. Factory visits were also conducted in two Mexican states, as well as at one plant's sister plant in Los Angeles, California. Both factories (which I refer to as Plant A and Plant B) are located in the same country (Mexico) and, therefore, operate in the same political and economic environment and are subject to the same labor regulations. Both plants interface with the same regional office of Nike (based in Mexico City), which is responsible for coordinating orders (sourcing) and compliance visits to the factories. In fact, the same compliance specialists audited both factories. Compliance scores for the two plants were almost identical. However, beneath these apparent similarities, very different realities in terms of working conditions and labor rights existed. By systematically comparing the two factories along a number of dimensions (wage systems, work hour regimes, employee representation, etc.), this chapter sheds light on the alternative approaches to capability-building deployed at these two plants and how these alternative approaches shaped differences in working conditions. Following an analysis of these differences, the chapter concludes by pondering the more general implications of this analysis for strategies aimed at enforcing labor standards in global supply chains.

A Tale of Two Factories

Plant A is located in the Estado de Mexico. It is situated in an industrial park where other garment factories are also operating. A Mexican family has owned the group that runs this plant since 1955. When the North American Free Trade Agreement was signed in 1994, the group began exporting. To support this new strategy, the company invested in state-of-the-art technology and trained its technical, operational, and administrative staff. At the time of our field research, the group exported 95 percent of its production to Europe, Asia, North America, and South America.

Plant B is located in a western Mexican state, 800 kilometers from the US border and 2,000 kilometers from the Nike regional office in Mexico City.[2] This has historically been an agricultural state, but in recent years, the state government has promoted economic development through foreign direct investment. Plant B is part of a Taiwanese group, which owns three other plants: one in Taiwan, one in the United States, and another in the same Mexican state.

---

[1] This chapter draws heavily on Richard M. Locke and Monica Romis, "The promise and perils of private voluntary regulation: Labor standards and work organization in two Mexican garment factories," *Review of International Political Economy* 17, no. 1 (February 2010): 45–74.
[2] The name of the state will remain anonymous to protect the identity of the plant.

TABLE 5.1. *Similarities between the Plants*

	Plant A	Plant B
Country location	Mexico	Mexico
Legal minimum wage	US$5.15/day	US$5.15/day
Structure	Part of a vertical group	Part of a vertical group
Product type	T-shirts, graphic T-shirts	T-shirts, seamless and high-tech T-shirts
Defect rate	1%	0.6%
Turnover rates	8%–10%	10%
System of promotion	Informal, based on skills	Informal, based on skills
Training	2 months	1 month (subsidized by state government)
Union	Mexican Workers Confederation (CTM)	Mexican Workers Confederation (CTM)

The plant in Taiwan manufactures fabrics and the other factory in Mexico produces garments for other brands. The group started producing for Nike in 1991 with its plant in the United States. In 1999, as production orders increased, the owner opened Plant B in Mexico, where a low-wage labor force and a bigger facility allowed the company to increase its production.

Both plants are part of larger, vertically integrated groups. Plant A belongs to a group that includes spinning, knitting, and finishing operations in the same location where the garment assembly (sewing) takes place. Plant B is also part of a vertically integrated group engaged in the same range of productive activities. Being part of a vertical group is crucial for selling products to global buyers. Global brands tend to prefer plants that can offer "full-package" services to avoid searching for material and component suppliers, which can increase the risk of poor product quality and late deliveries, as well as add to the compliance burden by increasing the number of factories that have to be monitored.

At the time of our research, both plants manufactured the same product (T-shirts) for Nike and other brands and had similar defect rates. Nike sets a 1.4 percent monthly defect rate ceiling for its contractors and considers both plants to be of high quality. Plant A had a 1 percent monthly defect rate and Plant B a 0.6 percent monthly defect rate. Finally, both plants paid the same legal minimum wage (US $5.15/day), had the same turnover rates (8–10 percent per year), and the same informal (based on skill) promotion policies. The labor forces in the two plants are both unionized. Table 5.1 describes the similarities between these two plants.

Notwithstanding their similarities, labor conditions at Plants A and B were, in practice, dramatically different, as illustrated through a more detailed comparison of wages, employee satisfaction, worker participation in production-related issues, work hours and over time, and worker voice/representation at these two plants.

TABLE 5.2. *Production Premiums in Sewing – Plant A*

Percent of Production	Premium (Mexican Pesos)	Premium (US$)*
70	2	0.18
81	25	2.22
86	35	3.11
91	46	4.09
96	60	5.34
100	70	6.23

* Exchange rate was calculated as $1US = 11.24 Mexican pesos at the time of our field research. *Source*: Plant A Management.

Two Worlds of Work

Wages

Workers in Plant A received higher wages than those in Plant B. Notwithstanding that both plants paid the same legal minimum wage, workers at Plant A earned on average a weekly salary that was 21 percent higher than what workers at Plant B earned. These differences in average wages could not be accounted for by differences in local wage rates since both plants are in the same region with respect to Mexican minimum wage laws. The National Commission of Minimum Wages, a division of the Federal Secretary of Labor and Social Welfare, divides Mexico into three geographic areas (A, B, and C) each with a distinct minimum wage. Plants A and B are located in the same (C) geographic area. Wage differences were instead due to different plant-level policies used to calculate worker wages.

In Plant A, workers were paid weekly. The factory opens a bank account for each worker and directly deposits his or her salaries into the account. Workers can withdraw money using an ATM card (there is an ATM station in the plant). At the time of our field research, production workers receive a fixed daily wage of 65 pesos (US$5.80). In addition, individual workers could receive premiums for attendance, punctuality, and overtime should they work extra hours. As a result, operators earned on average 644 pesos (US$57.60) per week plus any additional bonuses they may accrue. In each cell, workers also received productivity bonuses once they exceeded 70 percent of their production targets.

Table 5.2 shows the bonus schedule corresponding to different productivity levels in place at Plant A at the time of our research. Given that the productivity for most cells in Plant A was high, most workers earned close to, if not the entire, potential bonus. In other words, most operators earned their basic weekly wage of 644 pesos (US$ 57.60) plus a weekly bonus of 350 pesos (US$ 31.14) for a total of 994 pesos (US$ 84.52). Workers in other departments (i.e., ironing, quality control, and packaging) received similar bonuses.

In Plant B, workers were also paid weekly, also through direct deposits into their bank accounts. Workers at Plant B could also withdraw money from an

ATM machine located in the plant. Salary in Plant B was also determined through a mixed system that combined hourly wages and a piece rate system. However, the two systems varied in one fundamental way: in Plant A, productivity levels were calculated by cell; in Plant B, they were based on individual performance. Each garment produced at Plant B contained a ticket that reported the value of the individual piece. The value varied depending on the complexity or style of the individual piece. Over the course of the workweek, individual workers collected tickets from pieces they had worked on, and at the end of the week, they turned these into the accounting department, which calculated their earnings. The minimum expected of individual operators was between 300 and 400 pieces per day (depending on the complexity of the garment). At the time of our field research, this amounted to a base salary of 51 pesos per day. Weekly salaries in Plant B were thus the product of fixed daily salaries, productivity bonuses, and premiums for attendance and seniority. On average, at the time of our research, production workers at Plant B earned between 700 and 800 pesos per week.

Employee Satisfaction

Workers in Plant A were more satisfied with their work than were workers in Plant B. In Plant A, employees worked in teams, operated more than one type of sewing machine, and were responsible for routine maintenance of the equipment. Interviews conducted during the field research found that workers in Plant A appreciated job rotation. They valued knowing how to perform a variety of operations and claimed that this opportunity to work on several operations plus in teams significantly improved working conditions over what existed under the previous, more modular production system where they performed the same repetitive task.

In contrast, employees at Plant B worked in fixed, individual stations, were specialized in narrowly defined jobs, and thus performed the same operation over the course of the work day/week/year. The work was highly routinized and repetitive. Our interviews, however, revealed that although workers were not especially fulfilled by their jobs, they were not motivated to acquire new skills or perform a variety of operations. Instead, they preferred to stick with what they knew well so that they could earn more through increased productivity. This was consistent with the bonus system in place at Plant B. Productivity premiums significantly enhanced the base salaries of average production workers and thus, they avoided all change that threatened to undermine these bonuses.

Participation in Production Planning

Workers in Plant A participated in decisions affecting the production targets, scheduling, and even operations whereas workers in Plant B needed to follow orders from above and did not have the opportunity to give their input. During our field research, we observed that the relationship between supervisors and workers in Plant A appeared more collaborative than hierarchical. Supervisors in Plant A coordinated the work of different cells.[3] Every morning, supervisors communicated to each cell the style and quantity of items they needed to produce. Workers then got together and discussed how much they thought they were able to produce that day. Finally, the workers met again with the supervisor, shared their opinions, and together workers and supervisors reached a final agreement on the daily production target. Our field research indicated that these supervisors were inclined to accept input from the workers and establish mutually agreeable production targets. If workers or supervisors did not agree with a particular sequence of operations, or even with an entire operation, they could suggest changes to the production manager, who usually accepted these changes. In other words, workers could suggest alternative ways to perform an operation, rendering it quicker or easier. We found that the opportunity to participate in decisions related to work process had a strong and positive effect on work climate. It provided operators both with greater control over their work and with opportunities to express their creativity and ingenuity at work.

In Plant B, production orders were communicated from the top of the plant's hierarchy, and there was no place for worker participation. The plant manager planned production and distributed the orders to the area supervisors. Production in Plant B was divided into four areas, each consisting of six lines. Each area had one supervisor. Area supervisors received production orders from the plant manager, which they, in turn, divided up among the six lines under their control. The area supervisor was also in charge of explaining and teaching the operations involved in producing a given garment to production workers. Operators needed to follow the precise instructions that they were given. One of the workers we interviewed claimed: "We cannot change or suggest different ways to produce a garment because it is a chain and we need to follow what they tell us." Moreover, although there was no formal policy against workers talking with one another and diffusing work practice innovations during their shifts, many workers complained that they simply did not have the opportunity to share work process innovations among themselves because the pace of production was too fast and they were simply too busy to talk.

Work Hours and Overtime
Production workers at Plant A worked forty-eight hours every week, from 7:30 AM to 5:00 PM Monday through Friday. The cutting department had a

---

[3] Supervisors can oversee between five and eight cells, according to their experience. Thus, each supervisor may have thirty to forty-eight workers under his or her responsibility, which indicates a significant level of autonomy for workers. This also suggests that management trusts workers to do their jobs, based on clear expectations and peer monitoring within the teams. Supervisors are trained to work within this system of cell production. More specifically, they manage personnel, keep the workplace clean, and introduce continuous improvement in the production system. They are also responsible for ensuring that cells have all the material they need, when they need, to get their work done (just-in-time). A mistake in the timing could stop the whole production process in the cell.

different work schedule because it needed to stay three days ahead of the sewing operations. In cutting, there were two shifts in which employees worked six 8-hour days from Monday through Saturday, either from 6:00 AM to 2:00 PM or from 2:00 PM to 10:00 PM. Every two weeks, cutting department workers changed shifts. All workers had a 30-minute break for lunch. In Plant B, there were two shifts for all departments, and workers did not alternate shifts. The first shift began at 7:30 AM and went until 5:00 PM; the second shift started at 5:05 PM and ended at 11:50 PM, Monday through Friday. Both shifts included 30-minute breaks for lunch.

Nike, like most global brands, sets a maximum limit of sixty hours of work per week. Because Mexican law limits the regular workweek to forty-eight hours, workers in both plants could work no more than twelve hours of overtime per week. In both plants, overtime was paid according to Mexican law: for the first nine hours workers were paid twice their regular salary; for the subsequent three hours, they were paid three times their regular salary. However, the extent and form of overtime in the two plants was extremely different. When Plant A needed employees to work extra time, it made workers aware of this need and allowed them to "apply" to work extra hours (and earn extra wages). Overtime was voluntary.

At Plant B, forced overtime was the norm. Workers of the first shift reported that they often worked until 7 PM, sometimes even until 10 PM. This meant that when they worked overtime, they worked between 12 and 15 hours per day. During our interviews, several workers in Plant B reported that they actually worked more than sixty hours per week.[4] This was confirmed by the M-Audits Nike shared with us that documented persistent problems with excess work hours at this factory. Individual workers did not volunteer to work extra hours; the supervisor chose who had to stay longer. Supervisors explained that this is because they wanted their most experienced and efficient workers to work longer hours to reach their production targets sooner.

Worker Voice

Workers at both factories were affiliated with the main Mexican labor union, the Confederacion de Trabajadores Mexcianos. In addition to the legally mandated yearly collective bargaining agreements negotiated by union leaders and plant management, in Plant A, union representatives met more or less every week with the HR manager of the plant to discuss a variety of workplace issues. Relations between the HR managers and the union representatives were collaborative, and these frequent meetings provided a forum for workers to express their concerns. At the time of our field research, Plant B's union representatives also met on a weekly basis with the plant's HR department as well

---

[4] During our interviews, workers reported that they expect to work overtime and look forward to the increase in salary due to the overtime. Working extra hours is one of the ways that production workers can enhance their basic wages.

TABLE 5.3. *Workplace Differences*

	Plant A	Plant B
Average weekly wage	US$86/week	US$67.80/week
Team work	Yes	No
Job description	Multitasks	Single task
Job rotation	Yes	No
Worker participation in work-related decisions	Yes	No
Overtime	Voluntary and within limit	Mandatory and over limit

as with the plant's overall manager. However, these meetings were reported to be more formal, with issues being addressed and solved depending primarily on the desire and mood of the plant manager.

In addition to the union, workers had other channels through which to communicate their grievances and suggestions to management, but these practices as well, although apparently similar on paper, were very different in practice. For example, both plants had suggestion boxes that workers could use to voice grievances, ask questions, or even make suggestions to management. However, the implementation of this practice in the two plants varied significantly. In Plant A, workers' questions or comments remained anonymous and were dealt with in a nonpersonalized manner. In Plant B, management posted both the suggestions (including the name of the worker who wrote it) and its response in a public area on the shop floor, thus compromising the anonymity of the worker. Because some of these comments were of a personal nature (i.e., questions about discrepancies in individual paychecks, tensions between operators and their supervisors), this supposedly more transparent practice at times embarrassed individual workers and, as a result, discouraged them from using this system.

Both plants also possessed various "mixed commissions" composed of representatives from the workers and managers that focused on health and safety, training, first aid, and so on. These are required by Mexican labor law. In Plant A, these commissions were actively engaged in training and administration of first aid for minor injuries or checking to see that access to fire extinguishers and exits and the like were all up to code. Plant B also possessed similar commissions on paper but during our field research, we found no evidence that they were actually functioning.

In short, notwithstanding many apparent similarities, including almost identical scores on their M-Audits, working conditions at Plants A and B were in practice quite different. Table 5.3 summarizes these differences. In Plant A, workers were paid better; worked within the legal work-hour limits and had a choice of whether to work overtime; engaged in decisions affecting the pace, target, and mechanics of production; and participated in various fora that provide them voice at work. Workers in Plant B were paid less well, often worked longer hours, and had no voice in production decisions, let alone other aspects of life in the factory.

It is important to note that with the exception of excess overtime, Plant B was for the most part in compliance with Nike's Code of Conduct and local labor law and on certain issues (i.e., providing on-site day-care services for employees) provided benefits that Plant A did not offer its workers. Moreover, Plant A was not without its own issues. Aside from documentation problems, in the past, Plant A also had supervisors who verbally abused workers. The point of this comparison is not to present Plant A as "good" and Plant B as "bad" on all dimensions but rather to illustrate the very different working conditions manifest at these two plants. Plant B managers very much followed the letter of Mexican labor law as well as Nike's Code of Conduct. However, their approach to employment relations and labor standards differed significantly from the more substantive approach pursued by Plant A management.[5] These difference, in turn, shaped both the types of capability-building efforts promoted at these two plants as well as the consequences of these initiatives for workers employed at these two factories.

Explaining Differences in Working Conditions: Alternative Explanations Considered

Plants A and B were not perfectly matched. They were of different size, their ownership was of different nationality, and they dedicated different percentages of their production capacity to Nike. They were also situated in very different economic realities (labor markets) that may have also shaped their approach toward capability-building efforts and labor standards. The differences between the two plants are summarized in Table 5.4.

Of course, these differences mattered in shaping the strategies and behaviors of both managers and workers in these two plants. For example, workers employed in factories located near other, competing factories, during periods of labor shortage, could "vote with their feet" if conditions at their workplace were poor. This would create an incentive for managers to improve shop-floor conditions and workers to become more active in demanding these improvements. Likewise, proximity to Nike's regional office (and its compliance officers) could increase the likelihood of more frequent factory inspections, and this too could lead to better working conditions than those found in factories located further away from these compliance officers. In what follows, I examine the role each of these characteristics actually played in shaping the observed differences in working conditions in Plants A and B. The analysis is divided into three categories: factory characteristics, labor market differences, and alternative patterns of work organization and worker empowerment.

---

[5] For more on the differences stemming from managers behaving according the "letter" as opposed to the "substance" of the law, see various chapters in Silbey, 2011.

TABLE 5.4. *Differences between Plants A and B*

	Plant A	Plant B
Ownership	Local	Foreign
Proximity to Nike's regional office	Close (50 km)	Far away (2,000 km)
% of production for Nike	10	50
Surrounding environment	Industrialized	Agrarian, undeveloped
Production method	Lean (cell)	Modular (assembly lines)
Number of workers	487	1,100
Workforce nationality		
Managers	Mexican	Taiwanese
Supervisors	Mexican	Taiwanese
Production Workers	Mexican	90% Mexican
		10% Taiwanese

Factory Characteristics

The literature on globalization and labor standards suggests that a variety of factors – ownership, size of plant, type/complexity of product being manufactured – may all affect working conditions in the factories. Some have speculated that factories owned/managed by foreigners treat their workers less well (for a variety of linguistic and cultural reasons) than do factories where the ownership/management of the plants share the same nationality as the workers. Others have argued that plants that are owned/managed by particular nationalities (i.e., Korean and Taiwanese) employ less sophisticated personnel management policies and treat workers in "host" countries with less respect and fairness than do factories owned/managed by other nationalities (i.e., US, European).[6] Given that Plant A is owned/managed by Mexicans and Plant B is owned/managed by Taiwanese, perhaps this feature could explain the differences we observed at the two plants.

In addition, some scholars have claimed that larger, more bureaucratic, "modern" factories will be better able to introduce modern management and personnel systems, and thus, one would expect that larger factories would on average treat their workers better than smaller, less formally managed plants.[7] Given the differences in size between Plants A and B, perhaps this drove the divergent working conditions we observed. Finally, much has been written about the importance of skill and tacit knowledge in the production of high-value-added, differentiated products. From this we speculate that perhaps factories producing more complex (and expensive) products, which require greater skill and technology, will treat their workers as valuable assets for the

---

[6] Stephen J. Frenkel, "Globalization, athletic footwear commodity chains and employment relations in China," *Organization Studies* 22, no. 4 (2001): 531–62, 542.

[7] Theodore H. Moran, *Beyond Sweatshops: Foreign Direct Investment and Globalization in Developing Countries* (Washington, DC: Brookings Institution Press, 2002): 16.

TABLE 5.5. *Factory Characteristics and Working Conditions*

Characteristic	Expected Effect on Working Condition	Observed Working Condition between Plants
Size	Greater size, better working conditions	Not confirmed Smaller plant (A) possessed better working conditions
Nationality of ownership/ management	Foreign ownership (especially Taiwanese and Korean) treat workers less well than domestic owner-ship/management	Confirmed Domestically owned Plant A had better working conditions
Product complexity	More complex product/product mix, better working conditions	Not Confirmed Plant A with less complex product mix had better working conditions

factory.[8] Given that Plants A and B manufacture somewhat different mixes of products, with Plant B specializing in more high-tech performance T-shirts and Plant A concentrating on simpler, printed T-shirts, perhaps this also could explain the divergent working conditions observed across the two plants. Table 5.5 summarizes these various factory characteristics, their expected effects on working conditions, and what we actually observed during our field research.

Our field research in Plants A and B appears to contradict the expectations derived from the literature in terms of plant size and complexity of product mix. We found that workers in Plant A, the smaller facility manufacturing the less complex, lower-tech product, were paid better, worked less overtime, and enjoyed more voice at work than did workers in Plant B. However, our field research does appear to support the claim in the literature that foreign ownership/management negatively affects labor conditions in global supply chain factories.[9] Why this is so, especially given the long history of managers mistreating workers who were conationals and even working within the same nation-state, is unclear. Our field research suggested two possible explanations for these differences. The first concerns language differences and the difficulties in communication between the Taiwanese managers and Mexican workers on Plant B. Most of the managers in Plant B were not fluent in Spanish and thus

[8] Thomas A. Kochan, Harry C. Katz, and Robert B. McKersie, *The Transformation of American Industrial Relations* (New York: Basic Books, 1986); Michael J. Piore and Charles F. Sabel, *The Second Industrial Divide: Possibilities for Prosperity* (New York: Basic Books, 1984).

[9] In this chapter, we compare factories that are owned by people from different countries but do not investigate the modality of the relationship between these suppliers and the global buyers they work for. For a convincing argument for how ownership (as opposed to contracting) relations affect labor standards in these new centers of global production, see Mosley, 2011.

could not easily express themselves with the workers. Likewise, the workers found it nearly impossible to express their concerns or issues to plant management because of these same language barriers. This certainly contributed to some of the workplace tensions we observed at Plant B. A second, complementary explanation focuses on differences in commitment and time horizons by the owners of Plants A and B. Because Plant B was foreign owned, having been attracted to Mexico by various fiscal incentives and the promise of cheap labor, their commitment to improving working conditions was weaker than that of the owners/managers of Plant A, who were Mexican nationals and had been in business for several generations. For example, when asked how they would respond if labor costs increased at Plant B, the managers stated frankly that they would "return to Asia." In short, our interviews at both plants suggested that nationality differences between owners of Plants A and B did play some role in the alternative workplace practices observed at these two plants.

Labor Market Differences

Plants A and B also operate in very different labor markets, which, in turn, provide management in the two plants with varying degrees of leverage over their workers. Plant A is located in an industrial park close to Mexico City, which is home to a large number of other garment plants. This has two effects on Plant A. On the one hand, it provides Plant A with an abundant supply of skilled and experienced workers who are current or former employees of neighboring plants. On the other hand, these other firms compete with Plant A to hire the same workforce, especially the more skilled and experienced workers. This mixture of threat and opportunity creates an incentive for management at Plant A to seek to minimize turnover. Of course, all firms try to hold on to their most valued employees through higher wages and improved benefits, but Plant A also tries to tie workers to the firm through job enrichment and participation on the shop floor.

Plant B is the only garment factory in its locality and is therefore in a powerful position vis-à-vis its workers – all eager for employment in this underdeveloped state. Moreover, Plant B imports 10 percent of its workforce from Taiwan, ostensibly to train the local, inexperienced Mexican workers. These Taiwanese workers do not speak any Spanish and do not have any networks outside the factory. They conduct their lives exclusively in the factory, where they work, eat, and sleep (in the factory dorms). Under these conditions, it is unlikely, if not impossible, that these more experienced and skilled Taiwanese workers would find an alternative job in a different factory. There simply aren't any other factories (and thus available jobs) around, and Plant B uses this position to its advantage. In short, Plants A and B operate in very different local labor markets, providing their respective management teams with very different incentives and leverage over their workforces. These differences clearly account for some of the divergent patterns of working practices and conditions observed at the two plants. Yet, beyond differences in local labor market conditions and the nationality of the plants' managers/owners, our field research uncovered radically different approaches to the organization of work and the management of employees at these two factories. These differences in human resources management and work organization were central to the differences observed in working conditions and labor standards at these two plants.

Work Organization and Employment Relations on the Shop Floor: Alternative Approaches to Capability Building

To accommodate rapidly shifting consumer tastes, global brands are pushing their suppliers to reduce cycle times, produce varied products in smaller batches, and rapidly change production from one style to another. Suppliers are responding to these challenges in different ways. Plants A and B appear to have reacted to the same external market pressures by pursuing alternative approaches to capability building, especially as they related to work organization and human resource management policies. These alternative choices, in turn, generated significant consequences for working conditions at their respective establishments.

Plant A

Plant A responded to the challenges (and opportunities) presented by global buyers by introducing lean manufacturing processes within its facilities.[10] Workers were organized in groups of six "islands" or production "cells," each of which produced an entire garment. Each worker performed a variety of operations and worked on different machines. The machines were organized in a U-shape formation. The shop floor was clean and uncluttered by extra materials. Inventory was absent because the factory used a just in time system that did not permit excess inventory.

When this factory began manufacturing, it employed an assembly-line (bundle system) production system. In the mid-1990s, Plant A introduced a modular production system, but after ten years, it began to transition to lean manufacturing.[11] To transform the modules into cells, the factory had to extensively

---

[10] For a good, general description of lean manufacturing, see John F. Krafcik, "Triumph of the Lean Production System," *Sloan Management Review* 30, no. 1 (Fall 1988): 41–51.

[11] In 1995, the owners expanded their plant with another building. In the new structure, they adopted a modular production system to have a more flexible and shorter production cycle. However, in 2003, the owners of the factory attended a meeting with one of their global buyers and heard about lean manufacturing and its application in the footwear sector. They became interested and learned more about lean manufacturing. The following year, they decided to implement this new system in their plant. For more on the different systems of production in the apparel industry, see Frederick H. Abernathy, John T. Dunlop, Janice H. Hammond, and David Weil, *A Stitch in Time: Lean Retailing and the Transformation of Manufacturing – Lessons from the Apparel and Textile Industries* (New York: Oxford University Press, 1999);

retrain its workforce. All workers received twenty-five days (nine hours per day) of on-the-job training plus 10 hours of off-the-job training in preventive maintenance of their workstations. Training was carried out by the plant's human resource department, with the help of a process engineer. To motivate workers to participate and not exit the plant, workers were paid their daily salary plus a production bonus during this transition period.[12]

Adjustment to a new system of production can take time. After the shift to cell production, workers who were working at 100 percent productivity levels in the previous modular system dropped to 50 percent levels.[13] As we saw earlier, these productivity bonuses were a significant component of workers' wages. To facilitate the process of adjustment, Plant A management not only guaranteed a significant percentage of the productivity bonus (81 percent) for the entire transition period but also introduced a variety of nonmonetary rewards and incentives. For example, at the conclusion of the training, management organized a graduation ceremony attended by the owners and top managers of Plant A. All graduates received a T-shirt and a cake as a reward. Moreover, whenever particular cells achieved 100 percent productivity level under the new system, the cell was recognized with a small gift to celebrate the event and had their picture posted on the board at the factory entrance. At first, we thought that these rewards could not really make a difference and that workers would not value them. To our surprise, interviews with workers (conducted out of the presence of their supervisors or managers) indicated that, in fact, the small gifts or celebrations made them feel part of the company and created a more relaxed environment.

Overall, Plant A confirms what the literature on high performance work organizations suggests.[14] The HR manager indicated that the change from modular to lean production increased efficiency and quality.[15] By switching to lean manufacturing, the factory formed three cells (18 workers) from two lines (20 workers). With three cells, they were able to produce 2,700 T-shirts,

---

John. T. Dunlop and David Weil, "Diffusion and Performance of Modular Production in the US Apparel Industry," *Industrial Relations* 35, no. 3 (July 1996): 334–55.

[12] The production bonus was equal to 81 percent of worker productivity during their training period. Management chose a bonus corresponding to 81 percent productivity levels because it was the average bonus that operators were receiving under the previous, modular system of production in Plant A.

[13] Workers with more experience took less time to adapt to the new production method, but in general it took some time for an average worker to reach full productivity, and this can have a discouraging effect on the employees.

[14] Casey Ichniowski, Thomas A. Kochan, David Levine, Craig Olson and George Strauss, "What Works at Work: Overview and Assessment," *Industrial Relations* 35, no. 3 (Jul 1996): 299–333; Paul Osterman, "How Common is Workplace Transformation and Who Adopts It," *Industrial & Labor Relations Review* 47, no. 2 (January 1994): 173–88.

[15] At 100% level of productivity, one cell can produce 1,060 pieces/day for a basic T-shirt. This is equal to 181 pieces per person. For a more complex T-shirt, the cell can produce 782 pieces per day (132 per person).

TABLE 5.6. *Comparison between Old and New System of Production in Plant A*

	Old System (Module)	New System (Cell)
Number of workers	10	6
Number of T-shirts per day per module/cell	1,200 T-shirts/module	900 T-shirts/cell
Productivity per worker	120 T-shirts/day	150 T-shirts/day
Average weekly salary	US$68/week	US$86/week

whereas previously they used to produce 2,400 T-shirts with two lines. Quality improved as well. According to the head of operations, defect rates in sewing decreased by 40 percent. Achieving quality and output targets was considered a collective responsibility at Plant A, in which peer supervision and self-supervision played a large role. The production manager explained that each worker was accountable for quality at his or her workstation and that quality control was part of the basic job. Every worker had to check the quality of one out of every five T-shirts. Table 5.6 presents the differences between the two systems of production at the 80 percent productivity level. The numbers show that through cell production, workers increased both their productivity and their weekly salary. The salary increase was due to both a general wage increase at the factory and greater productivity bonuses for production workers.

This shift to lean production not only increased productivity, quality, and wages but also led to a new work system in which multiskilled workers operated a variety of machines and actively participated in key decisions affecting production and work orders. In other words, through the introduction of lean manufacturing techniques and high-performance work and employment practices, Plant A not only enhanced its competitiveness, it also improved working conditions.

Plant B
Plant B's response to increased buyer demands was to invest heavily in a modular system of production with assembly lines. The overall objective of modular production is to facilitate small shifts in large production runs with minimal delays in costs and without requiring specialized machinery. Modularization is one of the ways mass producers are able to increase efficiencies, cut costs, and achieve a modest amount of customization.[16] As the head of operations in Plant B reported, every style requires a specific set of machines and sequence of operations and requires a large area to set up the line.[17] This was different from

---

[16] For more on this system, see Jody Knauss, "Modular Mass Production: High Performance on the Low Road," *Politics & Society* 26, no. 2 (June 1998): 273–96.

[17] When a new style has to be produced, the factory needs to change the order of machines and operations. In a modular system, once the line is set up, it is hard to move the machines around. In addition, sometimes two or more machines are needed for the same operation because two

TABLE 5.7. *Comparison of Production Systems in Plant A and Plant B*

	Plant A	Plant B
Total no. of workers in one line or cell	6	10
T-shirts per day per line or cell	900 T-shirts/day	800 T-shirts/day
Daily wage (fixed salary + bonuses) per worker	US$17.20	US$13.60
T-Shirts per worker	150 T-shirts/worker	80 T-shirts/worker
Labor cost per T-shirt	US$0.11	US$0.18

Plant A where the layout of the machines was more flexible and people moved from one machine to another as they performed various operations. Cellular production is more conducive to rapid changes in styles and smaller batch production. In contrast, the modular system of production is especially good for producing large volumes because it does not require changes in machinery or plant layout.

Very much along the lines of Taylor's system of scientific management,[18] Plant B closely monitored and controlled its workers. In Plant B, production orders were communicated from the top of the plant's hierarchy, and there was no role for worker participation. The plant manager planned the production and distributed the production orders to the area supervisors, who, in turn, divided up the work among the six lines of workers under their control.

Table 5.7 compares the production systems in Plant A and Plant B. The table indicates that notwithstanding the high degree of worker specialization in Plant B and their efforts (incentives) to produce as much as they could, their daily productivity at the time of our field research was actually lower than that of workers in Plant A.

Plant A enjoyed higher productivity than Plant B, paid wages that were higher than those paid to workers in Plant B, and had lower unit labor costs than Plant B. Unit costs (along with quality and on time delivery) are what buyers really care about, which suggests that Plant A possessed both better working conditions *and* better business performance than Plant B. Moreover, its new production system permitted Plant A to more quickly respond to shifts in consumer tastes and buyer demands for smaller and more varied batches. In short, Plant A did not appear to be sacrificing profit for better working conditions. Instead, these two outcomes appear to go hand and hand.[19]

---

styles may differ only for slightly different operations. In these cases, it is more convenient for the factory to have only one line that can work on both styles. As a consequence, one line can get extremely long.

[18] Frederick Winslow Taylor, *The Principles of Scientific Management* (New York: W. W. Norton & Company, 1967).

[19] It is worth noting that this is a rough comparison. The comparison is made between a cell in Plant A and a line in Plant B that make comparable products (basic T-shirts), and it is based on information provided by the factories regarding the number of T-shirts produced by a cell or a

In sum, the differences in working conditions between Plants A and B were the product not solely of geographic location or nationality of ownership but also (and perhaps primarily) the result of very different ways that production and work were organized in these two factories. In Plant A, work was reorganized along the lines of lean production, which relies on multiskilled, autonomous work groups engaged in a variety of operations. This new system enhanced the plant's efficiency and quality, which allowed it to better schedule its workload (hence, avoid excessive overtime) and increase the wages of its workforce (share the efficiency gains). Plant B pursued a more scientific management approach, investing heavily in new plant and equipment. The goal of Plant B management was to increase productivity and quality through investments in new technology, strict control over the workforce, and various incentives (productivity bonuses) aimed at achieving ever-greater economies of scale.

Yet, we should be careful not to conflate particular production systems (lean vs. modular) with differences in workplace conditions. Although lean production lends itself to various human resource practices (increased training, autonomous work teams, etc.), there is no automatic link between this system of work organization and better working conditions. There is an extensive literature that shows that firms can (and do) actually mix elements of different production techniques with a variety of human resource management policies, generating mixed results.[20] This literature emphasizes the importance of bundling together particular systems of work organization with specific human resource management practices to achieve the greatest results for both companies and their workers.[21]

Closer examination of our two Mexican plants reveals the importance of different choices managers make in introducing new production techniques and management systems – choices that ultimately shape workplace conditions. In addition to introducing lean manufacturing, Plant A also employed various human resource management policies that provided workers with greater autonomy and power on the shop floor. For example, Plant A invested heavily in the training of its workers (in part to effectively implement lean manufacturing processes) and thus became wary of mistreating these highly skilled workers

---

line in a day, and workers' wages. A comparison between cells and lines that produce different types of T-shirts may provide different results.

[20] For more on this, see John Paul MacDuffie and John F. Krafcik, "Integrating Technology and Human Resources for High Performance Manufacturing: Evidence from the International Auto Industry," in Thomas A. Kochan and Michael Useem (Eds.), *Transforming Organizations* (New York: Oxford University Press, 1992), and Knauss, "Modular Mass Production: High Performance on the Low Road."

[21] For a good review of this literature, see John Paul MacDuffie, "Human-Resource Bundles and Manufacturing Performance: Organizational Logic and Flexible Production Systems in the World Auto Industry," *Industrial & Labor Relations Review* 48, no. 2 (January 1995): 197–221; Ichniowski, Kochan, Levine, Olson and Strauss, "What Works at Work: Overview and Assessment," *Industrial Relations*, 35, no. 3 (1996): 299–333.

for fear that they would lose their investments in these workers. Skilled but dissatisfied workers could easily leave and work for a competitor. These same workers, trained to stop production when they saw defects and who worked in autonomous production cells in which they actively participated in decisions affecting production targets and techniques, also became more empowered to resist management abuses on the shop floor. In the end, a virtuous cycle developed in which new forms of work organization and training led to enhanced competitiveness for the plant and improved working conditions for the workers, including greater discretion and participation over production decisions. Increased employee participation, in turn, generated operational innovations and efficiencies, which subsequently produced gains that could be shared by plant owners and workers alike.

Plant B pursued an alternative approach to capability building and the management of its workforce. Rather than invest in training and encourage worker autonomy/discretion, Plant B developed highly detailed work rules and maintained tight control over the shop floor. In contrast to Plant A, workers in Plant B were not seen as a resource for improving productivity and quality. Instead, management at Plant B considered workers a (variable) cost that needed to be reduced as much as possible. According to the head of operations at Plant B, "It's all about lowering the price of labor and increasing the quantity produced." For this reason, Plant B invested heavily in new process technologies and devised ever more specialized operations that less expensive, unskilled workers could perform under close supervision by factory managers. Increased productivity and quality resulted not from worker training and creativity but from new technologies, close supervision of the work process, and individual incentives that rewarded workers for ever-greater quantities of output and longer work hours.

Concluding Considerations

Almost a half-century ago, Douglas McGregor observed that the choices firms make in terms of how they organize work and manage their workforces are shaped by the assumptions managers hold about workers' motivations.[22] According to McGregor, workers could be seen as either variable costs to be reduced, reluctant contributors to the firm's prosperity and thus requiring constant supervision and control or as assets to be valued and developed, multifaceted individuals who are intrinsically motivated to work and contribute to their work organizations.[23] Clearly, the capability-building programs at Plants A and B reflect these opposing assumptions. At Plant A, management invested in training and empowered employees to work in autonomous cells. These workers often took initiative to solve various production-related

---

[22] Douglas Murray McGregor, *The Human Side of Enterprise* (New York: McGraw-Hill, 1960).
[23] Ibid.

problems. "We want people here to feel important," reported the owners during our interviews. In contrast, at Plant B, workers were seen as an "input" to be controlled, a "cost" to be reduced. When we asked the head of operations at Plant B what would happen if he could not continue to lower labor costs in the factory, he replied, "In that case we will move back to Asia."

However, managerial choices are shaped not only by previously held assumptions about human nature but also by the context within which managers operate.[24] This was evident at our two plants, especially in terms of the relationship between plant management and Nike's local staff. At Plant A, relations between factory management and Nike's local staff were collaborative and open. Nike managers would visit Plant A about once a month, and the owners of Plant A would also frequently visit Nike's regional office in Mexico City. Nike staff and plant managers reported that they often went out for dinner or played golf together. Over time, these frequent visits led to greater transparency and trust between Nike and Plant A management as well as joint problem solving. Whenever an issue related to workplace standards arose, both Nike compliance specialists and Plant A management worked together to quickly remediate the issue. Moreover, Nike production and quality managers were instrumental in supporting Plant A in its transition to lean manufacturing. They not only exchanged information and technical advice but also provided moral support to Plant A (in the form of an implicit agreement to continue to source from the plant during its transition) as it struggled to shift from a modular to a lean production system. Interviews with managers at Plant A indicated that they saw Nike as a partner with whom they could collaborate to improve both productivity and working conditions.

The relationship between Nike's regional office and Plant B management was more formal and distant. Plant B received fewer visits to its facilities (in part because of its geographic distance from Mexico City) and thus much of the communication between the local Nike office and Plant B occurred over the phone or through e-mail. Yet, Plant B was also one of Nike's "strategic partners." Strategic partners are those suppliers that Nike has designated as tier-one suppliers. Some of them (in footwear) are involved in collaborative design and product development processes. Others (in apparel) are permitted to source their own materials and are seen as long-term partners in the future. Nike organizes periodic meetings with its strategic partners to share with them various strategic directions or opportunities the company is pursuing. Strategic partners, in turn, are supposed to share "best practices" with one another, thus enhancing the competitiveness of the entire network of tier-one suppliers. Thus, one would expect greater trust and transparency between Plant B and Nike's regional office. However, this was not the case. Management at Plant B

[24] Mark S. Granovetter, "Strength of Weak Ties," *American Journal of Sociology* 78, no. 6 (May 1973): 1360–80; Richard M. Locke, *Remaking the Italian Economy*, Peter J. Katzenstein (Ed.), Cornell Studies in Political Economy (Ithaca, NY: Cornell University Press, 1995).

saw Nike as a buyer whose requirements and deadlines it needed to respect in order to receive future orders. Nike's local staff, in turn, viewed Plant B as a technically excellent manufacturer but whose commitment to labor standards was weak.

In many ways, the differences in relationships between Nike and the managers at the two Mexican plants resembled what Frenkel and Scott found in their study of supplier-buyer relations in China.[25] In that study, they argued that brands develop two distinct types of compliance relationships with their suppliers: a hands-on, cooperative relationship with some suppliers and an arm's length, more distrustful "compliance" relationship with others. These differences, according to Frenkel and Scott, shape not just the style but also the substance of compliance programs within factories.[26] The comparative study of two plants in Mexico presented in this chapter appears to support their findings. More frequent visits and more open communication between Nike's regional staff and management at Plant A led to the development of greater trust and a better working relationship between these two actors. This, in turn, contributed to the upgrading of Plant A's production system and its consequent positive impact on working conditions at the plant. Less frequent, more formal communication patterns between Nike's local staff and Plant B management appeared to have reinforced the arms-length nature of their relationship, in which Plant B sought to deliver product to Nike at the lowest cost (highest margin) and Nike tried to ensure compliance with both its technical and workplace standards through ever-more-sophisticated systems of policing and monitoring.

Unfortunately, the type of relationship between Plant B and Nike is the more common/typical relationship that exists between global buyers and their suppliers. As a result, these two actors are often locked in a low-trust trap in which suppliers claim that brands are sending them mixed messages, insisting on faster cycle times, better quality, and lower prices while policing and admonishing them for poor working conditions. Brands, in turn, argue that problems associated with both production and labor standards are the result of the lack of professionalism and short sightedness of their suppliers. The experience at Plant A shows that there is a way out of this trap. Through increased communication and interaction, more collaborative and transparent relations can be created.[27] This process takes time and requires investment on the part of both suppliers and global brands, but it promises to generate benefits for everyone involved, including the workers in these global supply chain factories. Whether

[25] Stephen J. Frenkel and Duncan Scott, "Compliance, Collaboration, and Codes of Labor Practice: The Adidas Connection," *California Management Review* 45, no. 1 (Fall 2002): 29–49.

[26] Ibid.

[27] For more on how trustlike relations are built, not inherited, see Richard M. Locke, "Building Trust," paper presented at Annual Meetings of the American Political Science Association, San Francisco (September 1, 2001).

these more collaborative relations can be sustained, let alone diffused, given then divergent and conflicting interests of the various supply chain actors is an open question. The case study presented in this chapter, as well as some of the capability-building initiatives analyzed in the previous chapter, illustrate that an alternative, more collaborative relationship between buyers and suppliers – one that benefits both companies and workers – *is* possible. The next chapter documents the enormous challenges this model faces given contemporary supply chain dynamics and traditional upstream business practices currently employed by global buyers and large retailers. Until these broader practices are reformed, collaborative buyer–supplier relations leading to improved labor standards will remain the exception rather than the rule in today's global supply chains.

6

Are We Looking in the Wrong Place?

Labor Standards and Upstream Business Practices in Global Supply Chains

Introduction

As we saw in the previous chapters, notwithstanding years of investment in private compliance programs by global brands and their lead suppliers, and even after some more recent, promising capability-building initiatives by global corporations, multistakeholder initiatives, and international organizations, poor working conditions, excessive work hours, precarious employment practices, and low wages persist in factories producing for global supply chains. This chapter seeks to explain why some of these problems continue by looking beyond the suppliers' factories and more broadly at the relationships among large retailers, global brands, lead suppliers, and factory workers in global supply chains. By taking this broader perspective, I hope to show that although better-designed private compliance systems and more encompassing capability-building programs would certainly help improve labor standards in these global supply chains, they are not in and of themselves sufficient to tackle these persistent workplace issues. This is because all of the interventions we have examined so far focus primarily on the locus of production, on the factories producing for global buyers. Although this focus on the workplace ostensibly makes sense given that this is where most labor standards violations are manifest, the reality is that many of the workplace problems we observe in global supply chains are not solely the product of poorly trained or unethical factory managers (hence in need of capability building or requiring careful auditing and policing) but also the result of a set of policies and practices designed and implemented *upstream* by large retailers and global buyers. In other words, global brands have responded to a business environment characterized by dynamic consumer demand, shorter product life cycles, and concentrated retail channels by reorganizing their supply chains to optimize efficiencies and minimize financial and reputational risks. Timely delivery of the latest products to the market is essential for global brands competing in these dynamic markets. As a result, global brands and their lead suppliers have developed production planning and manufacturing systems that minimize the financial and reputational risks of not meeting consumer demand in a timely manner.

Although these techniques allow for a broader selection of products, faster product introductions, and reduced inventory of poor-selling products for brands, they create all sorts of labor problems *downstream* for factories and their workers. The production architecture necessary to operate this more "lean" system exhibits high volatility at the point where products are assembled. As a result, order volatility in many supply chain factories is "managed" through a combination of rigid (Taylorist) work organization and flexible labor supply (often in the form of migrant workers who work long hours at low wages), which enables production to rapidly scale up and down but also creates a context prone to persistent labor standards violations.

The impact of these upstream business practices on the organization of work and employment relations in various global supply chains challenges much of our conventional wisdom on how best to address poor labor standards, especially in industries with short product life cycles and volatile consumer demand (i.e., many consumer goods industries). Yet, to date, there has been little systematic attention paid to the upstream sources of poor working conditions in these global supply chains.[1] This is mainly due to the way most labor scholars study and understand these issues. We focus on the workplaces and factories because this is, in fact, where workers are employed and where we observe the vast majority of the violations in labor standards and worker rights, and we "look under the lamppost" because of our own intellectual traditions and biases toward production (where people make things) as opposed to how these products are commercialized and consumed. Yet, upstream business policies and practices are provoking significant changes in supply chain governance, manufacturing practice, and ultimately employment conditions for the thousands of workers who make the goods each of us consume every day.[2]

This relationship between upstream business practices and factory-level labor conditions was foreshadowed in the previous chapters. Recall that suppliers that dedicated a significant percentage of their productive capacity to Nike had on average lower compliance scores than suppliers who were less dependent on Nike for their business. During our field research at these factories, my graduate students and I often heard plant managers lament that several of their labor problems, especially excessive working hours and mandatory overtime, were due to late or changed orders from Nike. Likewise, among ABC's suppliers

---

[1] With the exceptions, to be discussed later in this chapter, of Oxfam (2004), Clean Clothes Campaign (2008), and Raworth and Kidder, 2009.

[2] See Hamilton, Petrovic, and Senauer (2011) for a discussion of the role of large retailers in shaping consumer markets and supply chain practices in today's global economy.

in Central America, we saw how rapid replenishment and quick turnaround strategies provided an opportunity for some of these suppliers to continue to work with ABC and compete with lower cost but more distant Asian factories, but at the same time, these strategies created certain compliance problems (i.e., excess overtime) for these suppliers.

In recent years, several global brands have acknowledged that some of their own upstream business practices are driving poor labor conditions among their suppliers. Nike, for example, conducted an internal analysis of excessive overtime among its apparel suppliers and concluded:

One of the biggest root causes of excessive overtime in apparel manufacturing is the large number of styles factories produce. Every time a factory has to change a style, it reduces productivity and overall efficiency, adding to the total number of hours of work requested. Our analysis shows that, among the variables we have direct control over, asking factories to manufacture too many styles is one of the highest contributors to factory overtime in apparel. (Nike 2010a: 53)

In addition to the proliferation of styles, Nike's Corporate Responsibility Report goes on to list other upstream practices that also contribute to excessive working hours. These include last-minute changes in the colors or fabrics needed in product development, poor market forecasting for particular products, long approval processes in merchandising, and miscalculating the productive capacity of its suppliers (Nike 2010a: 54).[3] Timberland, a company with a very different reputation than Nike and competing in a very different market segment, admitted similar issues: "By taking a step back and reflecting on the effect internal procedures can have on our suppliers, we discovered that some of our procedures were making it difficult for factories to control working hours" (Timberland 2007: 4). These "internal procedures" included the number of styles being developed in Timberland's product line, which drove demand for samples to exceed capacity in the sample room; the simultaneous launch of several new products, which created learning curve-related drops in productivity among certain suppliers – inefficiencies that could only be recovered through increased working hours; and a mismatch between Timberland's overall orders and the total productive capacity of certain suppliers, especially during peak production months (Timberland 2007: 4–5).

The relationship between the upstream business practices of global brands and large retailers and poor labor conditions among their suppliers was also the focus of two major studies by nongovernmental organizations (NGOs) in recent years. In 2003–4, Oxfam International coordinated a research project on the supply chain practices of twenty companies spanning fifteen countries.

---

[3] Several of these same factors were discussed by Dusty Kidd, former director of compliance at Nike, in 2006. See Roseann Casey, "Meaningful Change: Raising the Bar in Supply Chain Workplace Standards," Working Paper # 29, Corporate Social Responsibility Initiative, John F. Kennedy School of Government, Harvard University, November 2006: 24–5.

The project included thousands of interviews with factory and farm work-ers, managers, government officials, union and NGO representatives, trading agents, importers, and staff from various major brands and large retailers. The study concluded that

current sourcing strategies designed to meet "just-in-time" delivery (premised on flexi-bility and fast turnaround), combined with the lowering of unit costs, are significantly contributing to the use of exploitative employment practices by suppliers. (Dhanarajan 2005: 531)

According to the authors of this study, lean production is "mimicked" rather than genuinely practiced when suppliers do not possess the managerial and technical tools to cope with the demands by global brands and large retailers for shorter production lead times, greater number of products/styles, and ever-lower unit prices. "As a result, it is most definitely the workers at the labor-intensive stage of production who are getting leaned on" (Raworth and Kidder 2009: 170). A subsequent study by the Clean Clothes Campaign of thirty plants located in Sri Lanka, Bangladesh, India, and Thailand, producing garments for several large retailers (Wal-Mart, Carrefour, and Tesco, to name a few) also found that the upstream business practices of these "giant retailers" and their demand for quick turnaround and lower unit costs were undermining the ability of their suppliers to respect their codes of conduct (Clean Clothes Campaign 2008).

These various studies – conducted both internally by global brands and externally by researchers affiliated with Oxfam and the Clean Clothes Cam-paign – suggest that promoting labor rights and improved working conditions in global supply chains requires more than compliance and capacity building: we need to reexamine the upstream business practices of the brands and the nature and terms of relations among the key actors in global supply chains, which is the focus of this chapter.

This chapter analyzes these broader supply chain dynamics and how they affect working conditions and labor rights on the shop floor by looking at HP and the global electronics industry. We might expect there to be higher degrees of compliance with labor standards in electronics because the suppliers operating in this industry are for the most part themselves large, multina-tional corporations, in some cases producing components that command high price premiums. Furthermore, whereas nearly all lead firms in previous stud-ies adopted supplier codes of conduct in response to consumer pressure or public scandal, HP anticipated these pressures and moved early to develop internal and industry-wide strategies for monitoring and improving conditions in the supply chain. As we saw earlier, the company also promoted various capability-building programs, an approach that appears to be more effective than traditional compliance practices, under certain conditions, at promoting improved working conditions. And yet even after all of these efforts, workplace problems and poor labor standards persist among HP's suppliers. This chapter first illustrates the impact of these upstream business practices on poor working conditions in various electronics plants supplying HP and then considers what might be done to redesign these practices and promote improved labor standards in global supply chains.

The Global Electronics Industry

The global electronics industry[4] is one of the largest and fastest growing manufacturing sectors, characterized by disaggregated production networks involving numerous suppliers located throughout the globe (United National Conference on Trade and Development 2004). In the late 1980s, leading electronics firms transitioned away from vertically integrated production structures to a new model of outsourced manufacturing, opting to concentrate almost exclusively on discrete competencies that rarely involved production. The vast majority of leading US electronics firms, including IBM, Nortel, Apple, 3Com, Hewlett-Packard (HP), Maxtor, and Lucent, followed this trend during these years (Sturgeon 2002; Sturgeon and Lester 2002; Gereffi, Humphrey, and Sturgeon 2005; Senauer and Reardon 2011). Many of these firms divested their manufacturing facilities during this period, resulting in the rapid growth of contract manufacturers. Much of this growth was concentrated among a small number of companies – most notably, Flextronics, Celestica, Sanmina, Jabil, and Foxconn. By 2000, leading contract manufacturers had production facilities in as many as seventy countries with the bulk of manufacturing activities occurring in two or three regions in the developing world (Luthje 2002; Ernst 2004).

The global electronics industry today is highly concentrated with a bifurcated structure involving a small number of international buyers and suppliers that control much of the market (Sturgeon and Lester 2002). Table 6.1 presents revenue, gross profit, and employment data for the leading electronics and contract manufacturing firms. Companies selling branded hardware largely control the industry's product definition, design, and innovation trajectories and thus continue to capture value associated with high-end markets and new technologies (Sturgeon 2002; Linden et al. 2009). There is, however, some evidence that this dynamic may be changing. Table 6.1 indicates that electronics suppliers such as Foxconn and Flextronics rival electronics lead firms like

---

[4] I use the term "electronics industry" to describe the population of firms that actively produce or manage the production of computer hardware. These firms directly manufacture or coordinate the assembly of computers, computer peripherals, communications equipment, repairs, and similar electronic products. Although these hardware firms may engage in other diversified technology services, a core aspect of their business focuses on the production of physical computer hardware. Lead firms in this industry almost always classify themselves within North American Industry Classification System (NAICS) codes for "Electronic Computer Manufacturing" (334111) and "Other Computer Peripheral Manufacturing" (334119).

TABLE 6.1. *Top Electronics Lead Firms and Suppliers by Revenue*

Rank	Firm	2011 Total Revenue (in billions)	2011 Gross Profit (in billions)	Employees
Electronics Firms Producing Computer Hardware				
1	Hewlett-Packard	$127.2	$29.7	324,600
2	Apple	$108.3	$43.8	60,400
3	IBM	$106.5	$46.0	426,751
4	Dell	$61.7	$11.4	100,300
5	Cisco	$43.7	$26.5	63,465
Electronics Suppliers				
1	Foxconn	$111.1	$2.2	920,000
2	Flextronics	$30.3	$1.6	200,000
3	Jabil Circuit	$16.8	$1.25	100,000
4	Celestica	$7.3	$0.1	35,000
5	Sanmina-SCI	$6.6	$0.1	48,000

The 2011 revenue and profit statistics are annual data, although it should be noted that company income statements report revenues as of different end periods in 2011. For the companies presented in this table, 2011 revenue and profit reflect annual data as of the following dates: September 24 (Apple), September 30 (Celestica, Flextronics, Foxconn, IBM), October 1 (Sanmina-SCIA), October 28 (Dell), October 29 (Cisco), October 31 (Hewlett-Packard), and November 30 (Jabil).

HP, Apple, or IBM in terms of revenue and employment. Moreover, several large and internationally diverse suppliers, such as ACER (2010 revenue of $20.1B with 7,757 employees) have recently begun to establish their own computer hardware brands. Notwithstanding these recent developments, much of the profit continues to be captured by branded lead firms rather than the suppliers responsible for production activities. While the five electronics lead firms present in Table 6.1 collectively produced 2011 gross profits of $157.4 billion, the industry's top five suppliers collectively achieved profits of $5.3 billion.

Fluctuating market demand and shorter product life cycles have produced a volatile manufacturing environment within the electronics sector (for a detailed review of risk factors specific to the electronics industry, see Sodhi and Lee 2007). Consistent advances in technology have led to the rapid obsolescence of consumer electronics (Byster and Smith 2006). According to one executive at Dell Computers, "Inventory has the shelf life of lettuce" (Catholic Agency for Overseas Development [CAFOD] 2004).

In response to variable demand and intense cost pressures, contract manufactures have adopted flexible employment policies. These work relationships are characterized by long work hours, contingent or temporary employment contracts, and high concentrations of women, minority, and migrant employees (CAFOD 2004; Smith et al. 2006; Chan and Peyer 2008). Many contract manufacturers employ significant numbers of contingent or agency workers to limit worker benefit coverage and enable suppliers to hire and fire employees rapidly in response to variations in production demand. A representative from the electronics supplier Foxconn went as far to say that "[Foxconn] believes that it would be better to hire all workers directly; unfortunately our variable manufacturing volumes do not allow us to do it" (Centre for Reflection and Action on Labour Issues 2007). This combination of low-skilled assembly work by large numbers of contingent and/or migrant workers has led to labor rights issues surrounding working hours, benefits, and safety (Smith, Sonnenfeld, and Pellow 2006; Schipper and de Haan 2007; Good Electronics 2009; SOMO 2009). The harsh working conditions in the electronics industry were most vividly manifest by the tragic worker suicides that began in 2010 within Chinese electronics facilities owned by Foxconn and producing for Apple.

In the 1990s, long before these most recent tragedies but still in response to poor labor and environmental conditions in the electronics industry, HP and other lead firms launched corporate social and environmental responsibility programs, and several prominent firms, such as HP, Dell, and IBM, established the Electronics Industry Citizenship Coalition and Code of Conduct (both commonly referred to as EICC), in an effort to promote a more collaborative approach to promoting improved labor and environmental standards among electronics suppliers. And yet despite these efforts, poor working conditions and labor rights abuses persist. To better understand why, we now turn to an in-depth case study of HP and its supply chain.

Hewlett-Packard

HP is a leading electronics firm with a globally dispersed supply base and a strong commitment to social and environmental responsibility. In fiscal year 2010, HP shipped in excess of 64 million personal computers and employed approximately 325,000 individuals in 170 countries. During fiscal year 2010, HP operated in more than 170 countries, contracting with approximately 1,000 suppliers in more than 1,200 locations. These suppliers provide product materials and components, in addition to manufacturing and distribution services. Most suppliers for HP are located in developing countries in four main geographical regions: Asia Pacific, Central and Eastern Europe, Greater China, and Latin America.

As described in Chapter 2, HP has been committed to social and environmental issues throughout its history. The "HP Way" refers to a management philosophy that emphasizes integrity, respect for individuals, teamwork, innovation, and contribution to customers and the community (Packard 2006). Although HP has a history of union avoidance at its facilities, it has exhibited a strong and long-standing commitment to social and environmental responsibility.[5] Consistent with this culture, HP became an early advocate of global labor standards. In 2002, the company developed its first supplier Code of Conduct. This was the first Code of Conduct in the electronics industry and provided an important foundation for the industry-wide standards that were later established through the Electronics Industry Citizens Coalition.

The EICC was established in 2004 when eight leading electronics firms, including HP, sought to improve the working conditions and environmental impacts of their suppliers through the development of an industry-wide Code of Conduct. By 2008, EICC membership had grown to include 45 firms with a collective 1.2 trillion in revenue, employing 3.4 million workers (EICC 2009). EICC-affiliated firms require their suppliers (and in some cases, their own facilities) to comply with the EICC code. The first EICC code was developed in 2004 and has since been revised three times, the most recent revision occurring in 2011.

The code is divided into seven sections; the first covers broad Code of Conduct compliance issues and is followed by six more specific sections addressing labor, health, the environment, labor management, environmental health and safety management, and ethics. Audits across suppliers and national settings are based on an evaluation of fifty-three EICC items that are independently assessed for compliance outcomes, and first-time audits usually take two days to complete. Depending on severity, issues may be flagged as a "major violation," "minor violation," or "observation." A major violation (also referred to as nonconformance) refers to the inability of a supplier's management system to comply with a core EICC standard. Select major nonconformances can also be denoted as zero-tolerance items. Such issues include the utilization of underage workers, forced labor, health and safety issues posing immediate danger or serious injury, and violation of environmental laws posing serious and immediate harm to the community. Minor violations refer to more isolated concerns such as a temporarily blocked emergency exit or missing safety equipment. Finally, observations are generally a recognition that a superior means of documenting or monitoring a process or procedure may exist. Audit items flagged as observations are not considered a code violations.

As part of this research project, HP shared more than 500 original reports from audits conducted between June 2004 and January 2009. This sample includes 276 unique facilities, 137 of which received multiple audits. These audits assessed supplier compliance with the HP and the Electronics Industry

---

[5] Although HP has avoided unionization of its own facilities, the firm mandates that its suppliers respect local laws pertaining to freedom of association and collective bargaining. HP's 2009 Code of Conduct (version 3.01) reads: "Participants are to respect the rights of workers as established by local law to associate freely on a voluntary basis, seek representation, join or be represented by Works Councils, and join or not join labor unions and bargain collectively as they choose" (Hewlett Packard 2009: 3).

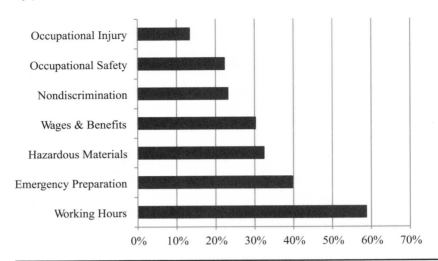

Major Code Violation	Audits with No Violations	Audits with Violations	Total Audits	Percent Audits in Violation
Working hours	204	290	494	59%
Emergency preparation	292	193	485	40%
Hazardous materials	322	155	477	32%
Wages and benefits	337	146	483	30%
Nondiscrimination	361	109	470	23%
Occupational safety	355	102	457	22%
Occupational injury	407	63	470	13%

FIGURE 6.1. Largest Code Violations by Total Audit Percentage, HP First-Tier Suppliers 2004–8 All Audits*
* All audits include 271 initial facility audits, and various follow-on audits.

Code of Conduct and were conducted by HP employees explicitly trained to evaluate suppliers' compliance with the code. Audits were performed onsite at supplier facilities and a subsection of audit reports were verified by an external organization to ensure the accuracy of assessments and enable improvements. As seen in Table 6.2, of the 276 facilities in our data set, only seven complied fully with all requirements included in the HP/EICC Code of Conduct at the time of their last audit.

Audit Results

Notwithstanding significant efforts by both HP and the EICC, an analysis of the audit reports reveals persistent problems. As seen in Figure 6.1, the top seven major code violations comprise three labor-related violations and four safety

TABLE 6.2. *Distribution of Fully Compliant Facilities (Last Audit) by National Setting and Issue*

	Asia Pacific		CE Europe		Greater China		Latin America	
	Total Facilities	% of Total	Total Facilities	% of Total	Total Facilities	% of Total	Total Facilities	% of Total
All sections (Full compliance)	4	6.06	1	4.00	1	0.67	1	2.78
All sections (No major violation)	21	31.82	9	36.00	2	1.34	13	36.11
Labor (Full compliance)	34	51.52	22	88.00	8	5.37	9	25.00
Labor (No major violation)	42	63.64	23	92.00	16	10.74	26	72.22
Health and safety (Full Compliance)	20	30.30	5	20.00	4	2.68	11	30.56
Health and safety (No major violation)	46	69.70	17	68.00	36	24.16	18	50.00
Environment (Full compliance)	26	39.39	12	48.00	14	9.40	14	38.89
Environment (No major violations)	47	71.21	21	84.00	62	41.61	22	61.11
Labor mgmt system (Full compliance)	26	39.39	14	56.00	17	11.41	5	13.89
Labor mgmt system (No major violations)	57	86.36	23	92.00	110	73.83	26	72.22
Health and safety mgmt system (Full compliance)	22	33.33	8	32.00	36	24.16	12	33.33
Health and safety mgmt system (No major violations)	55	83.33	23	92.00	119	79.87	30	83.33
Total	66	100	25	100	149	100	36	100

and health violations. Nearly 60 percent of audited facilities, including those with follow-up or periodic audits, had routine workweeks longer than sixty hours. Forty percent of audited plants, including those subjected to follow-up and periodic audits, had no or poor emergency planning, training, and evacuation procedures. Some had blocked fire escapes. Finally, 32.5 percent of audited firms had some troubles with their management of hazardous materials, and 30.2 percent exhibit problems with wages and benefits, indicating that wages may not have met local minimums and/or failed to include a premium for overtime work.

When the top four violations are examined by year of audit and by the number of audits conducted at particular plants, whether as follow-up audits or part of a periodic audit process, a clearer picture emerges of the situation at these factories. Analyzing these audit data by year of audit helps us explore the mechanisms that we examined in the previous chapters that should, theoretically, lead to improvements in audit results/factory conditions: increased compliance through more frequent inspections and policing; better working conditions through a plant's enhanced capabilities and management systems; plant management's growing appreciation of and ability to implement code requirements; and diffusion of best practices across the supply chain over time, to name a few. We would expect plants to demonstrate improvement as audits become more frequent and more recent, assuming that more recent audits would reveal better labor conditions as suppliers implemented various capability-building initiatives promoted by HP.

However, consistent with our previous discussion on the limitations of private compliance programs, Figure 6.2 shows the rate of failed audits in all four areas more or less increased between 2004 and 2008, with some improvements in wage and benefits requirements occurring more recently. A similar trend emerges when ordering audits by how often a particular plant was audited (Figure 6.3). In other words, although one would expect that facilities should improve as audits are repeated and learning takes place, other than wages and benefits, code violations actually increased. In fact, working hour violations occurred at nearly twice the rate as the next most common violation, emergency preparedness (67 percent vs. 35 percent).

To better understand the persistence of these workplace problems, let's examine the most frequent violation, excessive working hours, in greater detail. As we saw earlier in this chapter, excessive working hours was identified by both Nike and Timberland as a serious problem among their suppliers and a problem that both brands believe they contribute to through their own upstream business practices. NGOs, too, frequently cite working hour violations as an important and recurring issue (Verité 2004; Level Works 2006; Good Electronics 2009). As the HP data suggest, this problem is common in the global electronics industry as well. In fact, 90 percent of EICC members admitted that excessive working hours is an ongoing challenge for them (EICC 2009a), which is particularly noteworthy given that the EICC's working hours stipulation is

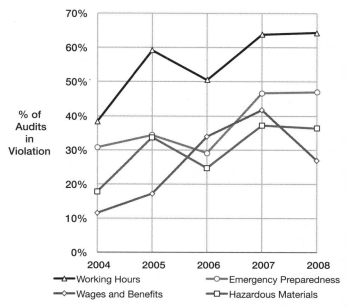

FIGURE 6.2. Largest Code Violations by Year of Audit, HP First-Tier Suppliers 2004–8 All Audits*

*All audits include 271 initial facility audits, and various follow-on audits.

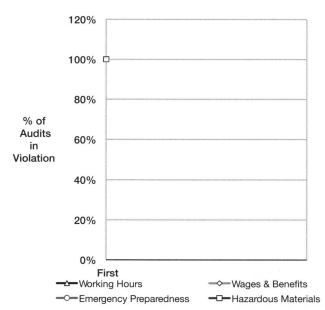

FIGURE 6.3. Largest code violations by audit number, Hewlett Packard (HP) first-tier suppliers 2004–8 first–third audits.*

*461–476 Audits: 260–271 first audits, 126–132 second audits, 70–73 third audits.

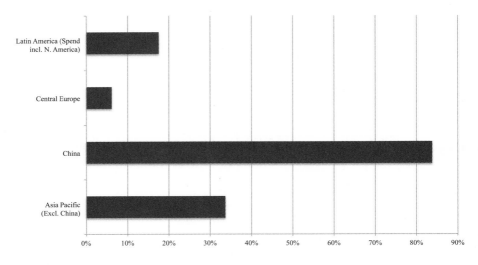

Percent of Total Annual HP Spend	HP Region	Audits with No Violations	Audits with Violations	Total Audits	Percent of Audits in Violation
75%	Asia Pacific (Excluding China)	63	32	95	34%
	China	48	248	296	84%
5%	Central Europe	46	3	49	6%
20%	Latin America (spend including N. America)	47	10	57	18%
100%	Total	204	293	497	59%

FIGURE 6.4. Working-hour violations by geographic region, Hewlett Packard (HP) first-tier suppliers 2004–8 all audits.

the only code item (out of 37 items) that specifically defines the standard: "a workweek should not be more than 60 hours per week, including overtime, except in emergency or unusual situations" (EICC 2009b, 2).

Consistent with the literature on Chinese labor issues (Ngai 2005; Yu 2008), and as seen in Figure 6.4, 83 percent of factories audited by HP in China had working-hour violations, as did 34 percent of the plants audited in Asia-Pacific, primarily Southeast Asia. Together, these two regions constitute 75 percent of HP's total purchases. In the Asia-Pacific region where purchasing is concentrated, we find violations do not vary significantly across countries with distinct economic profiles and very different institutional arrangements: in Malaysia, Singapore, and Thailand, notwithstanding their different levels

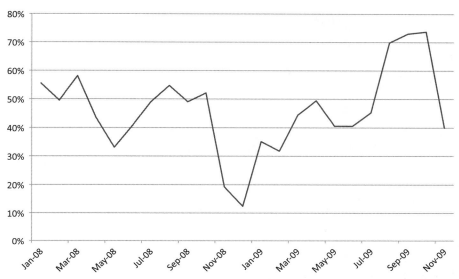

FIGURE 6.5. Hewlett Packard China supplier working-hour study 2008–9. Percent direct labor working more than 60 hours per week. *Source:* Hewlett-Packard China Working Hours Pilot Program (13 plants).

of industrial development and state capacity, 36 to 45 percent of all audits conducted reported excessive working-hour violations.[6]

Further highlighting the problems of excessive working hours are data from HP's pilot program of thirteen plants in China (presented in Figure 6.5), which sought to increase the managerial capabilities and systems of participating HP suppliers so that they could better tackle persistent labor problems like excess overtime. In January 2008, at the beginning of the HP pilot, 55 percent of the workers employed at the thirteen plants participating in the pilot study, worked more than the EICC maximum of sixty hours per week. By December 2008, after almost a year of engagement in this pilot, only 13 percent of these workers were working excess hours. However, this positive trend began to reverse by February 2009, when 50 percent of the employees at the pilot study plants were once again working above the EICC limit of 60 hours. By the summer of 2009, as new product ramp-up accelerated, more than 70 percent of employees at the thirteen plants were working above the EICC limit. Thus, the pilot program appears to have failed to sustainably reduce excessive working hours. Whether this was due to problems with the design and/or implementation

[6] An examination of the audit documents of Malaysian companies revealed that labor violations in Malaysia were underreported. This is because of the auditors' belief that the Malaysian national labor law (which allows 72 hours per week) took precedent over the EICC. The EICC states that working hours shall not exceed 60 hours per week, independent of national laws.

of the pilot program or to the seasonality of demand and orders for new products is difficult to determine with the data HP shared with us, but the way that excessive working hours at these 13 plants tracked closely to shifts in production orders and new product introductions suggests that what Nike and Timberland described as taking place within their respective supply chains may be true of HP as well.

Interestingly enough, code violations involving excessive working hours occurred not just in low-wage China – a country often depicted as lacking a strong commitment to enforcing labor regulations – but also in high-wage Singapore – an economy characterized by strong institutions, well-trained managers, and more stringent regulatory enforcement. How can we explain the persistence of poor working conditions and excessive working hours in electronics factories owned by different contract manufacturers, producing for different global buyers, and located in countries with distinct institutional arrangements?

To answer these questions, my graduate students and I not only analyzed HP's audit reports but also conducted field research in China, Mexico, the Czech Republic, Hungary, Malaysia, Singapore, Thailand, and the United States in 2009 and 2010.[7] For this chapter, I focus on seven HP first-tier supplier factories located in Malaysia, Singapore, and Thailand. Table 6.3 describes the characteristics of these seven plants.[8]

Explaining Persistent Workplace Violations

As we saw in the previous chapters, efforts to improve working conditions and labor standards in factories embedded in global supply chains, either through ever-more-sophisticated private compliance programs or through more targeted capability-building programs, appeared unable to fully tackle these workplace issues. Our study of HP and its globally dispersed suppliers confirmed these findings. For example, four of the plants analyzed in this chapter are owned by parent companies that are members of the EICC. Recall that the EICC is an industry-wide coalition that brings together global brands and lead suppliers and that members of the EICC coordinate audits and share information with one another. Leading contract manufacturers are by design actively engaged in this process. As such, the EICC's compliance program is

---

[7] The field research entailed visiting forty-five factories and conducting more than 200 interviews with plant managers, buyer representatives, contract manufacturing managers, CSR managers, NGO and union leaders, and government officials in China, the Czech Republic, Hungary, Mexico, Malaysia, Singapore, Thailand, and the United States. An overview of this research is presented in a companion paper. See Richard M. Locke, Gregory Distelhorst, Timea Pal, and Hiram Samel, "Production Goes Global, Standards Stay Local: Private Regulation in the Global Electronics Industry," MIT Political Science Working Paper # 2012-1 (2012).

[8] This section draws heavily from Richard M. Locke and Hiram M. Samel, "Looking in the Wrong Places?: Labor Standards and Upstream Business Practices in the Global Electronics Industry MIT Political Science Working Paper # 2012–18 (2012).

TABLE 6.3. *Hewlett Packard First-Tier Supplier Facilities Visited – Southeast Asia 2009*

	Company*						
	Alpha	Gamma	Epsilon	Kappa	Lambda	Sigma	Upsilon
Location	Thailand	Thailand	Thailand	Singapore	Singapore	Singapore	Malaysia
Parent HQ	Taiwan	US	Japan	Singapore	Canada	US	US
Publicly traded (Exchange)	Yes (Bangkok)	Yes (NYSE)	Yes (Tokyo)	Yes (Singapore)	Yes (NYSE)	Yes (NASDAQ)	Yes (NASDAQ)
Member EICC	No	Yes	No	No	Yes	Yes	Yes
ISO 14001 certified	Yes	Yes	Yes	Yes	Yes	Yes	Yes
Occupational Health and Safety Advisory Services 18001 certified	Yes	Yes	Yes	No	No	Yes	Yes
Has company Code of Conduct	Yes	Yes	Yes	No	Yes	Yes	Yes
Product	DC-DC Converters	2.5″ and 3.5″ Internal HDD	2.5″ Internal HDD	Mold making, injection molding	Inkjet cartridge dry/wet assembly	Rack mount servers	Inkjet printers, multifunction printers
Technology	SMT, Hand-Insertion	Man & Auto Assembly, Test	Auto Assembly, Test	CAD tool and die	Auto assembly	Box build	SMT, IM, Box-build
Employees at last audit	12,000	15,600	4,500	100	300	297	12,000

EICC, Electronics Industry Citizenship Coalition; ISO, International Organization for Standardization.

* For confidentiality reasons, we have used pseudonyms for these companies.

supposed to be more advanced than that found in other industries because it corrects for past problems with traditional compliance programs. Moreover, throughout the world, HP developed training and capability-building programs for its first-tier suppliers to probe root-cause issues and foster solutions. At many of these plants, management held regularly scheduled compliance meetings with HP's auditors in order to improve coordination between auditors and suppliers. All plants visited during our field research for this study claimed that HP auditors were very cooperative and helped build capability among their production staff. HP process engineers visited most of these plants on a regular basis and in some of the larger plants, HP maintained a full-time employee on site. HP and these suppliers shared detailed information and practiced root cause analysis. Yet still, all of these efforts failed to fully tackle certain workplace issues in these factories.

The Cascading Effect of Upstream Business Practices on Labor Standards in the Global Electronics Industry

Although better-designed compliance efforts and more comprehensive capability-building programs may certainly help improve working conditions and labor standards in numerous electronics factories, they appear unable in and of themselves to resolve persistent workplace issues in many of these same plants. This is consistent with what we found in our research on other global brands and their suppliers competing in very different industries. After years of analyzing audit reports, visiting factories, and interviewing hundreds of company managers, NGO leaders, local government officials, and union leaders throughout the world, I have realized that to truly understand the source of many workplace problems in global supply chain factories, we need to look not just at these plants but also more broadly at the entire value chain and how upstream business decisions shape supply chain practices, production architectures, and work organization *downstream* in the factories manufacturing these goods. Poor working conditions and weak labor standards are not only (or even primarily) the result of misguided managerial practices and behavior in the plants, but rather stem from the series of supply chain responses to dynamic market conditions that have become common among global buyers in an effort to mitigate their financial and reputation risks and meet demand for their products in a timely manner.

In seeking to minimize uncertainty, consumer electronics firms routinely utilize product design, demand-signaling, and production-planning practices that necessitate modularity of design and assembly, which allows for the building of buffer inventories of lower-cost standardized intermediates while postponing the final assembly of differentiated and much more costly finished goods. Although these practices diminish risk by producing only those goods demanded by consumers, they create labor problems by structurally constraining the supply chain's downstream production architecture and corresponding design of work organization. In what follows, I describe in detail the evolution of these upstream business practices and their consequences for work organization and working conditions in the factories.

The Starting Point: Increasing Industry Dependence on Consumer Markets

Since the advent of the personal computer, the electronics industry has evolved from being primarily a supplier to governments and large commercial organizations to one whose growth opportunities now originate in consumer markets. A 2008 survey of semiconductor firms found that integrated circuit manufacturers derived 60 percent of their revenues from chips that are placed in consumer electronics products (KPMG, Consumer Electronics Association, and Global Semiconductor Alliance 2008). Respondents further estimated that this would climb to 80 percent of revenues within five years. Consumer markets are continually subject to disruptive innovation, motivating firms to advance the technological frontier while reducing costs to prevent disruption from below (Christensen 1997). Increasing consumer technology-adoption rates have also shortened product life cycles.

To maximize market share over such short life cycles, large retailers engage in constant promotions that rapidly erode selling prices. This price erosion, along with the need to carry a broad product assortment, means that retailers do not like to carry large inventories. Instead, retailers opt for more frequent shipments, often by air cargo, to meet consumer demand (Leinbach and Bowen 2004). This allows them to avoid costly inventory but also keeps their shelves relatively well stocked with successful, high-selling products. At the same time, however, this practice puts enormous pressures on contract manufacturers to deliver these smaller, more customized batches of products as quickly and cheaply as possible.

This balancing act is complicated by the concentration of electronics retail channels that has occurred in recent years. As seen in Figure 6.6, the top four competitors in the US consumer electronics and computer retail distribution channels control close to 75 percent of their respective markets. Concentrated buying power allows retailers to maintain margins, thus forcing price drops on the brands as the electronics firms move products through their life cycles. Retailers also seek to differentiate products from their competitors in order to prevent consumers from price-shopping products, a process facilitated by the Internet.

As a result, brands often make small functionality changes to products to disguise any potential similarity between rival retail customers. Short product life cycles and the need for thinly differentiated products lead to a constant parade of new product introductions punctuated by rapid phaseouts. For example, in 2009, HP maintained more than 2,000 laser printer SKUs, more than 15,000

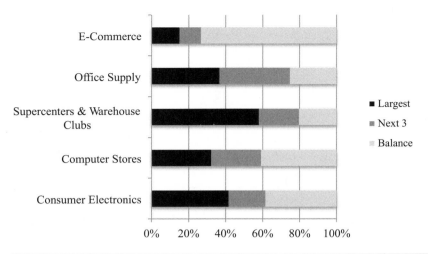

Retail Sector	Largest Retailer	Largest	Next 3	Balance
Consumer electronics	Best Buy	41.5%	20.0%	38.5%
Computer stores	Best Buy	32.2%	26.9%	40.9%
Supercenters and warehouse clubs	Wal-Mart	57.9%	21.8%	20.3%
Office supply	Staples	36.7%	38.0%	25.3%
E-commerce	Amazon	15.0%	11.7%	73.3%

FIGURE 6.6. US electronics market concentration by retail sector. Major concentration exists in all sectors except E-commerce. *Source:* Ibisworld 2010.

server and storage SKUs, and more than eight million possible configure-to-order combinations in its notebook and desktop product lines (Ward et al. 2010).

How the Electronics Industry Responds to Dynamic Consumer and Retail Markets

The result of these various practices generates great uncertainty within the industry. Buffeted by rapidly changing technology, volatile consumer demand, and powerful retail customers, brands are obligated to optimize supply chain management practices to remain competitive. Kaipia et al. looked at the demand and production volatility of another major (in this case, European) electronics manufacturer (Kaipia, Korhonen, and Hartiala 2006). As shown in Figure 6.7, even with a relatively linear demand (as evidenced by the retail channel sell-through), volatility is extreme at the contract manufacturer level, exhibiting production changes of 80 percent on a week-by-week basis. Kaipia, et al. present their case as a classic bullwhip effect, where amplification is progressive throughout the supply chain. The consequences of this bullwhip effect – excess inventories, low capacity utilization, late or unfulfilled deliveries – significantly add to costs and weaken brands' reputations.

FIGURE 6.7. Delivery quantities of one product through three echelons of a European electronics firm's supply chain. Thirty-week period incorporating introduction and maturity phase (Kaipia et al. 2006).

The electronics industry has sought to manage these supply chain challenges through three broad strategic responses: modular product design, creation of buffer inventories of intermediate components, and postponement of final assembly until signaled by pull-based ordering systems. Products are designed with standardized, substitutable components that can also be assembled when necessary into common modules. These modules and components, known as intermediates because of their unfinished state, have separate production schedules, allowing for the buildup of buffer inventories that can be easily reallocated among different products at final assembly, depending on consumer demand. Finally, assembly of finished goods is postponed until accurate demand signals are available. This is known as pull-based ordering because of its dependence on consumer demand (as evidenced by retail point of sales data) for releasing orders into a production system rather than production minimums, more

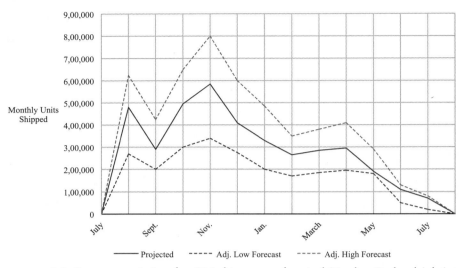

FIGURE 6.8. Forecast variation for CM shipments of typical Hewlett Packard ink jet printer. Twelve-month period reflects seasonality and price drop (Burruss and Kuettner 2002).

commonly employed during the era of Fordist mass-production. Final products have a significantly higher cost than the sum of their parts because of the threat of rapid obsolescence. This system works because postponement reduces the financial and reputational risks of unsold finished goods inventory.

To attenuate volatility during the production of intermediates and encourage the buildup of component inventory, brands choose to take the financial risk of maintaining ownership of and selling components to assemblers on an as-needed basis. In a series of articles, scholars working with HP planners laid out the logic for this practice, referred to as "price masking" (Ellram and Billington 2001; Amaral, Billington, and Tsay 2006). In addition to price masking, another feature of the electronics supply chain is pull-based ordering systems. A by-product of these systems is that demand volatility is magnified at the final point of assembly. Because brands want to avoid inventory of finished goods and thus postpone final assembly of their products for as long as possible, production volumes exhibit periodic spikes of 300 to 500 percent over baseline levels. This volatility, which is well known to brands and suppliers and is regularly optimized, can be further amplified by the timing of frequent new product introductions that require large ramp-ups. Figure 6.8 highlights the forecast volatility for the introduction of an inkjet printer by HP's planning department. In addition to the planned peak-trough volatility of 100 percent, adjusted low and high forecasts vary as much as 250 percent. For example, during the month of November, this differential was 500,000 units.

How these Policies and Practices Play Out on the Factory Floor

As seen in Table 6.4, four of the seven plants visited in Southeast Asia as part of this project (two in Singapore and two in Thailand) had working-hour violations in 2007. Three of these plants were reaudited in 2008 and once again failed to pass the audit. Closer plant-level analysis reveals that all of these violations occurred in plants with high unit volumes and relatively low product mix. Interviews with managers in five of these seven plants revealed that they believe managing working hour requirements is the most significant labor problem they face. All seven plants employ large numbers of agency or contract workers to help smooth production. These workers, who are overwhelmingly migrants, routinely exceeded 60 percent of a plant's total workforce.

All seven plants use manual labor for final assembly of modules and products, with six out of the seven employing conveyor assembly lines.[9] The six plants with conveyor assembly lines operate two 12-hour shifts, five to seven days a week, depending on orders. Managers at all of these plants claimed that it was often impossible to fulfill orders and meet the production schedules by working only five days a week.

Each assembly station involved work tasks requiring between 20 and 30 seconds to perform. Depending on the sophistication of the product being assembled, assembly lines can grow from 80 to 220 operators, each performing a very narrow task. Managers at all of these plants were well aware of alternative (cell) assembly options, and one plant employed both types of work organization whenever possible, yet 95 percent of employees worked on conveyor assembly lines. Plant managers claimed that they opt for this more Taylorist form of work organization because it permits short training periods for new operators. These managers indicated that this work organization (conveyor assembly) was independent of any specific brand they work with. Managers in almost every plant visited for this study reported that the vast majority of engineers in their plants were process engineers and focused on assembly-line efficiencies.

The conveyor assembly operations they use allow for both the quick absorption of new workers as well as the ability to rapidly shed these workers when demand suddenly drops, and so employee turnover at these plants is high and mobility between factories is facilitated by this common work organization. Most operators on the assembly lines are female migrant workers[10] hired on two-year contracts. Most migrant workers seek to maximize their earnings by working overtime whenever possible. Overtime hours are earned after an aggregate total is achieved,[11] so that workers can double their wages by

---

[9] In conveyor or linear assembly, the positions of operators are fixed and assembly occurs in a sequential manner as product travels past these operators on a conveying system.

[10] Migrant workers in China and Thailand are in country, whereas workers in Malaysia and Singapore are foreign.

[11] By contrast, this policy differs from those common in advanced industrialized countries where overtime can be achieved by working more than eight hours any day, independent of aggregate hours.

TABLE 6.4. *Product Market Demand Pressure and Work Organization Selection HP First-Tier Supplier Facilities Visited – SE Asia 2009*

		Company* Location						
		Alpha Thailand	Gamma Thailand	Epsilon Thailand	Kappa Singapore	Lambda Singapore	Sigma Singapore	Upsilon Malaysia
Produce		DC-DC converters	2.5″ and 3.5″ internal HDD	2.5″ internal HDD	Mold making, injection molding	Inkjet cartridge dry/wet assembly	Rack mount servers	Inkjet printers, multifunction printers
Intermediate or final assembly		Intermediate	Intermediate	Intermediate	Intermediate	Final	Final	Final
Approximate present HP of total plant production		5%	25%	25%	50%	100%	100%	95%
Product market demand pressures	Demand Volatility	Low	High	High	Medium	Low-Medium	Low	High
	Product Mix Volume	Low Medium	Low High (>8 million units monthly)	Low Low high (~3.8 million units monthly)	Medium Low	Low High (>7 million cartridges monthly)	High Low	Low High
	Buffer Inventories	No	Yes	Yes	No	No	Build to order	No

HP use of price-masking (as % of total components)	Yes (~80%)	Yes (~80%)	Yes, (100%) HP owns all equipment and components	No	Yes (n/a)	No or limited (has own magnetic operations)	Yes (n/a)
Production Line Change	Yes	Yes	Yes	Yes	Yes	No	n/a
Work organization selection — Requires HP approval type of assembly	Conveyer Yes	Cell Yes	Conveyor Yes	Cell Yes	Conveyor Yes	Conveyor Yes	Conveyor Yes
Kaizen/lean practices Employees in this facility 2008 (pre-recession)	12,000	297	550	570	8,500	28,000	8,800
Union	No	Branch of National Union	Branch of National Union	Branch of National Union	None, has Welfare Committee	No, believes in strategic HR	Company union
Use of contract workers	>60%	Dual market: 20%–30% of total workforce at lower wages	Dual market 55% of total workforce at lower wages	Dual market: 45% of total workforce at lower wages	77% of employees subcontractors before recession	Was 70% until 2008 when completely phased out	Phased out starting 2005

(continued)

TABLE 6.4 *(continued)*

	Company* Location						
	Alpha Thailand	Gamma Thailand	Epsilon Thailand	Kappa Singapore	Lambda Singapore	Sigma Singapore	Upsilon Malaysia
% of total employees and contract workers that are migrant	<5%	50% (in-country: Isan)	50% (in-country: Isan)	45% (mainly Malay and Chinese)	~60% (mainly Malay)	20%–30%	>50% (Bangladeshi, Nepali)
Women as % of total employees	84%	85%–90%	85%	n/a	85%	n/a	55%
Working-hour audit results	No violation	2007 – Yes	2007 – Yes	2007 – Yes	2007 – Yes	No violation	No violation
Number of shifts per day	2–12 hr (5 days on, 2 off)	2008-Yes 3–8 hr (6 days on, 1 off)	2008-No 2–12 hr (5 days on, 2 off)	2008-No 2–12 hr (5 days on, 2 off)	4–12 hr (4 days on, 3 off)	3–8 hr (5 days on, 2 off)	2–12 hr (5 days on, 2 off)

* For confidentiality reasons, we have used pseudonyms for these companies.

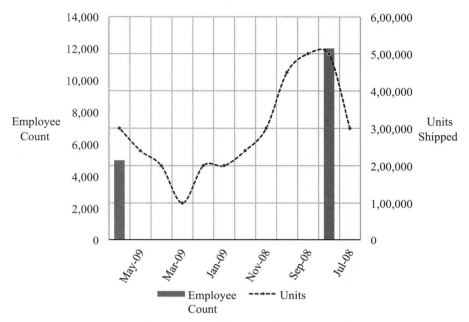

FIGURE 6.9. Ink jet shipments (all products) – Upsilon Plant 2008–9. Average product cycle = 9 months, 6–8 models.

working weekends.[12] Because production orders are highly volatile, factories break their labor contracts with these migrant workers on a regular basis (Good Electronics 2009; Bormann, Krishnan, and Neuner 2010). To illustrate this work system in greater detail, let's examine more closely one of the plants we visited, an inkjet printer manufacturer in Malaysia.

The Case of Inkjet Printers
The Upsilon[13] plant in Malaysia is a vertically integrated producer of inkjet printers that at its historic peak in 2007 produced one million units per month for HP. The plant exhibited the most extreme case of demand volatility among the seven Southeast Asian plants visited as part of this study. It currently produces six to eight models per year with an average product life of less than nine months. As seen in Figure 6.9, monthly volumes can increase by up to 250 percent, and employment levels can swing up and down by 58 percent.

To manage its highly volatile production schedules, the Upsilon plant regularly hires 60 percent of its workforce through Malaysian government-certified

[12] For a fascinating portrayal of working lives of such workers, see Leslie T. Chang, *Factory Girls* (New York: Spiegel and Grau, 2008).
[13] To protect the confidentiality of our respondents, we have disguised the actual name of the plant.

contract agencies. These agencies recruit Bangladeshi and Nepalese workers who sign two-year contracts with the agency and usually start work at the plant in June, in time for new product ramp-up. Even though the migrant workers have two-year employment contracts, the plant regularly lays off the vast majority of these workers six months later due to decreased production orders. Malaysian law allows for these contracts to be broken as long as workers receive a severance payment of one month's base wage. Thus, although this process of hiring and firing migrant workers on a regular basis is not a technical violation of the EICC (local labor law is being respected), this practice certainly violates the spirit of the industry's Code of Conduct.

Interestingly enough, our interviews at this plant revealed that management tries to be a "good" employer: both the plant and the dormitories housing the migrant workers are modern and clean; the facility promotes an extensive Kaizen program; production supervisors, whenever possible, promote cell assembly, although this is most often limited to low-volume, high-mix production (less than 5 percent of total production). Management clearly understands the value of skilled assembly workers and encourages teamwork, despite the length of its assembly lines (which can reach 220 workers or more). Thus, the issue at this plant is not one of managerial ill will, lack of technical know-how, or even inadequate management systems, but rather of various constraints that upstream business practices place on production and work organization practices on the shop floor. Given the highly volatile production orders they receive, plant managers at Upsilon claim that there is no other way they can profitably run their operations. They simply do not think that there is an alternative, more labor-friendly way to run their plant and deliver their products on time, at price, and with minimal defects, when demand is so volatile.

Volatility, Production Practices, and Labor Standards

Volatility and its disruptive effects on manufacturing practices and employment relations are not new but have a long history in an array of different industries.[14] But the way that volatility is being "managed" in today's electronics industry seems to create serious problems for workers manufacturing these products. Manufacturing practices in the electronics industry appears to be an odd amalgamation of lean manufacturing techniques and more traditional Taylorist work practices. On the one hand, the industry is characterized by a variety of practices – pull-based ordering, modular design and assembly, price masking, postponement of final assembly – that all appear to enhance efficiencies, reduce waste, and mitigate risks for both global brands and their lead suppliers. On the other hand, these "lean" practices are complemented by an organization of production and work (especially in plants with

---

[14] See Piore and Sabel (1984) for an historical overview for how both mass production and flexibly specialized firms responded to previous shifts in demand conditions. See Katz and Sabel (1985) for how volatility was "managed" historically in the US automobile industry.

high-volume/low-product mix production systems) that appears to be as Taylorist as factories of a bygone era (Lüthje 2002; McKay 2006; Smith, Sonnenfeld, and Pellow 2006). Pull-based ordering coupled with postponement of final assembly requires that plants have the ability to scale up and down quickly. Automation, although conceptually possible as a solution to volatility, runs the same risk that an earlier era of mass-production facilities faced: underutilization of capital-intensive equipment. Given the magnification of volatility through postponement as seen in Figures 6.8 and 6.9, where peak-trough volatility reaches 500 percent, final assembly plants would be burdened with unsustainably high fixed costs.

Instead, contract manufacturers employ large-scale hand-assembly coupled with lean manufacturing techniques. As we saw in the Malaysian factory, operators typically work on products in a sequential manner with each operation taking twenty to thirty seconds. Assembly lines average between 80 and 200 workers and can be reproduced in a rapid manner to respond to demand/production order volatility. Firms periodically hire and shed large numbers of readily available contingent workers, primarily rural (if domestic) or foreign migrants. Intentionally or unintentionally, work organized around Taylorist conveyor assembly is reinforced by the use of price-masking policies. Although brands may be absorbing contract manufacturers' inventory risk through this practice, they are also taking away some alternative opportunities for contract manufacturers to earn additional profit, thus forcing them to maximize labor efficiency as the main avenue for earning profits (Linden, Kraemer, and Dedrick 2009).[15] This drive to squeeze as much profit out of the work process inevitably leads to an array of different labor standards problems (excessive working hours, low wages, overreliance on contingent migrant workers, etc.).

Concluding Considerations: Collaborative Buyer–Supplier Relations as a Possible Solution?

Through a case study of Hewlett-Packard and the global electronics industry, this chapter has sought to demonstrate how some persistent labor problems originate in various upstream business practices. Although this situation may be especially pronounced in consumer electronics, where brands control up to 80 percent of the margins (Linden, Kraemer, and Dedrick 2009), similar patterns exist in the supply chains of other global brands (e.g., Nike and Timberland) that compete in very different industries. These findings suggest that if we are serious about improving working conditions and promoting labor rights in global supply chains, we need to look beyond compliance and/or capability-building programs directed at supply chain factories and begin to examine,

[15] Linden et al. (2009) estimate that Apple captures 79.5 percent of the total margin created in the production and sale of a 30 GB video iPod. The financial results of the largest brands and firms in Table 6.3 exhibit a similar pattern of value capture.

systematically, how upstream business practices impact workplace conditions in the factories producing the goods most of us purchase every day.

In the previous chapter, we saw that buyers and their suppliers can respond to market volatility in a more labor-friendly way. Recall, for instance, how Nike worked with its Mexican supplier (Plant A) to help it reorganize its production system and retrain its workforce so that it could respond to shifting patterns of consumer demand in a more flexible way. ABC played a similar role with its shirt supplier in Honduras, and others have documented similar patterns of collaborative buyer–supplier relations among IKEA's furniture suppliers in China (Ivarson and Alvstam 2010a, 2010b).[16] But these more collaborative relationships were not based solely on technical assistance but rather on a mutual recognition that each party had to gain from collaboration. In other words, Nike, ABC, IKEA, and other global corporations were able to establish more collaborative and labor-friendly relations with some (not all) of their suppliers because these buyer–supplier relations were based upon mutual gains, joint learning, and long-term commitments. Underlying these more collaborative relations was a fundamental understanding that both the risks and the rewards of doing business together would be distributed more or less fairly between the parties; the gains would not be captured nor the losses borne by one or the other party.

As Gary Herrigel has shown in his study of buyer–supplier relations in the United States, Germany, and Japan, this underlying sense of fairness and willingness to experiment together, learn from one another, and distribute the risks and rewards of doing business together is not a "natural" or even culturally determined feature of particular buyer–supplier relations, but rather something that was politically constructed over years of struggle and compromise. In other words, underlying these more collaborative buyer–supplier relations exists a set of distributive practices and policies, and institutional arrangements that support them, to promote both mutual benefits for both parties and, under certain conditions, more just labor practices at the suppliers' factories (Herrigel 2010).[17] Whether such distributive practices are stable or able to be diffused more broadly in today's volatile economy are open questions. But if history is any guide, perhaps there is hope that new competitive strategies supported by new, public or quasi-public institutions can be developed even in an economy shaped by global supply chains.

Historically, both in the United States, as well as in countries often characterized as "coordinated market economies," institutional arrangements existed to promote more stable buyer–supplier relations and less cutthroat competition

---

[16] For a more general discussion of these collaborative buyer–supplier relations, see Gary Herrigel, *Manufacturing Possibilities* (New York: Oxford University Press, 2010).

[17] See also Susan Helper, John Paul MacDuffie, and Mari Sako, "Determinants of Trust in Supplier Relations: Evidence from the Automotive Industry in Japan and the United States," *Journal of Economic Behavior and Organization* 34 (1998): 77–84.

among rival firms. Private firms still competed fiercely with one another, but the terms of competition were regulated (mostly self-regulated by the industry associations themselves) to protect standards for firms, their suppliers, and their workers. As a result of this greater coordination, rival firms shifted their competitive strategies away from increasing sales through pricing and toward more innovation-based and sustainable production and distribution practices (Hall and Soskice 2001; Trumball 2006; Whitman 2007; Berk 2009). Recent research on experimentalist governance (Sabel and Zeitlin 2012) suggests that similar arrangements are currently being developed in various national and regional economies. In these multilevel arrangements, government agencies, in collaboration with private firms, engage in a series of learning, standard-setting and benchmarking processes that ultimately promote innovative company strategies – strategies that are both adaptive to changing markets and respectful of labor and environmental standards.

Whether analogous institutional arrangements that are capable of shifting the terms of competition among global corporations competing in an array of different industries could be built in today's global economy, and if so, who would build them, are also open questions. But what is clear is that these questions cannot be addressed by focusing on individual factories or even supply chains and certainly not only by private actors, but rather by considering the appropriate mix of public (government) and private actions that are necessary to reform current supply chain practices. This is the focus of the next chapter and conclusion.

7

Complements or Substitutes?

Private Power, Public Regulation, and the Enforcement of Labor Standards in Global Supply Chains

Introduction

The previous chapters of this book have described both the promise and the limitations of various private efforts aimed at improving working conditions and promoting labor standards in global supply chains. Although corporate compliance programs were able to promote workplace improvements on some issues and among some suppliers, labor rights and working conditions stagnated or even deteriorated among other suppliers. Likewise, capability-building efforts by global brands, nongovernmental organizations (NGOs), and even the International Labor Organization were able to enhance the technical and managerial skills of factories participating in these various programs. But their impact on working hours, wages, and "enabling rights" was mixed. The previous chapter underscored the limitations of these private initiatives by showing how many workplace problems are the result not (or not solely) of misguided or unethical attitudes and behaviors by factory managers (hence, requiring ever-more-rigorous monitoring) nor even their poor managerial and technical skills (thus necessitating capability-building efforts); they are also the product of various upstream business practices by large retailers and global buyers that generate negative consequences downstream, among their suppliers. Until these practices among key actors within global supply chains are reformed, workplace-focused efforts aimed at improving working conditions and labor standards within global supply chains will always produce limited results.

The limitations of the various private initiatives I describe in the previous chapters will come as no surprise to critics of private voluntary regulation. Critics of private compliance programs and overly technocratic capability-building initiatives have long argued that they are designed not to protect labor rights or improve working conditions but rather to limit the legal liability of global brands and prevent damage to their reputations. Yet these critics argue that private voluntary regulation is not simply ineffective but also pernicious in that it displaces and undermines more thorough government regulation.[1] Former US Secretary of Labor, Robert Reich, nicely summarizes this line of argument:

It is easy to understand why big business has embraced corporate social responsibility with such verve. It makes for good press and reassures the public. A declaration of corporate commitment to social virtue may also forestall government legislation or regulation in an area of public concern where one or more companies have behaved badly, such as transporting oil carelessly and causing a major oil spill or flagrantly failing to respect human rights abroad. The soothing promise of responsibility can deflect public attention from the need for stricter laws and regulations or convince the public that there's no problem to begin with. (Reich 2007: 170)

Similar arguments about the negative effects of private initiatives, especially their crowding out of more stringent government regulation, have been made by a number of scholars working on an array of different industries and countries (O'Rourke 2003; Esbenshade 2004; Vogel 2005; Seidman 2007).

Yet, is this necessarily the case? Do private compliance and capability-building initiatives necessarily crowd out and displace state regulation or can these two approaches aimed at promoting labor standards in global supply chains complement and reinforce one another? Recent research on labor standards and working conditions in global supply chains has suggested that neither state regulation nor private voluntary initiatives function effectively in isolation but rather that a combination of private and public interventions are necessary to effectively tackle persistent labor problems in the new, globally dispersed centers of production (Utting 2005; Weil 2005; Graham, and Woods 2006; Amengual 2010). But to simply stress the importance of (potentially) complementary interventions and public-private partnerships fails to account for how these alternative forms of regulation actually interact on the ground. As Tim Bartley (2011) and David Trubek and Louise Trubek (2007) have argued, under certain circumstances, these different approaches to regulation can either complement one another or contradict and thus compromise the effectiveness of each other.

This chapter explores in greater detail how private and public forms of regulation interact on the ground through an examination of remediation efforts at two of HP's major suppliers.[2] As we saw in the last chapter, one of the

---

[1] For a review of the displacement hypothesis, see Tim Bartley, "Corporate Accountability and the Privatization of Labor Standards: Struggles over Codes of Conduct in the Apparel Industry," *Research in Political Sociology* 14 (2005): 211–44, and Jill L. Esbenshade, *Monitoring Sweat-shops: Workers, Consumers, and the Global Apparel Industry* (Philadelphia: Temple University Press, 2004).

[2] This section draws heavily on Richard M. Locke, Ben A. Rissing, and Timea Pal, "Complements or Substitutes?: Public vs. Private Regulation and the Improvement of Labor Standards in Global Supply Chains unpublished paper, Massachusetts Institute of Tecnology, July 2011.

leading compliance problems among electronics suppliers is the exploitation of migrant, contract workers.[3] In response to variable demand and intense cost pressures, contract manufactures have adopted flexible employment policies, characterized by low wages, long work hours, precarious or temporary work, and high concentrations of women, minority, and migrant employees (Catholic Agency for Overseas Development 2004; Smith et al. 2006; Chan and Peyer 2008). Additionally, many contract manufacturers outsource large portions of their workforce to limit worker benefit coverage and enable them to hire and fire employees rapidly in response to variations in production demand.

This chapter analyzes efforts to combine private and public regulation to redress these issues and improve working conditions for contract workers at two of HP's leading suppliers, Alpha Electronics and Beta Electronics,[4] in two very different national contexts, Mexico and the Czech Republic. Both suppliers are industry leaders with operations in several countries and strong brand reputations. In both Mexico and the Czech Republic, I compare facilities owned by these two manufacturers that contract with HP to perform similar functional roles: desktop assembly and repair work. By controlling for the same contract manufacturers performing the same tasks for the same lead firm (Hewlett Packard [HP]) but operating in different national settings, I seek to elucidate the processes through which private and public systems of regulation interact to redress the same labor problem. This structured comparison also helps to control for various factors – company ownership/culture, buyer–supplier relations, national socioeconomic and regulatory environment, and the particular labor issue being addressed – that may shape the outcomes described in this case study.

Alpha and Beta are suppliers of strategic importance for HP. Alpha is one of the largest manufacturers of electronics and computer components worldwide. In recent years, Alpha has established manufacturing plants in the United Kingdom, United States, Czech Republic, Hungary, Mexico, Brazil, India, and Vietnam, employing just under half a million workers in 2009. As a member of the Electronics Industry Citizenship Coalition (EICC), Alpha has an internal social and environmental responsibility committee to proactively work with stakeholders, including customers and NGOs. As a result of this committee's work, the company has dedicated significant resources and implemented a wide range of initiatives aimed at improving labor standards at its facilities across the globe.

---

[3] Contract workers are employees directly hired not by the assemblers/contract manufacturers supplying global brands like HP and Apple but rather by temporary staffing agencies. As such, they are referred to as both "contract" and "agency" workers. I use these terms interchangeably throughout this chapter.

[4] For purposes of confidentiality, I have disguised the identities of these two major electronics contract manufacturers.

Beta is an electronics contract manufacturer with operations in more than 30 countries. Also a member of the EICC, Beta has built on the principles and standards of the EICC and implemented its own corporate responsibility program. Internally, Beta has developed self-assessment tools and audit processes that are being deployed throughout all Beta sites and vertically down to its own supply base. These efforts enable Beta to engage in timely corrective actions to ensure continuous conformance to both internal and external (i.e., HP-mandated) corporate citizenship requirements.

The implementation of the Electronics Industry Code of Conduct through HP's Social and Environment Responsibility (SER) program and the improvements it generated played out very differently in Mexico and the Czech Republic. Although the content of the EICC and the rules regarding its implementation are uniform across all countries, differences in national context shaped the actual strategies employed by HP's SER team to address similar labor issues manifest among its suppliers located in different countries.

Interactions between private and public regulatory systems can take different forms. Complementary interactions emerge when private compliance and capability-building initiatives exist alongside active state enforcement efforts. In these settings, private efforts often focus on informing local suppliers about national labor laws and helping them comply with existing regulations, with the understanding that failure to comply with these laws and regulations will lead to sanctions by the relevant government authorities. Active state regulatory efforts are therefore bolstered (not undermined) through these additional private initiatives. In contrast, substitution occurs when private enforcement efforts intervene to address labor issues that are not being fully enforced by weak or ineffective government regulatory authorities. In these settings, private compliance initiatives rely on national laws to legitimate their activities but otherwise operate more or less independently and with little explicit coordination with government regulatory agencies.[5] The structured comparison presented in this chapter illustrates how the balance between private and public regulation, as well as the mode of interaction between them, depends on the relative capabilities and strategies of public regulatory authorities in different nation-states.

This chapter draws on both the unique data set of supplier audits that HP selectively administered to its network of global suppliers from 2003 through 2009 that we have discussed in previous chapters as well as field research in Mexico and the Czech Republic during the summer and fall of 2009. The fieldwork involved more than 70 interviews with HP managers; owners of supply chain factories; plant managers; production managers; human resources (HR) managers; environment, health, and safety representatives; and line supervisors. Access to suppliers was negotiated with support from HP, but my students and

---

[5] For an interesting description of how private and state regulatory efforts combine in different ways, see Matthew Amengual (2010).

I chose which facilities to study. Although we were able to interview managers (in different functions) at various suppliers, we chose not to interview factory line workers at these same suppliers because we could not guarantee that these workers would not be subsequently punished for sharing information. Given our concerns for these "human subjects," we chose to forego this important source of information. We did, however, assess working conditions through our own on-site visits to the factories and through our interviews with various labor-rights oriented NGOs in both Mexico and the Czech Republic.

Promoting Fair Employment Conditions for Contract Workers in Mexico and the Czech Republic

In recent years, electronics suppliers have increasingly relied on temporary employment agencies to meet their manufacturing staffing needs. This practice involves filling production jobs with workers who are formally employed by a separate and distinct staffing agency. Through the use of agency workers, manufacturers can maintain greater workforce flexibility, although this practice can lead to abuses surrounding working conditions and compensation practices for these "external" employees. The global electronics industry relies extensively on the use of agency workers and this form of employment has repeatedly been associated with low pay and precarious working conditions throughout the supply chain (Brown 2009; makeITfair 2009). In Mexico, an estimated 60 percent of employment in the electronics industry comprises agency workers, with some 240,000 workers employed by more than 60 temp agencies (Brown 2009; Centre for Reflection and Action on Labour Issues [CEREAL] 2007, 2009). Many Mexican electronics suppliers hire agency workers on multiple sequential short-term contracts so that workers fail to accumulate employment benefits afforded to full-time workers as required by the national labor code. Contracting with employees in this fashion is illegal in Mexico; however, this practice is used routinely in the country's electronics industry (CEREAL 2007). More than 80 percent of Mexican contract workers are employed for less than a year, which suggests that few accrue the nationally mandated benefits that they would otherwise be entitled to as full-time workers (Partida 2004).

Reliance on contract workers has increased significantly in recent years in the Czech Republic as well (International Confederation of Private Employment Agencies 2010). At the end of 2009, there were 2,212 registered temporary work agencies in the Czech Republic with the largest share of temporary workers employed in industrial sectors with high shares of foreign capital, including the automotive and electronics industries (Aleinik 2010; European Industrial Relations Observatory [EIRO] 2009). Sixty percent of the agency workers in the Czech Republic are employed for a time period shorter than three months (International Confederation of Private Employment Agencies 2010). Concerns surrounding equitable pay and fair benefits are significant issues affecting agency workforces in both countries.

The National Regulatory Frameworks Affecting Agency Work in the Czech Republic and Mexico

National labor legislation in Mexico, which has remained largely unchanged since 1970, offers few protections to contract workers. In contrast, revisions to Czech Republic labor laws in 2004 specifically address working conditions and compensation issues for these "temporary" agency workers. In Mexico, national labor law has remained largely inert for decades and is rarely enforced. Mexican law does allow for part-time positions (under a narrow set of circumstances) and provides substantial employment protections to safeguard full-time workers, including year-end bonuses and a three-month severance payment (see Article 35 of the Mexican Federal Labor Law).[6] However, these protectionist laws are in practice bypassed by many electronics firms, limiting the ability of workers to protect their wages and benefits. One strategy utilized by electronics suppliers has been to hire employees on short-term contracts with explicit end dates. By avoiding full-time employment contracts, these workers are generally ineligible for many federally mandated benefits such as year-end bonuses or severance payments. The use of agency workers has therefore developed in the shadow of the law, taking advantage of vague reporting structures, legal loopholes, and inadequate enforcement of national legislation. The full details of these working relationships are rarely disclosed to the Mexican labor authorities. One general manager interviewed for this project in Mexico portrayed the employment of agency workers as both "legal and illegal," depending on one's point of view.

Legislation pertaining to temporary employees in the Czech Republic was updated in late 2004 (and enacted in early 2005) to extend specific employment provisions to agency workers. Under these reformed laws, agency workers are entitled to employment conditions and compensation comparable to that offered to full-time employees.[7] Should suppliers be found in violation of these equal compensation/employment condition clauses, they must retroactively pay agency workers the differences they are due. Additionally, identical provisions with regard to sick pay and pension benefits extend to both agency workers and full-time employees. Fewer legal provisions are provided to temporary employees who work less than 100 hours in a given year (Ward et al. 2005; Coe et al. 2008). Finally, agency workers' employment in excess of twelve months is strictly regulated and restrictions exist on the hiring of agency workers

---

[6] Mandated benefits for full-time workers in Mexico are numerous and include paid time off, a national minimum wage, annual profit sharing, social security, retirement, and other special benefits surrounding medical conditions and pregnancy.

[7] The exact interpretation of this principle has been subject to debate at both the national and regional levels in the Czech Republic (EIRO 2009). Others have been critical of the licensing process that prospective temporary staffing agencies are subjected to by the Czech Ministry of Labor and Social Affairs, claiming that the current licensing process is overly lenient (makeITfair 2009).

to replace permanent employees on strike (European Foundation for the Improvement of Living and Working Conditions 2006).

Outdated and poorly enforced (in the case of Mexico) and recently revised and more stringent (in the case of the Czech Republic) labor regulation concerning agency work has led to very different regulatory contexts in these two countries. How labor standards are enforced – and especially the role private compliance initiatives play in this process – illustrates the different ways private and public regulation are layered together in Mexico and the Czech Republic.

Notes from the Field: The Conditions of Agency Workers at the Plant Level

Plant-level audit data obtained through HP revealed that notwithstanding these differences in national regulatory regimes, contract workers are vulnerable in both national contexts. Although the EICC code lacks specific provisions covering contract workers, a large number of the labor violations identified through HP's audits focused on this group of workers. These violations generally concerned agency workers' wages, benefits, and working hours.

In the Czech Republic, both the Alpha and Beta facilities relied extensively on agency workers at the time of our research. Employees hired through three agencies represented approximately 40 percent of the total workforce at Alpha and Beta plants. In 2007, HP audits revealed that agency workers at the Czech Republic Alpha facility were compensated only at the standard hourly rate for weekday overtime and weekend work, rather than receiving a 25 percent salary premium mandated by the Czech Labor Code. Although this issue was corrected, agency worker overtime compensation was still lower than that of core employees – 70 Czech crowns per hour (approximately $3.85) instead of 75 Czech crowns per hour (approximately $4.10). Moreover, agency workers at both of these facilities were not included in performance-based pay systems on an equal basis with permanent employees.

Alpha and Beta Electronics facilities in Mexico also used extensive numbers of contract workers at the time of our field research. Alpha outsourced the majority of its rank-and-file employees through external staffing agencies. In 2009, only the facility's managers, supervisors, and administrators were full-time employees. The remaining 75 percent of the facility's staff – all technicians, engineers, and operators – were agency workers. The Beta Electronics facility in Guadalajara also made significant use of agency workers, hiring more than 3,000 temporary workers from four different staffing agencies. Contract workers at Beta were also employed in the firm's cafeteria services, security, and maintenance operations.

A review of HP's audit records and several annual NGO reports revealed that Alpha and Beta experienced real issues surrounding the hiring, compensation, and training of agency workers. At Alpha's facility in Guadalajara, Mexico, temporary employees hired through staffing agencies experienced discriminatory hiring practices, including being subjected to mandatory preemployment pregnancy tests. Interviews conducted in 2006 by the NGO CEREAL indicated that agency workers at Alpha Electronics in Guadalajara were being concurrently fired and hired on short-term 15-day contracts in an effort to limit their tenure and subsequent full-time employee benefit eligibility. HP audits of both Alpha and Beta similarly found that although both firms had supplied their staffing agencies with a copy of the EICC, neither had a system in place to ensure that these vendors (which supplied most of the assembly line workers for Alpha and Beta) conformed to the code.

In both Mexico and the Czech Republic, the number of EICC audit violations that involved agency workers declined significantly over time between 2005 and 2009. These improvements at the Czech and Mexican facilities, however, were achieved through divergent pathways, shaped by the particularities of the institutional context in which these facilities were embedded.

Institutional Interactions and Divergent Pathways Toward Enforcement

Improvements in working conditions for contract workers in Mexico and the Czech Republic occurred through divergent pathways, involving alternative modes of interaction between private and public regulatory efforts. In Mexico, private actors – which included HP, its suppliers, local business associations, and labor-rights NGOs – developed a set of practices and institutional arrangements that substituted for ineffective government regulation. In the Czech Republic, private regulatory efforts were focused on helping suppliers comply with changing national legislation and assisting government labor inspectors understand the compensation issues related to contract work. As such, these private actions complemented public regulatory initiatives.

Improvements in Mexico through Private Substitution of Ineffective Public Regulation

Through the initiatives of multiple Mexican NGOs and HP, there were both immediate improvements in the treatment of agency workers as well as the creation of several long-term programs and new institutional arrangements designed to prevent the future abuse of workers in these temporary and contingent employment relationships. Initial improvements were achieved through HP's audits of Alpha and Beta facilities. At Alpha, HP objected to the use of pregnancy testing of potential new hires by the supplier's staffing agencies. Alpha in turn insisted that its staffing agencies discontinue these practices, and they were subsequently abandoned in December of 2005. Similarly, at both Alpha and Beta, pressure from HP led both suppliers to implement an auditing process of their respective staffing agencies to ensure that these firms met necessary EICC social and environmental responsibility requirements.

In an effort to address more fundamental concerns involving temporary worker tenure and benefit eligibility, significant change occurred through the joint efforts of several Mexican NGOs, working in collaboration with HP and its suppliers. These improvements were brought about through the actions of NGOs rather than union efforts. Neither Alpha nor Beta has a strong union presence, due in part to the fact that most workers are on temporary, short-term contracts and are employed not by Alpha or Beta but rather by external staffing agencies. This has largely precluded the use of strikes and collective action among these workers. One local NGO representative stated, "We haven't seen any unions in ten years. It's tough to establish them because of turnover." In 2006, the NGO CEREAL revealed that agency workers at Alpha were being concurrently hired and fired on short-term 15-day contracts, in an effort to limit the benefit eligibility of these workers. CEREAL reported this abusive practice to both HP and Alpha managers, and pressure from HP resulted in the cessation of this practice. It should also be noted that HP's first audit of Alpha, which occurred one year before these actions by CEREAL, had missed these abusive employment practices, which suggests that the EICC's lack of explicit attention to agency workers may have led this issue to be overlooked during their periodic audits.

More long-term change was brought about through the interactions of a local NGO, external pressure from HP, and the existence (on the books) of national labor regulations that were subsequently privately enforced. This corrective action was possible thanks to a unique relationship that developed among these actors in the Guadalajara electronics cluster, referred to by participants as "the Accord." The Accord is a novel dispute resolution system that was developed to respond to electronics workers' pay, benefits, and workplace grievances. Workers must bring their labor complaint to the courts within two months of its occurrence or they forfeit the right to initiate a labor dispute. Yet, aside from this initial filing, successful arbitrations are resolved without engaging Mexican legal authorities.

The Accord arose out of a standard naming and shaming campaign launched by CEREAL but evolved over time into a more collaborative arrangement pushed for by HP and that included not just CEREAL but also the Guadalajara electronics chamber of commerce (CANEITI) and a number of electronics suppliers in the Guadalajara region. As part of this agreement, CEREAL developed a more direct relationship with the HR managers of all local electronics plants. In the event that a worker approached CEREAL regarding a perceived labor violation, a representative from the NGO would contact the relevant factory's HR manager and discuss the issue directly. If the particular issue or complaint was not covered by either Mexican labor law or the industry Code of Conduct, CEREAL would inform the worker that his or her claim was invalid and would encourage the worker(s) to return to work. However, if the complaint violated either national labor law or the EICC, the HR manager would investigate and report back to CEREAL. If the complaint did turn out to be legitimate, the employer would compensate the workers in accordance with Mexican law. Cases that could not be resolved within the Accord could be escalated by involving the industry association CANEITI, or by initiating a formal lawsuit.

Before the Accord, workers had few options to seek remediation for labor grievances due to the absence of a strong union, few resources, and/or little knowledge of how to navigate the Mexican legal system. By 2007, CEREAL had addressed 237 total cases of labor violations, 78 percent of which were resolved through a dialogue between interested parties.[8] Four cases were escalated through the involvement of CEREAL, and forty-seven cases prompted lawsuits (CEREAL 2007). In 2008 and 2009, in excess of 4,000 workers approached CEREAL, and approximately 95 percent of them had claims related to temporary employment (Peterson 2010). According to CEREAL's internal records, in 2010, 60 percent of the cases brought forward through the Accord concerned issues relating to unfair dismissal, and a further 21 percent of cases pertained to unfair dismissal in conjunction with an additional issue (e.g., sexual harassment, failure to pay fair wages, etc.). Unfair dismissal cases in 2009 and 2010 frequently involved efforts to negotiate worker severance pay in accordance with Mexican national labor laws, although negotiations occasionally resulted in worker reinstatement (for more information, see also Salazar Salame 2011).

The Accord has substantially increased the speed with which worker labor grievances are being resolved. The staff at CEREAL described the pre-Accord situation as follows, "CEREAL has worked on hundreds of cases in courts, but it takes one to three years. Workers don't win. With [the Accord], we can win in one to three months." The efficiency of this system was lauded by both CEREAL and managers of various electronics suppliers – actors normally in disagreement over these issues. A senior manager at HP described his skepticism surrounding the Mexican government's process of grievance resolution, stating that "local authorities take years [to resolve grievances], and lawyers are the only ones that win." Describing the Accord, this manager went on to state: "we can solve these problems, we are mature people."

Building on the experience of the Accord, in 2009 a new Guadalajara institution emerged in a further effort to subject staffing agencies to greater oversight and thus protect the rights of temporary contract workers. Although HP has audited many of the local workforce staffing agencies, much of the content of the HP/EICC code does not apply to these organizations. Interviews with these staffing agencies indicated that responding to, and preparing for, these HP audits has been difficult and challenging. CADELEC, an offshoot of the Mexican electronics industry chamber of commerce (CANIETI), has introduced a certification system specifically targeting temporary staffing agencies. Although initially voluntary, HP managers interviewed for this project have expressed

---

[8] Of the 237 total cases reviewed by CEREAL in 2007, a subset of these involved agency workers.

their intention to mandate that all Mexican temporary staffing agencies used by their suppliers undergo CADELEC certification. External oversight through this new accreditation process is intended to ensure that agency workforce providers fully comply with legal mandates regarding the compensation, dismissal, and acceptable employment duration of agency workers. This emerging institution was borne of collaboration between HP and CADELEC in an effort to supplement the weak enforcement and inconsistent application of national labor law. Although the prospect of this emergent certification system is promising, it will take time to determine the effect it may have on firms' utilization of agency workers.

All of these developments contrast to accounts that argue that private voluntary regulation necessarily crowds out state regulation or worker voice (Esbenshade 2004; Bartley 2005; Reich 2007). The case of Alpha and Beta electronics in Mexico shows how private efforts can, under certain conditions – frequent interactions among buyers, suppliers, and local NGOs; the creation of new institutions that mediate conflicts between workers and their local employers; the layering of private voluntary initiatives on existing legal structures (labor courts, labor regulations) – promote an effective alternative to weak or absent state regulation. At the same time, it can provide a more efficient vehicle through which workers can actually exercise their citizenship rights.

Improvements in the Czech Republic through Complementary Private and Public Regulation

In contrast to Mexico, improvements in the working conditions of contract workers at Alpha and Beta Electronics facilities in the Czech Republic were achieved through complementary interactions between active national regulatory authorities and HP's private compliance team. These improvements focused primarily on providing contract workers with payment comparable to that of permanent employees.

At the Alpha Electronics plant in the Czech Republic, HP pressured management to disseminate the EICC code, hoping that this would increase awareness of labor rights among all employees. Staffing agencies were also asked to include information about the EICC in their training programs for all new recruits. According to the HR manager at this facility, the failure to include operators, consisting mostly of contract workers, in the bonus system was to a great extent due to the company's lack of awareness that the comparable pay principle mandated by the Czech Labor Code includes also performance-based rewards and not just basic compensation. At the insistence of HP's auditors, Alpha modified its bonus system to include agency workers in addition to full-time employees.

The porous organizational boundary between Beta's plant and the temporary staffing firms that supplied Beta with agency workers presented significant challenges to monitoring legal and fair payment practices for the large number of agency employees working at Beta. Although these contractors worked at

Beta's facility, their working hours were tracked (on paper) by the temporary staffing firms that directly employed them. This mismatch created a variety of problems concerning the underreporting (and thus underpaying) of overtime and weekend work by these agency workers. Once these violations were detected by HP's auditors, however, Beta worked with its staffing agencies to compensate their temporary workers in compliance with the law.

However, to more permanently correct this situation, Beta and its staffing agencies introduced electronic record keeping that could accurately track working hours and shift schedules for contract workers, thus enhancing the accuracy and transparency of working hours and work schedules for both the individual workers as well as for the temporary staffing agency that employed them. These more transparent records were also used by Beta Electronics, HP auditors, and even government labor inspectors to ensure compliance with Czech labor law. The introduction of electronic records was supplemented by HP's efforts to encourage Beta to monitor its own subcontractors to guarantee that they were in compliance with the EICC. As a result, the HR department at Beta was trained and encouraged to audit the staffing agencies on a regular basis, as well as frequently exchange information regarding employee work hours and wages with these second-tier suppliers. This increased coordination between Beta and its staffing agencies (engineered by HP) led to greater compliance with the EICC as well as with Czech labor law, which stipulates that staffing agencies and their clients are jointly responsible for ensuring that agency workers' working conditions and pay are comparable with those of the client company's permanent employees.

Although the facility adjusted the pay rates of temporary workers and their weekend and overtime compensation with relatively little resistance, the inclusion of temporary workers in the performance-based bonus system proved to be more problematic and was addressed more gradually. Insistence on complying with the comparable pay and working conditions principle stipulated by Czech labor law was essential in establishing a pilot project to expand the performance based payment system to agency workers that operate in the Personal Computer section of the facility.

Labor inspections take place at this facility on a regular basis. In the context of significant concerns regarding human trafficking and forced labor in the Czech Republic (Aleinik 2010), however, the inspections conducted by the local labor inspectorate focused primarily on ensuring that the documentation of migrant workers was in order and that their fundamental human rights were not violated through their employment at the facility. The expertise of HP auditors was key in exposing the unequal labor practices surrounding agency workers and staffing agencies and insisting upon improvements. Once the government labor inspectors were focused on these issues, remediation quickly took place. However, the fact that improvements were limited to issues regulated by national law reveals both the opportunities and limitations of this complementary approach to labor regulation.

In both the Czech Republic and Mexico, EICC violations linked to contract workers at all four factories analyzed in this chapter declined substantially over time. The reasons for and processes underlying these improvements are particularly important because labor code violations affecting agency workers are frequently overlooked in both private and public systems of regulation (Barrientos and Smith 2006). This chapter illustrates that even when a particular issue is of similar importance in two national settings – as is in the case of working conditions for contract workers – the pathways toward improvement can differ significantly given the institutional context and interest constellation in which suppliers are embedded. In Mexico, workplace and labor rights improvements were enabled through the presence of a strong worker advocacy organization active in the region and aligned with HP's own efforts to improve labor standards among its electronics suppliers. The NGO CEREAL, through its familiarity with local labor practices, accessibility to local employers, and legitimacy in the eyes of workers, complemented HP's activities and thus encouraged local industry leaders to cooperate with them in both the initial Accord and the subsequent certification initiative. In contrast, in the absence of local organizations to represent the interests of contract workers in the Czech Republic, HP's monitoring efforts, even if imperfect, were essential in bringing compensation issues related to contract workers to the attention of both factory managers and government labor inspectors (who were focused on other issues). Improved conditions for contract workers in the Czech Republic were possible only through a strict interpretation of national legislation and greater cooperation with government labor inspectors.

Common across these two national contexts was the role of private regulation, which although key in promoting improvements in working conditions, wages, and employment contracts for contract workers in both Mexico and the Czech Republic, was nonetheless enabled, legitimated, and shaped by the particularities of the respective national regulatory frameworks and the constellation of interest groups in the two settings. Thus, the particular ways private and public regulation combined in Mexico and the Czech Republic was determined not solely (or even primarily) by the attitudes, behaviors, or even capabilities of private actors (HP and its suppliers) to comply with the EICC and local labor laws but rather by the institutional capabilities of the labor inspectorates and the constellation of local civil society groups in these two countries. Notwithstanding these differences, however, the case study presented here shows how persistent labor issues affecting temporary, migrant workers – some of the least skilled and most marginalized workers toiling in today's global supply chains – can be redressed, even in industries characterized by volatile demand and "fissured" work organization. But these improvements came about only by combining private and public regulation and through the development of more collaborative relationships among key actors in these settings – HP auditors and managers, NGOs, local factory managers, and in the case of the Czech republic, government labor inspectors.

This collaborative process, linking together private compliance officers, government regulators, labor-rights-oriented NGOs, and other actors involved in promoting labor rights in global supply chains is not limited only to private compliance initiatives but also characterizes some of the more innovative experiments with government regulation as well. As discussed at the beginning of this chapter, the limitations of private voluntary programs has led in recent years to growing demands for more effective and legitimate interventions by the state and as a result, a number of new or reformed public regulatory initiatives aimed at promoting greater compliance with labor laws, health and safety standards, and the ability of workers in supply chain factories to freely organize themselves into independent unions have been launched. We now turn to an examination of some of these efforts by national governments to enforce their domestic labor and employment laws to assess their effectiveness. Through this analysis, I show that although the revival of labor inspection and the promotion of innovative regulatory initiatives in an array of different countries have certainly helped improve working conditions and labor rights in these countries, these efforts also suffer various limitations – limitations in their organizational capacities and ability to adequately inspect, let alone redress, violations in all workplaces under their jurisdiction – that can also only be addressed by combining with and complementing private initiatives.

Regulatory Renaissance and the Need for Complementary Public and Private Action

In just about every country hosting global supply chains, national governments have passed strong laws that regulate the conditions of employment and protect the citizenship rights of workers. However, in many of these countries, these labor laws and regulations are often violated, and the labor inspectorates/ministries charged with inspecting workplaces and enforcing labor laws are weak, underfunded, and at times, prone to politicization or even corruption. In addition to these organizational limitations, which reduce the ability of the state to adequately enforce its domestic laws, exist other concerns regarding the mismatch between the "highly legalistic" and rigid enforcement practices of government regulatory agencies and the dynamic and evolving reality of supply chain factories. As such, many observers have argued that traditional government approaches to labor inspection/enforcement are inadequate at promoting workplace improvements and labor rights in today's emerging centers of production (Kagan and Scholz 1984; Ayers and Braithwaite 1992; Gunningham, Kagan, and Thorton 2003; Lee 2005; Coslovsky, Pires, and Silbey 2011).

In response to these limitations of both private initiatives and traditional government regulation, a number of scholars and policymakers alike have become engaged in regulatory reform and innovative government programs aimed at enhancing enforcement of labor laws and employment standards. According to Michael Piore and Andrew Schrank, "a regulatory renaissance" is underway in a host of developing and already developed nation-states. Significant expansions of labor inspectorates and labor ministries are reported in countries as diverse as Argentina, Brazil, Costa Rica, El Salvador, France, Honduras, Spain, Morocco, and Uruguay (Piore and Schrank 2008: 3). More than simply increasing the size and budgets of these respective government bureaucracies, various scholars describe an array of innovative strategies pursued by labor inspectors (sometimes, public prosecutors) in Brazil (Pires 2008, 2011; Coslovsky 2011), the Dominican Republic (Schrank 2009), Cambodia (Polaski 2006; Rossi and Robertson 2011), China (Gallagher, Jing, and Trieu 2010), and even the United States (Weil 2010). These innovations range from the increased professionalization of, and increased discretion given to, labor inspectors in the Dominican Republic so that they can more thoroughly enforce labor laws (Schrank 2009), to the development of sector-based enforcement strategies by the Wage and Hour Division of the US Department of Labor that enable labor inspectors to more effectively regulate labor practices in industries characterized by "fissured" work organization (Weil 2010), to experiments by activist labor inspectors in Brazil that combine both old and new forms of enforcement – deterrence (fines and sanctions) with pedagogy (providing technical, financial, and legal advice) – so that noncompliant firms can gradually move toward compliance with national labor and environmental laws without compromising their competitiveness (Pires 2008, 2011; Coslovsky 2011).

Perhaps the most well known of these innovative experiments with regulatory enforcement is the Better Factories Cambodia (BFC) program. Better Factories Cambodia grew out of the 1999 US-Cambodia bilateral trade agreement in which increased access to the US market (quota) was linked to demonstrated improvements in working conditions in Cambodia's garment sector. Because the Cambodian labor ministry and labor inspectorate did not, at the time of the agreement, possess the organizational capacities to accurately audit garment factories throughout the country, the ILO was asked by both the US and Cambodian governments to monitor and report on industry-wide compliance with ILO labor standards. Audit reports were used by both the US government to determine whether to grant quota increases to Cambodian apparel exporters and by global buyers who used this same information to shape their sourcing decisions (Polaski 2006). At the same time, the ILO sought to enhance the capabilities of domestic actors and institutions by hiring and training local Cambodians to conduct the factory audits. Through these various mechanisms, this agreement sought to promote economic development, generate employment, improve working conditions in the garment sector and to help develop the institutional capabilities of the Cambodian state to enforce its own laws.

Although textile and garment quotas were eliminated with the end of the Multi-Fiber Arrangement (MFA) in January 2005, the Better Factories Cambodia program has continued to operate by employing different incentives and sanctioning mechanisms. If before 2005, access to the US market created the necessary incentives for Cambodian garment manufacturers to participate in the BFC and comply with ILO labor standards, following the demise of the MFA, the Cambodian government has granted export licenses only to factories that continue to participate in the BFC. Moreover, although individual factory audit reports are not made public, global buyers can and do request these reports and use them to determine whether to continue sourcing from these suppliers. In sum, it appears that even in Cambodia – a country ravaged by war, genocide, underdevelopment, and weak political institutions – experiments with new forms of labor regulation have taken shape and appear to be working. If such developments can occur even in Cambodia, then the prospects for a regulatory renaissance in other rapidly growing emerging markets may also be possible.

Interestingly enough, more recent research on Cambodia's Better Factory program, as well as on other cases of "regulatory renaissance" reveal that successful enforcement of labor laws and employment standards is the product not solely of enlarged, better funded, more professionalized state bureaucracies but rather arise from a combination of (often, collaborative) private and public regulatory interventions. Using audit data collected by ILO monitors of export-oriented garment factories in Cambodia from January 2006 to December 2008 (covering 344 individual factories), Oka (2010a, 2010b) shows that compliance with ILO standards among Cambodian garment factories is, in fact, uneven, and that in the continuing absence of a well-funded labor inspectorate, reputation-conscious global buyers appear to be driving improved compliance with ILO labor standards. According to Oka, reputation-conscious buyers use the factory audit reports to determine whether to continue sourcing from individual factories, and they share this information with other reputation-conscious buyers. In fact, Oka shows that the greater the number of reputation-conscious buyers sourcing from any one factory, the higher its compliance record. Thus, it is clear that without the continuing role of private codes of conduct and the insistence by private actors (reputation-conscious global buyers) that their suppliers continue to participate in and report progress on compliance with ILO labor standards, the Better Factories Cambodia program would not achieve anything close to its well-reported success. In fact, Cambodian garment factories not producing for reputation-conscious global buyers manifest greater labor code violations and worse working conditions (see also Robertson, Dehejia, Brown, and Ang 2010; Rossi and Robertson 2011; and Wetterberg 2011 for similar findings using the same and other, additional data sources). The absence of these same private initiatives, able to complement government- and ILO-run programs, may also explain the difficulties the Better Factory Program has experienced as it has sought to expand to other countries: Jordan (Kolben 2010) and Lesotho (Seidman 2009).

Complementary private and public regulation also appears to be at work in the Dominican Republic and Brazil as well. Notwithstanding the very real and important efforts by the Dominican Republic's labor inspectorate to expand

and professionalize its staff, it still appears unable to fully inspect all work-places, both in the export-oriented and domestic-focused sectors of the economy. As a result, a tacit and "uncoordinated" division of labor has developed in which private auditors focus on factories operating within the country's export-processing zones while state inspectors concentrate their scarce resources on redressing labor problems in the domestic-focused sectors of the economy (e.g., agriculture, construction, and small and medium-sized firms producing for the domestic market) (Amengual 2010). But more than simply divide up the national territory into separate and distinct regulatory spheres, Amengual shows how private and public forms of labor rights enforcement complement one another even within the same export-oriented zones. Private auditors rely on national laws and regulations to provide them with the legitimacy to demand certain changes in workplace practices among their suppliers. Likewise, by insisting on better employment and wage records, private compliance managers help state labor inspectors by providing them with up-to-date documentation on wages, work hours, working age of employees – documentation that is essential to assess whether or not a particular export-oriented factory is complying with national labor legislation. As a result, private and public regulation complement one another not simply by increasing the reach of regulation throughout the country but also by building off one another and enhancing the respective effectiveness of each form of regulation. Similar public-private partnerships have been documented in Brazil as well, where activist labor inspectors and public prosecutors work with individual firms, local banks, trade associations, and local governments in order to "stitch together" a strategy that both encourages and enables firms to comply with labor and environmental regulation (Coslovsky 2011; Pires 2011). Given the continuing problems (personnel shortages, budget cuts, difficulties in tracking labor conditions for highly mobile workers or in increasingly complex supply chains) experienced by most national labor inspectorates,[9] it should come as no surprise that the most effective efforts aimed at promoting improved working conditions and labor rights in global supply chains are precisely those that blend together private and public regulation.

Conclusion

Through a detailed case study of efforts to improve working conditions for contract workers employed at two of HP's suppliers in Mexico and the Czech Republic, this chapter has sought to show that private voluntary regulatory efforts do not necessarily crowd out or undermine state enforcement of labor laws and employment standards but rather, under certain circumstance, can complement and even enhance the effectiveness of government enforcement

---

[9] See the ILO 2011 for more on the difficulties national labor ministries and labor inspectorates face in the current economic environment.

efforts. Yet, this positive synergy between public and private forms of labor regulation is not unique to HP's Mexican and Czech suppliers. In a companion study, my graduate students and I found similar associations in our broader analysis of HP's compliance program. Electronics suppliers located in countries with stronger national institutions and greater rule of law consistently performed better on the Electronics Industry Code of Conduct audits than factories located in countries with weaker institutions and rule of law (Locke, Distelhorst, Pal, and Samel 2011). As we saw in Chapter 2, Nike's private compliance program also worked best in countries with more developed labor inspectorates and strong rule of law. Other researchers working on both labor and environmental standards have found similar findings, showing that differences in state policy shape the efficacy of private compliance programs in an array of different countries (Seidman 2007; Bartley 2011). According to David Graham and Ngaire Woods (2006), governments, both in developed and developing countries, can enhance the effectiveness of corporate self-regulation by insisting on (perhaps even legislating) greater transparency and accountability by global buyers and their suppliers and that the rights of workers to organize and mobilize to advance their claims be protected. Only in these circumstances can the promise of private voluntary regulation be fulfilled. Moreover, collaboration between private compliance officers and state regulators also underlie the most innovative experiments with regulatory reform and labor enforcement in a number of developing countries (Brazil, Cambodia, the Dominican Republic). How best to promote these forms of collaboration both among private supply chain actors as well as between them and state authorities is the focus of the Conclusion.

Conclusion

Collaboration, Compliance, and the Construction of New Institutions in a World of Global Supply Chains

This book has analyzed multiple private voluntary initiatives, across different countries and economic sectors, all aimed at improving working conditions and enforcing labor standards in an economy shaped by global supply chains. Chapters 2 and 3 evaluated the compliance programs of several major global corporations – Nike, ABC, Hewlett-Packard – and showed that although each of these companies had spent years developing ever-more-comprehensive monitoring tools, hiring growing numbers of internal compliance specialists, conducting hundreds of factory audits, and collaborating with external consultants and nongovernmental organizations (NGOs), working conditions and labor rights had improved somewhat among some of their suppliers but had stagnated or even deteriorated in many other supplier factories. After more than a decade of concerted efforts by global brands and labor rights NGOs alike, private compliance programs appear unable to deliver on their promise of enforcing labor standards in today's new centers of global production. This does not mean that private compliance efforts have not delivered on any improvements in working conditions. As the data presented on the Nike case in Chapter 3 illustrate, it clearly has. The point is that these improvements seem to have hit a ceiling: basic improvements have been achieved in some areas (e.g., health and safety) but not in others (e.g., freedom of association, excessive working hours). Moreover, these improvements appear to be unstable in the sense that many factories cycle in and out of compliance over time. This pattern of mixed and unstable compliance is not unique to Nike but characterizes the compliance programs of the other global brands analyzed in this book. Similar patterns have been described by other scholars studying labor standards in a variety of sectors throughout the world (Barrientos & Smith 2007; Egels-Zandén 2007; Korovkin and Sanmiguel-Valderrama 2007; Yu 2008; Nadvi et al. 2011).

As the shortcomings of these private compliance programs became increasingly apparent, global corporations, NGOs, and even international organizations began to promote an alternative (but still private, nongovernmental) approach to combating poor labor standards in global supply chains, built around the concept of capability building. The capability-building model rests on the observation that supply chain factories throughout the developing world often lack the resources, technical expertise, and management systems necessary to address the root causes of compliance failures. Whereas traditional compliance programs sought to deter Code of Conduct violations by policing and penalizing factories, capability-building initiatives seek to **prevent** violations by providing the skills, technology, and organizational capabilities necessary to enable factories to enforce labor standards and improve working conditions on their own. Rather than treating suppliers as immoral agents motivated by a desire to cheat their way through inspections, the capability-building approach conceives of them as willing partners who simply lack certain organizational skills for effective Code of Conduct enforcement.

Chapters 4 and 5 analyzed an array of capability-building initiatives across multiple industries (apparel, electronics, metalworking) and in different countries (Mexico, Honduras, the Dominican Republic, Vietnam, India, and China). Notwithstanding significant improvements over traditional compliance programs, many (but not all) capability-building initiatives analyzed in this book suffered from their own shortcomings, especially their inability to address certain distributive issues and overcome various political hurdles necessary to achieve labor rights enforcement. Although capability-building programs generated marked improvements in productivity and quality for participating factories, and for some workers, better health and safety conditions, these same initiatives – precisely because of their overly technocratic approach – eschewed more difficult, distributive issues (e.g., living wages) and the enforcement of "enabling rights" so that workers could organize to demand higher wages and better working conditions. The case study of two Nike apparel suppliers presented in Chapter 5 highlighted the importance of alternative approaches to capability building. When these programs are designed and implemented in ways that engage and empower workers, both business-related outcomes (i.e., productivity, quality) and labor standards improve. However, when these programs are designed or implemented in a more top-down, technocratic fashion, workers' rights are rarely strengthened.

Chapter 6 described why poor working conditions, precarious employment practices, low wages, excessive work hours, and weak labor rights persist in global supply chains by looking beyond the suppliers' factories and more broadly at the "upstream" business practices of large retailers and global brands and their "downstream" effects on suppliers and their workers. In that chapter, I documented how global brands have responded to a business environment characterized by dynamic consumer demand, shorter product life cycles, and concentrated retail channels by reorganizing their supply chains to optimize efficiencies and minimize financial and reputational risks. Although these techniques allowed major retail chains and global brands to offer a broader selection of products, introduce new products in a more timely fashion, and reduce inventory of poor-selling items, these same practices created various labor problems – excessive work hours, low wages, exploitation of migrant (contract) workers – at supplier factories. Chapter 6 argued that although better-designed private compliance systems and more capacious capability-building programs would certainly help improve labor standards in global supply chain factories, they could not, in and of themselves, adequately tackle these persistent workplace problems because the root cause of many of these labor issues lies in the structure of relations among large retailers, global brands, lead suppliers, and their factories. Until these relations, this broader structure, is reformed, interventions focused primarily on the factories will have limited impact.

In response to both the limitations of these private voluntary programs, and growing demands for more effective state enforcement of already existing labor and employment laws designed to protect workers employed in the factories and farms supplying global buyers, a number of new and/or reformed public regulatory initiatives aimed at promoting greater compliance with labor, environmental, and health and safety standards have been launched in recent years. Chapter 7 examined some of these efforts by national governments to enforce their domestic laws to assess their effectiveness. The analysis revealed that although the revival of labor inspection and the promotion of innovative regulatory initiatives in an array of different countries have certainly helped improve working conditions and labor rights in these countries, these efforts also suffer from various limitations – limitations in their organizational capacities and ability to adequately inspect, let alone redress violations in all workplaces under their jurisdiction. These organizational limitations could, however, be overcome through complementary interactions with private voluntary initiatives. To illustrate the positive potential of this complementary private/public regulatory approach, Chapter 7 revisited the case of contract work in the electronics industry and showed how these two systems of regulation combined in novel ways, in different national settings, to correct various labor code violations impacting temporary, migrant, contract workers – among the least skilled, least organized, and most vulnerable workers employed in global supply chains. The goal of that chapter was to show how labor rights and working conditions can be improved, even for these marginalized workers employed in a sector characterized by volatile demand and fissured employment, when private and public forms of regulation combine in complementary and mutually reinforcing ways.

In many ways, the various strategies analyzed in this book reflect the evolution of thinking and practice among key actors engaged in promoting labor standards in global supply chains. Private compliance programs emerged as a response to pressures and campaigns by consumer activists and NGOs to address significant labor abuses discovered among the suppliers producing goods for several reputation-conscious brands. And the global corporations analyzed in this book have invested considerable organizational resources into developing and monitoring their codes of conduct, building up their compliance staffs, and working with external compliance specialists to monitor their suppliers more effectively. The data generated by these processes are important because they reveal both the improvements taking place among some suppliers and on some issues, as well as the continuing difficulties most suppliers experience in redressing persistent problems like excess overtime, low wages, and irregular employment contracts. Yet, collecting data through factory audits is not enough because this process alone does not lead to changes in behaviors and practices at most supply chain factories.

In an effort to change these practices and behaviors, private corporations, labor-rights NGOs, and even international organizations promoted a series of capability-building initiatives, aimed at providing factory managers with the managerial and technical skills necessary to tackle the "root causes" underlying many labor issues manifest in global supply chains. Yet, most of these capability-building initiatives are targeted at the shop floor, at the suppliers' factories, and not at the upstream business practices that are, in fact, driving some of these unfair labor practices among suppliers. Moreover, many of these capability-building initiatives eschew particular issues like living wages and "enabling rights" for workers to organize freely and collectively – issues that are difficult to resolve either through technical capability-building efforts or by convincing factory managers (let alone company directors) that it is in their own self-interest (the so-called business case) to pay workers higher wages and embrace independent unions. This is why government regulation is required because only the state has the authority and legitimacy to enforce labor legislation and promote/protect citizenship rights.

Yet, given the limited capacities and scale of most labor ministries and labor inspectorates in both developing and already developed countries, public regulation alone is unable to fully address the myriad labor issues surrounding global supply chains. This is why public and private regulatory efforts need to work with and build off of one another. Taken together, the findings of this study of labor conditions among the suppliers of several major global brands, competing in different industries, and operating across many countries, suggest the need for a multifaceted approach to improving working conditions and labor standards in today's global supply chains. Each of the strategies analyzed in this book – private compliance efforts, capability-building initiatives, and even innovative state enforcement strategies – are necessary and important components to this strategy but none alone is sufficient to tackle this complex set of issues.

While recognizing the limits of generalizing from the experiences of a few reputation-conscious global buyers and their suppliers, the results of this study suggest the value of thinking about how these seemingly alternative strategies might fit together and complement one another in an integrated system for improving working conditions and labor standards in global supply chains. As we saw in each of the previous chapters, notwithstanding the limitations of private compliance, capability-building, and state enforcement strategies, fragments of an alternative set of practices, behaviors and institutional arrangements were visible within each of the case studies we analyzed. Recall, for instance, how Nike worked with some of its suppliers to help them reorganize their production systems and retrain their workers so that they could better respond to shifting patterns of consumer demand in a more flexible way. ABC and HP played similar roles with some of their suppliers as well, and others have documented analogous patterns of collaborative buyer–supplier relations in the automobile, footwear, furniture, metalworking, and steel industries – in a host of different countries (Sabel 1994; Helper, MacDuffie & Sako 1998; Frenkel & Scott 2002; Herrigel 2010; Ivarson & Alvstam 2010a). These more collaborative relationships were not based (or not solely based) on the technical assistance provided by global buyers to their suppliers but rather on the mutual recognition that each party had to gain from collaboration. In other words, Nike, ABC, HP, and other global corporations were able to establish more collaborative and labor-friendly relations with some of their suppliers because these buyer–supplier arrangements were based upon mutual gains, joint learning, long-term commitments, and even trust. Underlying these more collaborative relations was a fundamental understanding that both the risks and rewards (costs and benefits) of doing business together would be distributed more or less fairly between the parties. Can these collaborative, mutually dependent, trust-like relations be diffused more broadly, across multiple actors with divergent and competing interests, in today's global supply chains?

Earlier, I argued that the inherent problem with private voluntary initiatives seeking to enforce labor standards is their inability to reconcile diverse and conflicting interests and thus promote solutions that require collective action among the myriad actors involved in global supply chains. In the various case studies presented in this book, I showed how, under certain conditions, (long-term relations, frequent interactions, and mutually beneficial economic arrangements between buyers and suppliers) private voluntary initiatives *could* succeed by tapping into and aligning the interests and incentives of private firms (by reducing information and transaction costs, developing new capabilities, promoting process and product innovations that enhance the competitiveness of both buyers and suppliers) while also generating improved working conditions and wages for workers through new work and production processes in the supplier factories. I also showed that several of these initiatives relied, in one way or another, on government regulation and agents to legitimize and support their activities.

Building on recent research on "experimentalist governance" and "collaborative manufacturing," I argue that we can replicate these cases of labor-friendly supply chain practices through an iterative process that blends together the "encapsulated self-interest" (Hardin 2001) of the various actors engaged in global supply chains, innovative forms of government regulation, and the development of mechanisms for learning, self-governance, and monitoring by the actors themselves (Ostrom 1990; Greif 1997; Sabel and Zeitlin 2012). Like Hardin (2001), I too believe that collaborative behavior among utility-maximizing actors begins with self-interest. Although some actors collaborate and/or act in a trustworthy fashion out of affection or moral commitment, the vast majority of actors, especially market-driven private actors, collaborate because they believe that it is in their self-interest to do so.

Yet, there are limits to this form of collaboration. Most of us will be inclined to cooperate only with people we know, or who are sufficiently like us, or even who have good reputations based on their prior records. In many real-world situations, especially the world of global supply chains, however, complete information about other, potential partners is not available, nor is there much certainty about the circumstances surrounding our interactions. Often, our potential partners are numerous and may be not only different from us but also different from one another (heterogeneous). Moreover, sometimes, cooperation among small groups of like-minded actors can lead to cartels, which may benefit cartel members but damage the rest of us. Given that we are interested in promoting labor-friendly supply chain practices throughout the globe – practices that benefit not just a few powerful private actors but also (especially) workers employed in these supply chain factories, we need to avoid these limitations. This is why we need government regulation and intervention even for the most promising private initiatives.

Cohen and Rogers (1992, 1995) have argued that secondary associations with certain attributes (leadership accountability, inclusiveness of group membership, cooperative modes of interaction with other groups) are more likely to effectively aggregate and represent interests and thus facilitate efficient democratic governance than are other groups with qualitatively different features (hierarchical intra-group relations, parochial concerns, conflictual politics). They also suggest that government can use an array of selective incentives to artifactually shape groups and associations along these lines. In their work on "experimentalist governance," Sabel and Zeitlin (2012) have shown how various public authorities can shape interactions both among private actors and between the private and public sector in ways that promote innovation, the diffusion of best practices, and the enhancement of standards. Building on both bodies of research, as well as the field research conducted over the last several years, I argue that collaborative efforts initiated by self-interested actors are more likely to become responsive to worker concerns and demands for labor standards when government authorities intervene, in a variety of ways, to reinforce this more encompassing behavior. As we saw in the analysis of the Better Factories Cambodia program, as well as other innovative cases of complementary private-public regulation in Brazil, the Czech Republic, the Dominican Republic and Mexico, government played an important role in shaping the way private actors addressed labor standards issues. There was no standard government policy or intervention that cut across all of these different examples. In many ways, government regulatory authorities were learning and experimenting with different practices at the same time, and often in collaboration with, the private actors they were ostensibly regulating. But in all cases, government regulation not only legitimated private initiatives but also structured them in ways that were consistent with broader, societal concerns.

Yet, external government intervention is insufficient in guaranteeing the continuing functioning of these collaborative endeavors. As novel initiatives like the Better Factories Cambodia program or any of the other initiatives we analyzed in this book become transformed from relatively small experiments into larger and certainly more internally diverse and heterogeneous programs, the possibilities for shirking, cheating, and other opportunistic behavior by individual members increases significantly. This opportunistic behavior threatens to undermine the whole cooperative effort. Building on the insights of Ostrom (1990), I agree that government does not have the know-how, let alone capacity to intervene and continually monitor the behavior of all global suppliers located within its jurisdiction. Instead, the interested actors must develop their own self-governance mechanisms to ensure that their members continue to behave in a collaborative manner. As a result, the development of a set of internal self-governance and monitoring mechanisms that ensure the stability and longevity of these collaborative efforts is key to their continuing success and diffusion.

What the various examples of more labor-friendly buyer–supplier relations documented in this book share is the *process* through which mutually beneficial collaboration was built among them. Although the initial challenges facing Nike's high-performing Mexican t-shirt supplier, ABC's garment suppliers in India and Central America, HP's electronics contract manufacturers in the Czech Republic and Mexico, and even the garment manufacturers participating in Better Factories Cambodia were different, the underlying thrust of their problems was the same: failure to develop more efficient and more labor compliant business practices would undermine their ability to continue to do business with reputation-conscious buyers. As a result, these suppliers began to engage in a series of experiments aimed at reorganizing their work practices and address their labor code violations. They did this not simply because they suddenly discovered the virtues of lean manufacturing or high-performance work systems but rather out of self-interest, because they saw that these changes in practices were necessary for them to continue their business. In the process of reconfiguring their operations and redressing various labor code violations, they developed not only new organizational and technical capabilities but also more collaborative relations with their buyers. They became increasingly engaged in joint problem solving, information exchange, and mutual learning that strengthened both their operations and their employment practices.

Yet, many of these private initiatives could not have occurred had it not been for the legitimacy and authority they received from government regulatory authorities. Although private actors were key in monitoring and designing remediation plans for thousands of supply chain factories throughout the world, their authority ultimately rested on their insistence that individual factories respect domestic labor and employment laws. Very seldom did these private compliance officers advocate that suppliers go beyond the law of the land. Likewise, the development of innovative institutional arrangements like the Accord in Mexico or the Better Factories Cambodia program relied on state labor laws and regulations to operate effectively. Without the Cambodia government's decision to grant export licenses only to factories participating in the BFC, this program could never have continued after the demise of the Multi-Fiber Arrangement. Likewise, without its strict reliance on Mexican labor law, the elaborate grievance procedures developed through the Accord, could never have withstood legal challenges.

Finally, the continuing pressure and campaigns by NGOs and consumer groups on the various global brands analyzed in this book pushed all of them to develop elaborate monitoring systems aimed at tracking performance on various labor issues. Yet, among some of these compliance officers, a new form of auditing/monitoring process developed. At various factories visited for this research project, my graduate students and I observed auditors who developed more cooperative, less antagonistic relationships with the suppliers they inspected. These auditors were frequent visitors to these factories, and they had been visiting these same factories for several years. Rather than act as "inspectors" whose job focused primarily on uncovering Code of Conduct violations and punishing management for these infractions, these auditors acted more like consultants by engaging in joint problem solving, information sharing, and the diffusion of best practices that were in the mutual self-interest of the suppliers and aligned with the policies of the global buyers. And although the threat of sanction was still present in these settings, it served less to force the suppliers to comply with the various codes of conduct and more as a background condition or fallback mechanism aimed at fostering the joint problem solving initiatives underway at these factories.

Together, the self-interest of the various parties, the role of government in legitimating and reinforcing certain practices, and the constant engagement by external and internal actors led to the development of collaborative relations among some of the suppliers and buyers analyzed in this book and the development of novel institutional practices that promoted both compliance and competitiveness. If mutually beneficial collaboration and the development of new institutional arrangements aimed at promoting/supporting more labor-friendly practices can be constructed among actors within the highly competitive and volatile and underinstitutionalized settings analyzed for this book, then surely there is reason to hope that it can be built among other actors within and across other global supply chains.

Bibliography

Aleinik, M. 2010. "Employment Agencies – The Open Door for Migrant Workers: Recruitment Mechanisms and Working Conditions of Russian speaking Female Migrants in the Czech Republic." Open Society Institute & Soros Foundation Network Report.

Amaral, J., Billington, C. A., & Tsay, A. A. 2006. "Safeguarding the promise of production outsourcing." *Interfaces*, 36(3): 220–33.

Amengual, M. 2010. "Complementary Labor Regulation: The Uncoordinated Combination of State and Private Regulators in the Dominican Republic." *World Development*, 38(3): 405–14.

Amengual, M. 2011. "Enforcement without Autonomy: The Politics of Labor and Environmental Regulations in Agentina." PhD dissertation, Massachusetts Institute of Technology.

Amsden, A. H. 1989. *Asia's Next Giant: South Korea and Late Industrialization.* New York: Oxford University Press.

Amsden, A. H., & Chu, W. 2003. *Beyond Late Development: Taiwan's Upgrading Policies.* Cambridge, MA: MIT Press.

Anderson, M. B., & Woodrow, P. J. 1989. *Rising from the Ashes: Development Strategies in Times of Disaster.* Boulder, CO:San Francisco: Westview Press.

Anner, M. S. 2011. *Solidarity Transformed: Labor Responses to Globalization and Crisis in Latin America.* Ithaca, NY: Cornell University Press.

Apple. 2009. "Supplier Responsibility Progress Report." Retrieved from http://www.apple.com/supplierresponsibility.

Apple. 2011. "Apple Supplier Responsibility: 2011 Progress Report." Retrieved August 12, 2011.

Apple. 2012. "Apple Supplier Responsibility: 2012 Progress Report." Retrieved from http://images.apple.com/supplierresponsibility/pdf/Apple_SR_2012_Progress_Report.pdf.

Armbruster-Sandoval, R. 1999. "Globalization and Cross-Border labor Organizing: The Guatemalan Maquiladora Industry and the Phillips Van Heusen Workers' Movement." *Latin American Perspectives*, 26(2).

Armbruster-Sandoval, R. 2003. "Globalization and Transnational Labor Organizing: The Hondoran Maquiladora Industry and the Kimi Campaign." *Social Science History*, 27(4): 551–76.

Armbruster-Sandoval, R. 2005. *Globalization and Cross-Border Labor Solidarity in the Americas: The Anti-Sweatshop Movement and the Struggle for Social Justice.* New York: Routledge.

Axelrod, R. 1984. *The Evolution of Cooperation.* New York: Basic Books.

Ayers, I. and Braithwaite, J. 1992 "Responsive Regulation: Transcending the Deregulation Debate" Oxford, UK: Oxford University Press.

Baccaro, L. 2001. *Civil Society, NGOs, and Decent Work Policies: Sorting out the Issues.* International Labor Organization (International Institute for Labour Studies). Geneva: IILS Publications. Retrieved from http://ilo.org/public/english/bureau/inst/publications/discussion/dp12701.pdf.

Bair, J., & Gereffi, G. 2001. "Local Clusters in Global Chains: The Causes and Consequences of Export Dynamism in Torreon's Blue Jeans Industry." *World Development*, 29(11): 1885–903.

Barboza, D. 2011. "Workers Sickened at Apple Supplier in China." *The New York Times.* February 23, p. B1.

Bardach, E., & Kagan, R. A. 1982. *Going by the Book: The Problem of Regulatory Unreasonableness.* Philadelphia: Temple University Press.

Barrientos, S., & Smith, S. 2006. "The ETI Code of Labour Practice: Do Workers Really Benefit?" Sussex, UK: Ethical Trading Initiative.

Barrientos, S., & Smith, S. 2007. "Do Workers Benefit from Ethical Trade? Assessing Codes of Labour Practice in Global Production Systems." *Third World Quarterly*, 28: 713–29.

Barrientos, S., Gereffi, G., & Rossi, A. 2010. "Economic and Social upgrading in Global Production Networks: Developing a Framework for Analysis." Working Paper #1020/03, Institute for Development Policy & Management, University of Manchester, UK.

Bartley, T. 2005. "Corporate Accountability and the Privatization of Labor Standards: Struggles over Codes of Conduct in the Apparel Industry." In Harland Prechel (Ed.), *Politics and the Corporation*, Vol. 14 (Research in Political Sociology), Greenwich, CO; Oxford: JAI Press: 211–44.

Bartley, T. 2007. "Institutional Emergence in an Era of Globalization: The Rise of Transnational Private Regulation of Labor and Environmental Conditions." *The American Journal of Sociology*, 113: 297–351.

Bartley, T. 2010. "Transnational Private Regulation in Practice: The Limits of Forest and Labor Standards Certification in Indonesia," *Berkeley Electronic Press.* Retrieved from http://www.bepress.com/bap/vol12/iss3/art7.

Bartley, T. 2011. "Transnational Governance as the Layering of Rules: Intersections of Public and Private Standards." *Theoretical Inquiries in Law*, 12(2): 6.

BBC. n.d. "The History of Running Shoes." Retrieved from http://news.bbc.co.uk/sportacademy/hi/sa/athletics/features/newsid_3935000/3935703.stm.

Becker, G. S. 1968. "Crime and Punishment: An Economic Approach." *The Journal of Political Economy*, 76(2): 169–217.

Berger, S. 2006. *How We Compete: What Companies around the World Are Doing to Make It in Today's Global Economy.* New York: Doubleday.

Berman, S. 1997. "Civil Society and the Collapse of the Weimar Republic." *World Politics*, 49(3): 401–29.

Berk, G. 2009. *Louis D. Brandeis and the Making of Regulated Competition, 1900–1932*. New York: Cambridge University Press.

Bhagwati, J. 1995. "Trade liberalisation and 'fair trade' demands: addressing the environmental and labour standards issues." *The World Economy*, 18(6): 745–59.

Billington, C., & Ellram, L. 2001. "Purchasing Leverage Considerations in the Out-sourcing Decision." *European Journal of Purchasing and Supply Management*, 7(1): 15–27.

Bloom, N., Eifert, B., Mahajan, A., McKenzie, D., & Roberts, J. December 2010. "Does management matter: evidence from India," with Benn Eifert, Aprajit Mahajan, David McKenzie, & John Roberts, Stanford Graduate Business School Research Paper No. 2074.

Blowfield, M. 2007. "Reasons to Be Cheerful? What We Know about CSR's Impact." *Third World Quarterly*, 284: 683–95.

Bormann, S., Krishnan, P., & Neuner, M. E. 2010. *Migration in a Digital Age: Migrant Workers in the Malaysian Electronics Industry*. Berlin: World Economy, Ecology and Development.

Bormann, S., & Plank, L. 2010. "Under Pressure: Working Conditions and Economic Development in Central and Eastern Europe." *WEED – World Economy, Ecology and Development Report 2010*.

Bowman, J. R. 1985. "The Politics of the Market: Economic Competition and the Organization of Capitalists." *Political Power and Social Theory*, 5: 35–88.

Braithwaite, J. 2006. "Responsive Regulation and Developing Economies." *World Development*, 34(5): 884–98.

Braithewaite, V., & Levi, M., eds. 1998. *Trust and Governance*. New York: Russell Sage Foundation.

Brown, D. L. 2005. "Challenges and Opportunities for the Fair Labor Association in the Post-MFA Period." Prepared under the supervision of Professor Richard Locke for The Fair Labor Association (FLA) Strategic Planning Meeting, July 26–27, at MIT Sloan School of Management, Cambridge, MA.

Brown, G. 2009. "Global Electronics Industry: Poster Child of 21st Century Sweatshops and Despoiler of the Environment?" EHS Today, pp. 45–8. Retrieved from: http://mhssn.igc.org/EHSToday-Sept09_GBrown.pdf.

Burruss, J., & Kuettner, D. 2002. "Forecasting For Short-Lived Products: Hewlett-Packard's Journey." *Journal of Business Forecasting Methods and Systems*, 21(4): 9–14.

Byster L., & Smith, T. 2006. "The Electronics Production Life Cycle. From Toxics to Sustainability: Getting Off the Toxic Treadmill." In T. Smith, D. Sonnenfeld, and N. Pellow (Eds.), *Challenging the Chip: Labor Rights and Environmental Justice in the Global Electronics Industry*. Philadelphia: Temple University Press.

Carrillo, J. 1998. "Third-generation Maquiladoras? The Delphi-General Motors case." *Journal of Borderlands Studies*, 13(1): 79–97.

Carrillo, J. 2005. "Cooperation without Trust? Reflections on the FLA's Efforts to Promote Collaboration Among Its Members and with Other MSIs." Prepared under the supervision of Professor Richard Locke for The Fair Labor Association (FLA)

Strategic Planning Meeting, July 26–27, at MIT Sloan School of Management, Cambridge, MA.

Casey, R. 2006. *Meaningful Change: Raising the Bar in Supply Chain Workplace Standards.* Working Paper # 29, Corporate Social Responsibility Initiative, John F. Kennedy School of Government, Harvard University, November 2006: 24–5.

Catholic Agency for Overseas Development. 2004. *Clean up your computer: working conditions in the electronics sector.*

Centre for Reflection and Action on Labour Issues. 2007. *Electronics, Multinationals, and Labour Rights in Mexico.*

Centre for Reflection and Action on Labour Issues. 2009. *Labour Rights in a Time of Crisis.* J. Barajas.

Chakrabarty, S., & Grote, U. 2009, "Child Labor in Carpet Weaving: Impact of Social Labeling in India and Nepal." *World Development*, 37(10): 1683–93.

Chambers, R. 1983. *Rural Development: Putting the Last First.* New York: Longman.

Chambers, R. 1994. "The Origins and Practice of Participatory Rural Appraisal." *World Development*, 22(7): 953–69.

Chan, J., & Peyer, C. 2008. "High Tech – No Rights? A One Year Follow Up Report on Working Conditions in China's Electronic Hardware Sector." SACOM. p. 62.

Chan, J., & Pun, N. 2010. "Suicide as Protest for the New Generation of Chinese Migrant Workers: Foxconn, Global Capital, and the State." *The Asia-Pacific Journal*, 37(2) 1–11.

Chan, J., de Haan, E., Nordbrand, S., & Torstenson, A. 2008. "Silenced to Deliver: Mobile Phone manufacturing in China and the Philippines." SOMO & SwedWatch, available at www.SwedWatch.org.

Chang, L. T. 2008. *Factory Girls.* New York: Spiegel and Grau.

Channel News Asia. 2008. "The Olympics: It's All about the Shoes." Originally aired May 28, 2008.

Charnovitz, S. 1987. "The Influence of International Labour Standards on the World Trading Regime: A Historical Overview." *International Labour Review*, 126(5): 565–84.

Charnovitz, S. 2001. "Rethinking WTO Trade Sanctions," *The American Journal of International Law*, 94(4): 792–832.

Christensen, C. M. 1997. *The Innovator's Dilemma: When New Technologies Cause Great Firms to Fail.* Boston: Harvard Business School Press.

Christensen, C. R., & Rikert D.C. October 16, 1984. "Nike (A)." Harvard Business School Case, No. 9-385-025: 1–31.

Claudia, S., & Castilleja, L. 2005. "The Maquiladora Electronics Industry and the Environment along Mexico's Northern Border." Research Paper prepared for the Third North American Symposium on Assessing the Environmental Effects of Trade, November 2005. Retrieved from http://www.cec.org/Storage/58/5077-Final-Schatan-T-E-Symposium05-Paper_en.pdf.

Clean Clothes Campaign. 2008. "Cashing In: Giant Retailers, Purchasing Practices, and Working Conditions in the Garment Industry." Retrieved from http://www.cleanclothes.org.

Coe, N. M., Johns, J., & Ward, K. 2008. "Flexibility in Action: The Temporary Staffing Industry in the Czech Republic and Poland. *Enforcement and Planning*, 40: 1391–415.

Cohen, J., & Rogers, J. 1992. "Secondary Associations and Democratic Governance." *Politics and Society*, December: 393–472.

Cohen, J., & Rogers, J. 2003. "Power and Reason." In Archon Fung and Erik Olin Wright, eds., *Deepening Democracy: Institutional Innovations in Empowered Participatory Governance* (pp. 237–255). London: Verso.

Cohen, J., & Sabel, C. 2006. "Extra Republicam Nulla Justita?" *Philosophy & Public Affairs*, 34(2): 147–75.

Cole, R. E. 1999. "Market Pressures and Institutional Forces: The Early Years of the Quality Movement." In R. E. Cole & W. R. Scott (Eds.), *The Quality Movement and Organizational Theory* (pp. 67–88). Thousand Oaks, CA: Sage.

Collier, P., & Dollar, D. 2002. *Globalization, Growth, and Poverty: Building an Inclusive World Economy*. Washington, DC: World Bank/Oxford University Press.

Collins, J., & Packard, D. 2005. "Foreword to the HP Way." In D. Kirby & K. Lewis (Eds.), *The HP Way* (xi–xviii). New York: HarperCollins.

Compa, L., & Vogt, J. S. 2001. "Labor Rights in the Generalized System of Preferences: A 20-Year Review." *Comparative Labor Law and Policy Journal* 22(2/3): 199–238.

Connor, T., & Dent K. 2006. *Offside! Labor Rights and Sportswear Production in Asia*. Oxfam International. Retrieved from http://www.oxfam.org/en/policy/policy/offside_labor_report.

Consumers International. 2009. "The Real Deal: Running Costs." Retrieved from http://www.consumersinternational.org/media/105607/realdealrunningshoes-finalfinal300609.pdf.

Cooney, S. "Dynamism and Stasis: Regulating Working Conditions in China." Unpublished manuscript, University of Melbourne Law School.

Cooney, S. 2007. "China's Labour Law, Compliance and Flaws in Implementing Institutions." *Industrial Relations Society of Australia*, 49: 673.

Coslovsky, S. 2011. "Relational Regulation in the Brazilian Ministério Publico: The Organizational Basis of Regulatory Responsiveness." *Regulation & Governance*, 5(1): 70–89.

Coslovsky, S., & Locke, R. M. 2011. "Enforcing Labor Standards in the Sugar Supply Chain: The Brazilian Experience." Unpublished manuscript.

Coslovsky, S., Pires, R., & Silbey, S. 2011. *The Politics of Regulatory Compliance and and Enforcement* (Handbook on the Politics of Regulation, David Levi-Faur, Ed.) London: Edward Elgar Publishers.

Czech Environmental Inspectorate. 2006/2007/2009. Annual Report 2006, 2007, 2009. Retrieved from http://www.cizp.cz/1362_Annual-Report-2007; http://www.cizp.cz/2667_Annual-Report-2009.

Danish Commerce and Companies Agency. 2008. "Small Suppliers in Global Supply Chains." Retrieved from http://www.dcca.dk/graphics/publikationer/CSR/Small%20Suppliers%20in%20Global%20Supply%20Chains.pdf.

Dean, J., & Tsai, T. 2010, May 27. "Suicides Spark Inquiries: Apple, H-P to Examine Asian Supplier After String of Deaths at Factory." Retrieved from online.wsj.com/.

Dedrick, J., & Kraemer, K. L. 2011. "Market Making in the Personal Computer Industry." *The Market Makers: How Retailers Are Reshaping the Global Economy*. Oxford: Oxford University Press: 291–310.

Devlin, R., Estevadeordal, A., & Rodríguez-Clare, A. (Eds.). 2006. *The Emergence of China: Opportunities and Challenges for Latin America and the Caribbean*.

Washington, DC: Inter-American Development Bank; Cambridge, MA: David Rockefeller Center for Latin American Studies, Harvard University, Harvard University Press.

Dhanarajan, S. 2005. "Managing Ethical Standards: When Rhetoric Meets Reality. *Development in Practice*, 15(3/4): 529–38.

Dobbin, F., & Sutton, J. R. 1998, September. "The Strength of a Weak State: The Rights Revolution and the Rise of Human Resources Management Divisions." *American Journal of Sociology*, 104(2): 441–76.

Dong, J. 2002, April 10. "The Rise and Fall of the HP Way." *Palo Alto Weekly*. Retrieved from http://www.paloaltoonline.com/weekly/morgue/2002/2002_04_10 .hpway10.html.

Doumbia-Henry, C., & Gravel, E. 2006. "Free Trade Agreements and Labour Rights: Recent Developments." *International Labour Review*, 145(3): 185–205.

Dubin, C. December 2009. "Snapshot: Footware." Retrieved from http://www.inboundlogistics.com/cms/article/snapshot-footwear.

Duhigg, C., & Barboza, D. 2012, January 25. "In China, Human Costs Are Built into an iPad." *New York Times*. Retrieved from http://www.nytimes.com/2012/01/26/business/ieconomy-apples-ipad-and-the-human-costs-for-workers-in-china.html?pagewanted=all.

Duhigg, C., & Bradsher, K. 2012, January 21. "How the US Lost Out on iPhone Work." *New York Times*. Retrieved from http://www.nytimes.com/2012/01/22/business/apple-america-and-a-squeezed-middle-class.html?pagewanted=all.

Duhigg, C., & Greenhouse, S. 2012, March 29. "Electronic Giant Vowing Reforms in China Plants," *The New York Times*. Retrieved from http://www.nytimes.com/2012/03/30/business/apple-supplier-in-china-pledges-changes-in-working-conditions.html?pagewanted=all&_r=0.

Eade, D. 1997. *Capacity-building: An Approach to People-centered Development*. Oxfam United Kingdom.

Eckstein, H. 1991. "Case Study and Theory in Political Science." In H. Eckstein (Ed.), *Regarding Politics: Essays on Political Theory, Stability, and Change* (pp. 117–76). Berkeley: University of California Press.

Edwards, M., & Hulme, D. 1996b. "Introduction: NGO Performance and Accountability." In M. Edwards & D. Hulme (Eds.), *Beyond the Magic Bullet-NGO Performance and Accountability in the Post-Cold World* (pp. 1–12). Save the Children. West Hartford, CT: Kumarian Press.

Egels-Zandén, N. 2007. "Suppliers' Compliance with MNC's Codes of Conduct: Behind the Scenes at Chinese Toy Suppliers." *Journal of Business Ethics*, 75: 45–62.

Electronics Industry Citizenship Coalition. 2009a. "Electronic Industry Citizenship Coalition: 2008 Annual Report." Electronic Industry Citizenship Coalition.

Electronics Industry Citizenship Coalition. 2009b. "Electronic Industry Code of Conduct: Version 3.01."

Elliott, K. A., & Freeman, R. B. 2001. "White Hats or Don Quixotes? Human Rights Vigilantes in the Global Economy." National Bureau for Economic Research.

Elliott, K. A., & Freeman, R. B. 2003. *Can Standards Improve under Globalization?* Washington, DC: Institute for International Economics.

Ellram, L., & Billington, C. 2001. "Purchasing leverage considerations in the outsourcing decision." *European Journal of Purchasing and Supply Management*, 7(1): 15–27.

Environmental Law Service. 2006. "LG Philips Displays in Hranice." Retrieved from http://www.responsibility.cz/index.php?id=173.

Evans, P. 1995. *Embedded Autonomy: States and Industrial Transformation*. Princeton, NJ: Princeton University Press.

Ernst, D. 2004. "Global Production Networks in East Asia's Electronics Industry and Upgrading Prospects in Malaysia." In S. Yusuf, M. S. Altaf, & K. Nabeshima (Eds.), *Global Production Networking and Technological Change in East Asia* (pp. 89–157). Washington, DC: World Bank/Oxford University Press.

Esbenshade, J. 2001. "The Social Accountability Contract: Private Monitoring from Los Angeles to the Global Apparel Industry." *Labor Studies Journal* (Spring): 98–120.

Esbenshade, J. 2004. *Monitoring Sweatshops: Workers, Consumers, and the Global Apparel Industry*. Philadelphia: Temple University Press.

Espach, R. H. 2009. *Private Environmental Regimes in Developing Countries: Globally Sown, Locally Grown*. New York: Macmillan.

Estache, A., & Wren-Lewis, L. 2009. "Toward a theory of regulation for developing countries: Following Jean-Jacque Laffont's lead." *Journal of Economic Literature*, 47(3): 729–70.

Esty, D., & Porter, M. E. 2000. "Ranking National Environmental Regulation and Performance: A Leading Indicator of Future Competitiveness?" In M. E. Porter, J. Sachs, & A. M. Warner (Eds.), *Global Competitiveness Report of 2000*. New York: Oxford University Press.

European Foundation for the Improvement of Living and Working Conditions. Temporary Agency Work in an Enlarged European Union, Dublin, Ireland, 2006.

European Industrial Relations Observatory. 2009. Country Profiles. Retrieved http://www.eurofound.europa.eu.

Evans, P. 2004. "Development as Institutional Change: The Pitfalls of Monocropping and the Potentials of Deliberation." *Studies in Comparative International Development* (SCID), 38(4): 30–52.

Fair Labor Association. "FLA 3.0 – Toward Sustainable Compliance." Retrieved from http://www.fairlabor.org/fla/go.asp?u=/pub/mp&Page=FLA3.

Fair Labor Association. 2011. "Wages along the Supply Chain: Trends, Progress and Looking Ahead." Conference report, June 2011.

Fair Labor Association. 2012, March. "Independent Investigation of Apple Supplier, Foxconn." Retrieved from http://www.fairlabor.org/sites/default/files/documents/reports/foxconn_investigation_report.pdf.

Farrell, Henry, 2009. *The Political Economy of Trust: Institutions, Interests, and Inter-Firm Cooperation in Italy and Germany*. New York: Cambridge University Press.

Frank, T. A. 2008. "Confessions of a Sweatshop Inspector." *Washington Monthly*, 40(4): 34–7.

Fraser, S. 1991. *Labor Will Rule: Sidney Hillman and the Rise of American Labor*. Ithaca, NY: Cornell University Press.

Fitter, R., & Kaplinsky, R. 2001. "Who Gains from Product Rents as the Coffee Market Becomes More Differentiated?" A Value Chain Analysis IDS Bulletin Special Issue on The Value of Value Chains, 32(3): 69–82.

Freidman, E. 2012. "Getting through Hard Times Together?: Chinese Workers and Unions Respond to the Eonomic Crisis," *Journal of Industrial Relations*, 54(4): 1–17.

Freire, P. 2005. *Education for Critical Consciousness*. New York: Continuum. Original work published 1973.

Freire, P. 2007. *Pedagogy of the Oppressed*. New York: Continuum. Original work published 1972.

Frenkel, S. J., & Scott, D. 2002. "Compliance, Collaboration, and Codes of Labor Practice: The Adidas Connection." *California Management Review*, 45(1): 29–49.

Frenkel, S. J. 2001. "Globalization, Athletic Footwear Commodity Chains and Employment Relations in China." *Organization Studies*, 22(4): 531–62.

Frundt, H. J. 2001. "The Impact of Private Codes and the Union Movement." Paper presented at XXIII International Congress of the Latin American Studies Association, Washington, DC.

Frundt, H. J. 2002. "Central American Union in the Era of Globalization." *Latin American Research Review*, 37(3): 7–53.

Fukuyama, F. 1995. *Trust: The Social Virtues and the Creation of Prosperity*. New York: Free Press.

Fung, A., O'Rourke, D., & Sabel, C. F. 2001. *Can We Put an End to Sweatshops? A New Democracy Forum on Raising Global Labor Standards*. Boston: Beacon Press.

Gallagher, K. P., & Zarsky, L. 2007. *The Enclave Economy: Foreign Investment and Sustainable Development in Mexico's Silicon Valley*. Cambridge, MA; London: The MIT Press.

Gallagher, M. 2012. "Changes in the World's Workshop: The Demographic, Social, and Political Factors Behind China's Labor Movement." Unpublished Manuscript.

Gallagher, M. E., Jing, S., & Trieu, H. 2010. "Industrial Relations in the World's Workshop: Participatory Legislation, Bottom-Up Law Enforcement and Firm Behavior." Paper presented at the Annual Meeting of the American Political Science Association, September 2–5, 2010, Washington, DC.

Gambetta, D. 1998. *Trust: Making and Breaking Cooperative Relations*. Oxford, UK: Blackwell.

Gelman, A., & Hill, J. 2007. *Data Analysis Using Regression and Multilevel/ Hierarchical Models*. Cambridge, UK: Cambridge University Press.

• Gereffi, G. 1999. "International Trade and Industrial Upgrading in the Apparel Commodity Chain." *Journal of International Economics*, 48(1): 37–70.

◢ Gereffi, G. 2005. The Global Economy: Organization, Governance, and Development. In N. J. Smelser & R. Swedberg (Eds.), *The Handbook of Economic Sociology* (pp. 160–182). Princeton, NJ: Princeton University Press.

• Gereffi, G., Humphrey, J., & Sturgeon, T. 2005. "The Governance of Global Value Chains." In *Review of International Political Economy*, 12(1): 78–104.

• Gereffi, G., & Korzeniewicz, M. 1994. *Commodity Chains and Global Capitalism*. Westport, CT; London: Praeger.

Gibbons, R. 2001. "Trust in Social Structures: Hobbes and Coase Meet Repeated Games." In K. Cook (Ed.), *Trust in Society*. New York: Russell Sage Foundation.

Glaeser, E., Johnson, S., & Shleifer, A. 2001. "Coase Versus the Coasians." *The Quarterly Journal of Economics*, 116: 853–99.

Global Production. 2008, January. "Footwear: trends in global production and trade." Retrieved from http://www.global-production.com/footwear/trendstudy/index.htm.

Good Electronics. December 2009. Newsletter (8th ed). Retrieved http://goodelectronics.org/news-en/Newsletter/archive-newsletter.

Good Electronics. 2009. *Reset: Corporate Social Responsibility in the Global Electronics Supply Chain*. Amsterdam: Good Electronics MVO Platform.

Graham, D., & Woods, N. 2006. "Making Corporate Self-Regulation Effective in Developing Countries." *World Development*, 34(5): 868–83.

Granovetter, M. 1973. "The Strength of Weak Ties." *American Journal of Sociology*, 78: 1360–80.

Greif, A. 1998. "Self-Enforcing Political System and Economic Growth: Late Medieval Genoa." In R. Bates, A. Greif, M. Levi, J.-L. Rosenthal, and B. Weingast (Eds.), *Analytic Narratives*. Princeton, NJ: Princeton University Press: 23–63.

Grossman, E. 2010, November. "200 People per Shoe: Making Footwear in Tangerang, Indonesia." Retrieved from http://scienceblogs.com/thepumphandle/2010/11/200_people_per_shoe_making_n.php.

Gunningham, N., Kagan, R., & Thornton, D. 2003. *Shades of Green: Business, Regulation and Environment*. Palo Alto, CA: Stanford University Press.

Gupta, P., & Chan, E. 2012, March 29. "Apple, Foxconn revamp China work conditions." *Reuters*.

Hainmueller, J., Hiscox, M., & Sequeira, S. 2011. "Consumer Demand for the Fair Trade Label: Evidence from a Field Experiment." *SSRN eLibrary*. Retrieved from http://ssrn.com/paper=1801942.

Hainmueller, J., & Hiscox, M. J. 2012, June 3. "The Socially Conscious Consumer? Field Experimental Tests of Consumer Support for Labor Standards." MIT Political Science Department Working Paper Series, No. 2012–15.

Hall, P., & Soskice, D. 2001. *Varieties of Capitalism: The Institutional Foundations of Comparative Advantage*. Oxford: Oxford University Press.

Hamilton, G. G., Petrovic, M., & Senauer, B. (Eds.). 2011. *The Market Makers: How Retailers Are Reshaping the Global Economy*. Oxford, UK: Oxford University Press.

Hardin, R. 2001. "Conceptions and Explanations of Trust." In Karen Cook, ed., *Trust in Society*. New York: Russell Sage Foundation.

Haufler, V. 2001. *A Public Role for the Private Sector: Industry Self-regulation in a Global Economy*. Washington, DC: Carnegie Endowment for International Peace.

Helper, S., MacDuffie, J. P., and Sako, M. 1998. "Determinants of Trust in Supplier Relations. Evidence from the Automotive Industry in Japan and the United States." *Journal of Economic Behavior and Organization*, 34: 77–84.

Heritier, A., A. K. Mueller-Debus, & C. R. Thauer 2009. "The Firm as an Inspector: Private Ordering and Political Rules." *Business and Politics*, 11(4): Article 2.

Herrigel, G. 2010. *Manufacturing Possibilities*. New York: Oxford University Press.

Herrigel, G., and Volker, W. 2010. "Mutually Beneficial Upgrading? China's Changing Relationship With Developed Country Manufacturing Multinationals," Presented at The Beijing Forum, Beijing, China, November 5–7, 2010.

Hewlett-Packard. 2009, March. "Global Citizenship Customer Report 2008." Hewlett-Packard Development Company, Palo Alto, California.

Hewlett-Packard. 2010. "2009 HP Global Citizenship Report." Hewlett-Packard Development Company, Palo Alto, California.

Hewlett-Packard. 2011. "A Connected World: The Impact of HP Global Citizenship in 2010 – and Beyond." Hewlett-Packard Development Company.

Hiscox, M., Broukhim, M., & Litwin, C. 2011. "Consumer Demand for Fair Trade: New Evidence from a Field Experiment Using eBay Auctions of Fresh Roasted Coffee." unpublished.

Hiscox, M., & Smyth, N. 2012. "Is There Consumer Demand for Improved Labor Standards? Evidence from Field Experiments in Social Labeling." Journal of Business Ethics. Unpublished manuscript:School of Government, Harvard University. Cambridge, Massachusetts.

Humphrey, J., & Schmitz, H. 1996. *Trust and Economic Development, Discussion Paper 355*. Brighton, UK: Institute of Development Studies.

Humphrey, J., & Schmitz, H. 2002. "How Does Insertion in Global Value Chains Affect Upgrading in Industrial Clusters?" *Regional Studies*, 36: 1017–27.

Ichniowski, C., Kochan, T. A., Levine, D. I., Olson, C. A., & Strauss, G. (1996). "What Works at Work: Overview and Assessment." *Industrial Relations*, 35(3): 299–333.

Interfaith Center on Corporate Responsibility. 2010. "Investor Statement Regarding Suicides and Working Conditions at Electronics Manufacturing Facilities." Retrieved from http://www.iccr.org/news/press_releases/072110InvestorStatementon WorkingConditions.pdf.

International Confederation of Private Employment Agencies. 2009. The agency work industry around the world. Retrieved from http://www.ciett.org.

International Labor Orgaization. 2006. "Strategies and Practice for Labour Inspection (GB.297/ESP/3)." ILO, *Labour Administration and Labour Inspection*. Geneva: International Labour Conference, 100 Session.

International Labor Organization. 2007. "Monitoring Process Brochure." Retrieved from http://www.betterfactories.org/content/documents/1/Monitoring%20Process% 20Brochure%20(en).pdf.

International Labor Organization. 2008a. *Global Employment Trends*, Geneva: ILO.

International Labor Organization. 2008b. "Child Labor." Retrieved from http://www. ilo.org/global/topics/child-labour/lang-en/index.htm.

International Labor Organization. 2008c. "Eradicating Forced Labour from Global Supply Chains." Retrieved from: http://www.ilo.org/empent/Eventsandmeetings/ WCMS_165497/lang-/index.htm.

International Labor Organization. 2008d. "Safety and Health at Work." Retrieved from: http://www.ilo.org/global/topics/safety-and-health-at-work/lang-en/index.htm.

International Labor Organization. 2011. "Labor Administration and Labor Inspection." Presented at the International Labour Conference, 100th Session.

Ivarsson, I., & Alvstam, C.G. 2009. "Local Technology Linkages and Supplier Upgrading in Global Value Chains: The Case of Swedish Engineering TNCs in Emerging Markets." *Competition & Change*, 13(4): 368–88.

Ivarsson, I., & Alvstam, C. G. 2010a. "Supplier Upgrading in the Home-furnishing Value Chain: An Empirical Study of IKEA's Sourcing in China and South East Asia." *World Development*, 38(11): 1575–87.

Ivarsson, I., & Alvstam, C. G. 2010b. "Upgrading in Global Value-Chains: A Case Study of Technology-Learning Among IKEA-Suppliers in China and Southeast Asia." *Journal of Economic Geography*, 10(2): 731–52.

Jack, E. P., & Raturi, A. 2002. "Sources of Volume Flexibility and Their Impact on Performance." *Journal of Operations Management*, 20(5): 519–48.

Jenkins, R. April 2001. "Corporate Codes of Conduct: Self-Regulation in a Global Economy," United Nations Research Institute for Social Development. Retrieved from http://www.eldis.org/static/DOC9199.htm; http://www.unrisd.org/unrisd/website/document.nsf/(httpPublications)/E3B3E78BAB9A886F80256B5-E00344278?OpenDocument.

Johnson, S., McMillan, J., & Woodruff, C. 2000. "Courts and Relational Contracts." Unpublished manuscript, MIT, Cambridge, MA.

Justice, D. W. 2005. "The Corporate Social Responsibility Concept and Phenomenon: Challenges and Opportunities for Trade Unionists." Presented at the ILO Training Seminar in Kuala Lumpur, November 28–December 3, 2005.

Kagan, R., & Scholz, J. 1984. "The Criminology of the Corporation and Regulatory Enforcement Strategies." In K. Hawkins & J. M. Thomas (Eds.), *Enforcing Regulation*. Boston: Kluwer-Nijhoff Publishing.

Kaipia, R., Korhonen, H., & Hartiala, H. 2006. "Planning Nervousness in a Demand Supply Network: An Empirical Study." *International Journal of Logistics Management*, 17(1): 95–113.

Kane, T,Holmes, K. R., & O'Grady, M. A. 2007. *2007 Index of Economic Freedom: The Link Between Economic Opportunity and Prosperity*. Washington, DC: The Heritage Foundation.

Kaplinsky, R. 2000. "Globalisation and Unequalisation: What Can Be Learned from Value Chain Analysis?" *Journal of Development Studies*, 37(2): 117–46.

Kaplinsky, R. 2005. *Globalization, Poverty and Inequality: Between a Rock and a Hard Place*. Cambridge, UK: Polity Press.

Katz, H., & Sabel, C. 1985. "Industrial Relations & Industrial Adjustment in the Car Industry." *Industrial Relations: A Journal of Economy and Society*, 24(3): 295–315.

Kaufmann, D., Kraay, A., & Mastruzzi, M. 2006. *Governance Matters III: Governance Research Indicator Country Snapshot (GRICS), 1996–2002*. The World Bank. Retrieved from http://www.worldbank.org/wbi/governance/pubs/govmatters3.html.

Keck, M. E., & Sikkink, K. 1998. *Activists Beyond Borders: Advocacy Networks in International Politics*. Ithaca, NY: Cornell University Press.

Keck, M. E., & Sikkink, K. 2007. *Activists Beyond Borders: Advocacy Networks in International Politics*. Ithaca, NY: Cornell University Press.

Kelman, S. 1981. *Regulating America, Regulating Sweden: A Comparative Study of Occupational Safety and Health Policy*. Cambridge, MA: MIT Press.

Kernaghan, C. 2006. "US-Jordan Free Trade Agreement: Descends Into Human Trafficking & Involuntary Servitude." The National Labor Committee, New York.

Knauss, J. 1998. "Modular Mass Production: High Performance on the Low Road." *Politics and Society*, 26(2): 273–96.

Knight, Jack, 1992. *Institutions and Social Conflict*, Cambridge, UK: Cambridge University Press

Kochan, T. A., Katz, H. C., & McKersie, R. B. 1986. *The Transformation of American Industrial Relations*. New York: Basic Books.

Kolben, K. 2007. "Integrative Linkage: Combining Public and Private Regulatory Approaches in the Design of Trade and Labor Regimes." *Harvard International Law Journal*, 48(1): 203.

Kolben, K. 2010. "Better Work Jordan: A Case Study." Unpublished manuscript.

Korovkin, T., & Sanmiguel-Valderrama, O. 2007. "Labour Standards, Global Markets and Non-State Initiatives: Columbia's and Ecuador's Flower Industries in Comparative Perspectives." *Third World Quarterly*, 28(1): 117–35.

Korzeniewicz, M. 1994. "Commodity Chains and Marketing Strategies: Nike and the Global Athletic Footwear Industry." In G. Gereffi & M. Korzeniewicz (Eds.), *Commodity Chains and Global Capitalism* (pp. 247–66). Westport, CT: Greenwood.

KPMG, Consumer Electronics Association, and Global Semiconductor Alliance. 2008. "The Consumer Electronics Boom: How Semiconductor and Consumer Electronics Companies Can Improve Cost, Time-to-Market, and Product Quality." Retrieved from http://www.kpmg.com/au/en/issuesandinsights/articlespublications/pages/the-consumer-electronics-boom.aspx.

Kuhn, P. J., & Shen, K. December 2009. "Employers' Preferences for Gender, Age, Height and Beauty: Direct Evidence." NBER Working Paper No. 15564.

Laffont, J., & Tirole, J. 1993. *A Theory of Incentives in Procurement and Regulation.* Cambridge, MA; London: The MIT Press.

Lake, H. 2006. "Production and Principles: A Study of Work Organization in the South Indian Apparel Industry." PhD dissertation, Tufts University.

Lee, E. 2005. "Why Did They Comply while Others Did Not?" (Ph.D. dissertation, Massachusetts Institute of Technology).

Leinbach, T. R., & Bowen, J. T. 2004. "Air Cargo Services and the Electronics Industry in Southeast Asia." *Journal of Economic Geography*, 4(3): 299–321.

Level Works. 2006. *Wages, Benefits and Work Hours in the Peoples Republic of China.* San Francisco, CA: Level Works Limited.

Levi, M., & Linton, A. 2003. "Fair Trade: A Cup at a Time?" *Politics & Society*, 31(3): 407–32.

Levy, B. 1991. "Transaction Costs, the Size of Firms and Industrial Policy: Lessons from a Comparative Case Study of the Footwear Industry in Korea and Taiwan." *Journal of Development Economics* (November): 151–78.

Linden, G., Kraemer, K. L., & Dedrick, J. 2009. "Who Captures Value in a Global Innovation Network? The Case of Apple's iPod." *Communications of the ACM*, 52(3): 140–4.

Locke, R. M. 2003. "The Promise and Perils of Globalization: The Case of Nike, Inc." In T. A. Kochan & R. Schmalensee (Eds.), *Management: Inventing and Delivering Its Future* (pp. 39–70). Cambridge, MA; London: The MIT Press.

Locke, R. M., Amengual, M., & Mangla, A. 2009. "Virtue out of Necessity? Compliance, Commitment, and the Improvement of Labor Conditions in Global Supply Chains." *Politics & Society*, 37(3): 319–51.

Locke, R. M., Distelhorst, G., Pal, T., & Samel, H. 2012. "Production Goes Global, Standards Stay Local: Private Labor Regulation in the Global Electronics Industry." Working paper.

Locke, R. M., Kochan, T., Romis, M., & Qin, F. 2007. "Beyond Corporate Codes of Conduct: Work Organization and Labour Standards at Nike's Suppliers." *International Labour Review*, 146(1–2): 21–40.

Locke, R. M., Qin, F., & Brause, A. 2007. "Does Monitoring Improve Labor Standards? Lessons from Nike." *Industrial and Labor Relations Review*, 61(1): 3–31.

Locke, R. M., & Romis, M. 2007. "Improving Work Conditions in a Global Supply Chain." *MIT Sloan Management Review*, 48(2): 54–62.

Locke, R. M., Rissing, B. A., & Pal, T. 2011. "Complements or Substitutes? Public vs. Private Regulation and the Improvement of Labor Standards in Global Supply Chains." Working paper.

Locke, R. M., & Samel, H. 2012. "Looking in the Wrong Places?: Labor Standards and Upstream Business Practices in the Global Electronics Industry MIT Political Science Working Paper #2012–18.

Lowi, T. J. 1964. "American Government, 1933–1963: Fission and Confusion in Theory and Research." *The American Political Science Review*, 58(3): 589–99.

Lowi, T. J. 1972. "Four Systems of Policy, Politics, and Choice." *Public Administration Review*, 32(4): 298–310.

Lu, J. 2009. "Employment Discrimination in China: The Current Situation and Principle Challenges." *Hamline Law Review*, 32(1): 133.

Luthje, B. 2002. "Electronics Contract Manufacturing: Global Production and the International Division of Labor in the Age of the Internet." *Industry & Innovation*, 9(3): 227–47.

MacDuffie, J. P. 1995. "Human-Resource Bundles and Manufacturing Performance: Organizational Logic and Flexible Production Systems in the World Auto Industry." *Industrial & Labor Relations Review*, 48(2): 197–221.

MacDuffie, J. P., & Krafcik, J. F. 1992. "Integrating Technology and Human Resources for High-Performance Manufacturing: Evidence from the International Auto Industry." In T. A. Kochan & M. Useem (Eds.), *Transforming Organizations* (pp. 206–26). New York: Oxford University Press.

makeITfair. November 2009. On the Move: Electronics Industry in Central and Eastern Europe. http://makeitfair.org/en/the-facts/reports/2007-2009.

Mamic, I. 2004. *Implementing Codes of Conduct: How Businesses Manage Social Performance in Global Supply Chains*. Geneva: International Labor Organization.

Matten, D., & Crane, A. 2005. "Corporate Citizenship: Toward an Extended Theoretical Conceptualization." *Academy of Management Review*, 30(10): 166–79.

Mayer, M., & Gereffi, G. 2010. "Regulation and Economic Globalization: Prospects and Limits of Private Governance." *Berkeley Electronic Press*, 12(3).

McGregor, D. M. 1960. *The Human Side of Enterprise*. New York: McGraw-Hill.

McKay, S. C. 2006. "Hard Drives and Glass Ceilings – Gender Stratification in high-tech production." *Gender & Society*, 20: 207–35.

Miller, G. 2001. "Why Is Trust Necessary Organizations? The Moral Hazard of Profit Maximization." In Karen Cook, ed., *Trust in Society*. New York: Russell Sage Foundation.

Ministry of the Environment of the Czech Republic. 2004. "State Environmental Policy of the Czech Republic 2004–2010." Retrieved from http://www.cenia.cz/web/www/web-pub-en.nsf/$pid/MZPMSFJAIK01.

Ministry of the Environment of the Czech Republic. 2005. Report on the Environment in the Czech Republic in 2005. Retrieved from: http://www.mzp.cz/osv/edice.nsf/D6D4FAF979DB843AC125728E003A8B1B/$file/Report2005.pdf.

Minnich, D., & Maier, F. 2007. "Responsiveness and Efficiency of Pull-Based and Push-Based Planning Systems in the High-Tech Electronics Industry."

Moran, T. H. 2002. *Beyond Sweatshops: Foreign Direct Investment and Globalization in Developing Countries*. Washington, DC: Brookings Institution Press.

Morrison, A., Pietrobelli, C., & Rabellotti, R. 2008. "Global Value Chains and Technological Capabilities: A Framework to Study Learning and Innovation in Developing
Countries." *Oxford Development Studies*, 36(1): 39–58.

Mosley, L. 2010. *Labor Rights and Multinational Production*. New York: Cambridge
University Press.

Mosley, L., & Saika U. 2007, August. Racing to the Bottom or Climbing to the Top?:
Economic Globalization and Collective Labor Rights," *Comparative Political Studies*,
40(8): 023–048.

Marine Stewardship Council. 2011. "MSC in Numbers." Retrieved from http://www.
msc.org/business-support/key-facts-about-msc.

Murakami, Y. 1987. "The Japanese Model of Political Economy." In K. Yamamura &
Y. Yasuba (Eds.), *The Political Economy of Japan: The Domestic Transformation*
(Vol. 1, pp. 33–90). Stanford, CA: Stanford University Press.

Nadvi, K. 2008. "Global Standards, Global Governance and the Organization of Global
Value Chains." *Journal of Economic Geography*, 8: 323–43.

Nadvi, K., Lund-Thomsen, P., Xue, H., & Khara, N. 2011. "Playing against China:
Global Value Chains and Labour Standards in the International Sports Good Industry." *Global Networks*, 11(3): 334–54.

Nadvi, K., & Wältring, F. 2004. "Making Sense of Global Standards." In H. Schmitz
(Ed.), *Local Enterprises in the Global Economy: Issues of Governance and Upgrading*
(pp. 53–94). Northampton: Edward Elgar.

National Research Council. 2004. *Monitoring International Labor Standards:
Techniques and Sources of Information*, Washington, DC: National Academies
Press.

National Sporting Goods Association. 2005. Retrieved from http://www.sbrnet.com.

National Sporting Goods Association. 2010. Retrieved from http://www.nsga.org/i4a/
pages/index.cfm?pageid=3506.

Navas-Alemán, L., & Bazan, L. 2003. "Local Implementation of Quality, Labour and
Environmental Standards: Opportunities for Upgrading in the Footwear Industry."
SEED Working Paper No. 45. Geneva: International Labour Organization.

Navas-Alemán, L., & Bazan, L. 2005. "Making Value Chain Governance Work for the
Implementation of Quality, Labor and Environmental Standards: Upgrading Challenges in the Footwear Industry." In E. Giuliani, R. Rabellotti, & M. P. van Dijk
(Eds.), *Clusters Facing Competition: The Importance of External Linkages* (pp. 39–
60). Aldershot, UK: Ashgate.

Nelson, V., Martin, A., & Ewert, J. 2007. "The Impacts of Codes of Practice on Worker
Livelihoods: Empirical Evidence from the South African Wine and Kenyan Cut Flower
Industries." *The Journal of Corporate Citizenship*, Winter, 28: 61.

Ngai, P. 2005. "Global Production, Company Codes of Conduct, and Labor Conditions
in China: A Case Study of Two Factories." *China Journal*, 54: 101–13.

Ngai, P., & Jenny Chan. 2010. "Global Capital, the State, and Chinese Workers: The
Foxconn Experience." *Modern China*, 38(4): 383–410.

Nike, Inc. 2005, March. FY04 Corporate Responsibility Report. Beaverton, OR:
Nike. Retrieved from http://www.nike.com/nikebiz/nikebiz.jhtml?page=29&item=
fy04.

Nike, Inc. 2007, May. "Innovate for a Better World: FY05–06 Corporate Responsibility
Report." Beaverton, OR: Nike, Inc., pp. 39–42.

Nike, Inc. January 2010a. Corporate Responsibility Report. Beaverton, OR: Nike, Inc. Retrieved from http://nikeinc.com/news/nike-outlines-global-strategy-for-creating-a-more-sustainable-business.

Nike, Inc. July 2010b. Annual Report. Retrieved from http://www.nikebiz.com.

Nike, Inc. May 2012. FY10–11 Sustainable Business Performance Summary. Beaverton, OR: Nike, Inc. Retrieved from http://nikeinc.com/news/nike-inc-introduces-new-targets-elevating-sustainable-innovation-within-business-strategy.

North, D. 1990. *Institutions, Institutional Change and Economic Performance*. Cambridge, UK: Cambridge University Press.

Organization for Economic Cooperation and Development. 2008. "OECD Information Technology Outlook 2008: Highlights." http://www.oecd.org/dataoecd/37/26/41895578.pdf.

Oka, C. 2010a. "Accounting for the Gaps in Labour Standard Compliance: The Role of Reputation-Conscious Buyers in the Cambodian Garment District." *European Journal of Development Research*, 22(1): 59–78.

Oka, C. 2010b. "Channels of Buyer Influence and Labor Standard Compliance: The Case of Cambodia's Garment Sector." *Advances in Industrial and Labor Relations*, 17: 153–83.

Ōno, T. 1988. *Toyota Production System: Beyond Large-scale Production*. Portland, OR: Productivity Press. Original work published 1978.

O'Rourke, D. 1997. "Smoke from a Hired Gun: A Critique of Nike's Labor and Environmental Auditing in Vietnam as performed by Ernst & Young." San Francisco: Transnational Resource Action Center, 1997. Retrieved from http://www.corpwatch.org/articla.php?id=966.

O'Rourke, D. 2000, September 28. "Monitoring the Monitors: A Critique of PriceWaterhouseCoopers Labor Monitoring." Unpublished manuscript, MIT, Cambridge, MA.

O'Rourke, D. 2002. "Monitoring the Monitors: A Critique of Corporate Third-party Labor Monitoring." In R. Jenkins, R. Pearson, & G. Seyfang (Eds.), *Corporate Responsibility and Labour Rights: Codes of Conduct in the Global Economy* (pp. 196–208). London: Earthscan.

O'Rourke, D. 2003, February. "Outsourcing Regulation: Analyzing Nongovernmental Systems of Labor Standards and Monitoring." *Policy Studies Journal*, 31(1): 1–30.

O'Rourke, D. 2007. "Bringing in Social Actors: Accountability and Regulation in the Global Textiles and Apparel Industry." In D. Brown & N. Woods (Eds.), *Making Global Self-Regulation Effective in Developing Countries*. Oxford: Oxford University Press. 113–148.

O'Rourke, D. 2011. "Citizen Consumer." *Boston Review*, November/December: 12–19.

Osterman, P. 1994. "How Common Is Workplace Transformation and Who Adopts It?" *Industrial and Labor Relations Review*, 47(2): 173–88.

Ostrom, E. 1990, November. *Governing the Commons: The Evolutuion of Institutions for Active Action*. New York, New York: Cambridge University Press.

Overeem, P. 2009. "Reset. Corporate Social Responsibility in the Global Electronics Supply Chain." Amsterdam: Good Electronics MVO Platform.

Oxfam International. 2004. "Trading Away Our Rights: Women Working in Global Supply Chains."

Packard, D. 2006. *The HP Way: How Bill Hewlett and I Built Our Company*. New York: HarperBusiness.

Partida, R. E. 2004. "Efectos de los Tratados de Libre Comercio suscritos con otros paises sobre los salarios y empleo (NAFTA, Union Europea)." Universidad de Guadalajara, Guadalajara, Mexique.

Pattberg, P. H. 2005. "The Forest Stewardship Council: Risk and the Potential of Private Frest Governance." *Journal of Environment and Development*, 14(3): 356–74.

Pay, E. 2009. "The Market for Organic and Fair-Trade Coffee." United Nations, Food and Agriculture Organization, Rome, Italy. Retrieved from http://www.fao.org/fileadmin/templates/organicexports/docs/Market_Organic_FT_Cofee.pdf.

Pessoa, A. 2006. "Public-Private Sector Partnerships in Developing Countries: Prospects and Drawbacks." *FEP Working Papers* 228, Universidade do Porto, Faculdade de Economia do Porto.

Peterson, K. 2010. "Temping Down Labor Rights: The Manpowerization of Mexico." *CorpWatch*. Retrieved from http://www.corpwatch.org/article.php?id=15496.

Petrecca, L., & Howard, T. 2005, August 4. "Adidas-Reebok Merger Lets Rivals Nip at Nike's Heels." *USA Today*, p. B1.

Piore, M. J. 2005. "Looking for Flexible Workplace Regulation in Latin America and the United States." Conference paper for Workshop on Labour Standards Application: A Compared Perspective, November 28–30, Buenos Aires, Argentina.

Piore, M. J., & Sabel, C. F. 1984. *The Second Industrial Divide: Possibilities for Prosperity*. New York: Basic Books.

Piore, M. J., & Schrank, A. 2008. "Toward Managed Flexibility: The Revival of Labour Inspection in the Latin World." *International Labour Review*, 147(1): 1–23.

Pires, R. 2008. "Promoting sustainable compliance: Styles of labour inspection and compliance outcomes in Brazil." *International Labour Review*, 147(2–3): 199–229.

Pires, R. 2011. "Beyond the Fear of Discretion: Flexibility, Performance, and Accountability in the Management of Regulatory Bureaucracies." *Regulation & Governance*, 5(1): 43–69.

Polaski, S. 2004. "Protecting Labor Rights through Trade Agreements: An Analytical Guide." *U.C. Davis Journal of International Law & Policy*, 13: 13–25.

Polaski, S. 2006. "Combining global and local forces: The Case of Labor Rights in Cambodia." *World Development*, 34(5): 919–32.

Posthuma, A., & Nathan, D. 2010. *Labour in Global Production Networks*, Cambridge UK: Oxford University Press.

Potoski, M., & Prakash, A. 2004. "The Regulation Dilemma: Cooperation and Conflict in Environmental Governance. *Publication Administration Review*, 64(2): 137–48.

Power, M. 1997. *The Audit Society: Rituals of Verification*. New York: Oxford University Press.

Prakash, A., & Potoski, M. 2007. "Investing Up: FDI and the Cross-Country Diffusion of ISO 14001 Management Systems." *International Studies Quarterly*, 51: 723–44.

Prakash, A., & Potoski, M. 2006a. "Racing to the Bottom? Trade, Environmental Governance, and ISO 14001," *American Journal of Political Science*, 50(2): 350–64.

Prakash, A., & Potoski, M. 2006b. *The Voluntary Environmentalists: Green Clubs, ISO 14001, and Voluntary Environmental Regulations*. Cambridge, UK: Cambridge University Press.

Program on International Policy Attitudes. 2000. Retrieved from http://www.pipa.org.

Putnam, R. 1993. *Making Democracy Work: Civic Traditions in Modern Italy*. Princeton, NJ: Princeton University Press.

Pruett, D. 2005, November. "Looking for a Quick Fix: How Weak Social Auditing Is Keeping Workers in Sweatshops." Clean Clothes Campaign. Retrieved from http://www.cleanclothes.org/ftp/05-quick_fix.pdf.

Raworth, K., & Kidder, T. 2009. "Mimicking 'Lean' in Global Value Chains: It's the Workers Who Get Leaned On." (Jennifer Bair, Ed.) *Frontiers of Commodity Chain Research* (pp. 165–189). Stanford, CA: Stanford University Press.

Reich, R. B. 2007. *Supercapitalism: The Transformation of Business, Democracy and Everyday Life*. New York: Knopf.

Reinhardt, Forest. 1999. "Market Failure and the Environmental Policies of Firms: Economic Rationales for "Beyond Compliance" Behavior," *Journal of Industrial Economy*, 3(1): 9–21.

Renard, M. C. 2005. "Quality Certification, Regulation and Power in Fair Trade." *Journal of Rural Studies*, 21(4): 419–31.

Rivoli, P. 2005. *The Travels of a T-Shirt in the Global Economy: An Economist Examines the Markets, Power, and Politics of World Trade*. Hoboken, NJ: John Wiley & Sons.

Riisgaard, L. 2009. "Global Value Chains, Labor Organization and Private Social Standards: Lessons from East African Cut Flower Industries." *World Development*, 37(2): 326–40.

Robertson, R., Dehejia, R., Brown, D., & Ang, D. 2010. "Labor Law Compliance and Human Resource Management Innovation: Better Factories Cambodia." Geneva, IlO: Working paper.

Rodriguez-Garavito, C. A. 2005. "Global Governance and Labor Rights: Codes of Conduct and Anti-Sweatshop Struggles in Global Apparel Factories in Mexico and Guatemala." *Politics and Society*, 33(2): 203–33.

Rosenzweig, P. M. July 14, 1994. "International Sourcing in Athletic Footwear: Nike and Reebok." *Harvard Business School Case*, No. 9-394-189: 1–17.

Rossi, A., & Robertson, R. 2011. "Better Factories Cambodia: An Instrument for Improving Industrial Relations in a Transnational Context." Washington D.C. *Center for Global Development*. Unpublished manuscript.

Ruggie, J. G. 2003. "Taking Embedded Liberalism Global: The Corporate Connection." In D. Held & M. Koenig-Archibugi, *Taming Globalization: Frontiers of Governance*. Cambridge: Polity Press.

Ruggie, J. G. 2003. "The United Nations and Globalization: Patterns and Limits of Institutional Adaptation." *Global Governance*, 9: 301.

Ryan, J., and Thein, A. 1998. *Stuff: The Secret Lives of Everyday Things*. Seattle, WA: Northwest Environment Watch. Retrieved from www.worldwatch.org/system/files/EP112C.pdf.

Sabel, C. F. 1982. *Work and Politics*. New York: Cambridge University Press.

Sabel, C. F. 1994. "Learning by Monitoring: The Institutions of Economic Development." In N. J. Smelser & R. Swedberg (Eds.), *The Handbook of Economic Sociology* (pp. 137–65). Princeton, NJ: Princeton University Press.

Sabel, C. F., & Zeitlin, J. 2004. "Neither Modularity nor Relational Contracting: Inter-Firm Collaboration in the New Economy." *Enterprise & Society*, 5(3): 388–403.

Sabel, C. F., 7 Zeitlin, J. 2012. "Experimental Governance" (David Levi-Faur, Ed.). *The Oxford Handbook of Governance*. Oxford: Oxford University Press.

Salazar Salame, H. 2011. *Worker Rights Protection in Mexico's Silicon Valley: Confronting Low-Road Labor Practices in High-Tech Manufacturing through Antagonistic Collaboration* (master's thesis). Retrieved from DSpace@mit. Retrieved from http://hdl.handle.net/1721.1/69456.

Schatan, C., & Castilleja, L. 2005. "The Maquiladora Electronics Industry and the Environment along Mexico's Northern Border." Third North American Symposium on Assessing the Environmental Effects of Trade, Working Paper 05.

Scherer, A. G., Palazzo, G., & Baumann, D. 2006. "Global Rules and Private Actors: Toward a New Role of the Transnational Corporation in Global Governance." *Business Ethics Quarterly*, 16: 505–32.

Schipper, I, & de Haan, E. 2007. *Hard (Disk) Labour: Research Report on Labour Conditions in the Thai Electronics Sector*. Amsterdam: Stichting Onderzoek Multinationale Ondernemingen (SOMO).

Schon, D., & Rein, M. 1994. *Frame Reflection: Toward the Resolution of Intractable Policy Controversies*. New York: Basic Books.

Schrage, E. J. 2004, January. *Promoting International Worker Rights through Private Voluntary Initiatives: Public Relations or Public Policy?* University of Iowa Center for Human Rights. Retrieved from http://www.uiowa.edu/~uichr/publications/documents/gwri_report_000.pdf.

Schrank, A. 2005. "Professionalization and Probity in the Predatory State: Labor Law Enforcement in the Dominican Republic." Paper presented for the MIT Institute for Work and Employment Relations Seminar, February 8, Cambridge, MA.

Schrank, A. 2007. "Labor Standards and Human Resources: A Natural Experiment in an Unlikely Laboratory." Paper presented at the annual meeting of the International Studies Association 48th Annual Convention, January 28, Hilton Chicago, Chicago, IL.

Schrank, A. 2009. "Professionalization and Probity in a Patrimonial State: Labor Inspectors in the Dominican Republic." *Latin American Politics and Society*, 51(2): 91–115.

Seidman, G. W. September, 2003. "Monitoring Multinationals: Lessons from the Anti-Apartheid Era." *Politics & Society*, 31(3): 381–406.

Seidman, G. W. 2007. *Beyond the Boycott: Labor Rights, Human Rights, and Transnational Activism*. New York: Russell Sage Foundation.

Seidman, G.W. 2009. "Labouring under an Illusion? Lesotho's 'sweat-free' label." *Third World Quarterly*, 30(3): 581–98.

SEMARNAT (Secretaría del Medio Ambiente, Recursos Naturales y Pesca). 2000. *Informe 1995–2000*. Mexico City, Mexico: SEMARNAT.

SEMARNAT (Secretaría del Medio Ambiente, Recursos Naturales). 2003. *Informe Anual PROFEPA, 2002*, Mexico City, Mexico: SEMARNAT.

Sen, A. 1999. *Development as Freedom*. New York: Anchor.

Senauer, B., & Reardon, T. 2011. "The Global Spread of Modern Food Retailing." In G. G. Hamilton, M. Petrovic, B. Senauer (Eds.), *The Market Makers* (pp. 271–90). New York: Oxford University Press.

Shamir, R. 2004. "The De-Radicalization of Corporate Social Responsibility." *Critical Sociology*, 3: 669–89.

Sharma, A., Sharma, R., & Raj, N. 2000. "The Impact of Social Labelling on Child Labour in India's Carpet Industry." ILO/IPEC Working Paper. New Delhi, Institute for Human Development.

Shiba, S., Graham, A., & Walden, D. 1993. *A New American TQM: Four Practical Revolutions in Management.* Cambridge: Productivity Press, Inc.

Silbey, S., Huising, R., & Vinocur Coslovsky, S. 2009 "The 'Sociological Citizen': Related Interdependence in Law and Organizations," *L'Annee* Sociologique, 59(1): 201–29.

Silbey, S. (Editor of Special Issue) 2011. "The Sociological citizen: Pragmatic and relational regulation in law and organizations," *Regulation and Governance*, 5(1): 1–164.

Smith, G., & Feldman, D. 2003, October. *Company Codes of Conduct and International Standards: An Analytical Comparison. Part I of II: Apparel, Footware and Light Manufacturing; Agribusiness; Tourism.* The World Bank. Retrieved from http://siteresources.worldbank.org/INTPSD/Resources/CSR/Company_Codes_of_Conduct.pdf.

Smith, T., Sonnenfeld, D., & Pellow, D. 2006. *Challenging the Chip: Labor Rights and Environmental Justice in the Global Electronics Industry.* Philadelphia: Temple University Press.

Sodhi, M. S., & Lee, S. 2007. "An Analysis of Sources of Risk in the Consumer Electronics Industry." *Journal of the Operational Research Society*, 58(11): 1430–9.

SOMO. (2009). "On the Move: The Electronics Industry in Central and Eastern Europe" Make IT Fair Publication. Retrieved from makeitfair.org/en/the-facts/reports/on-the-move/at_download/file.

Standing, G. 2007. "Decent Workplaces, Self-Regulation and CSR: From Puff to Stuff?" *Working Papers* (62). United Nations, Department of Economics and Social Affairs.

Stavins, R. N. 2003. "Experience with market-based environmental policy instruments." In K. G. Mäler & J. R. Vincent (Eds.), *Handbook of Environmental Economics* (Vol. 1, pp. 355–435). Amsterdam, NL: Elsevier.

Steinfeld, E. S. 2004. "China's Shallow Integration: Networked Production and the New Challenges for Late Industrialization." *World Development*, 32(11): 1971–87.

Strasser, J. B., & Becklund, L. 1993. *Swoosh: The Unauthorized Story of Nike and the Men Who Played There.* San Diego, CA: Harcourt Brace Jovanovich.

Strathern, M. 2000. *Audit Cultures.* London: Routledge.

Streeck, W. 1987, September. "The Uncertainties of Management in the Management of Uncertainty: Employers, Labor Relations and Industrial Adjustment in the 1980s." *Work, Employment & Society*, 1(3): 281–308.

Streeck, W. 1991. "On the Institutional Conditions of Diversified Quality Production." In E. Matzner & S. Wolfgang (Eds.), *Beyond Keynesianism: The Socio-Economics of Production and Employment* (pp. 21–61). London: Edward Elgar.

Streeck, W. 2009. *Re-forming Capitalism: Institutional Change in the German Political Economy.* Oxford: Oxford University Press.

Sturgeon, T. J. 2002. "Modular Production Networks: A New American Model of Industrial Organization." *Industrial and Corporate Change*, 11(3): 451–96.

Sturgeon, T. J., & Lester, R. 2002. *The New Global Supply Base: New Challenges for Local Suppliers in East Asia.* Cambridge MA: MIT Industrial Performance Center.

SwedWatch, SACOM, and SOMO. 2008. "Silenced to Deliver: Mobile Phone Manufacturing in China and the Philippines."

Swenson, P. 1991, July. "Bringing Capital Back in, or Social Democracy Reconsidered: Employer Power, Cross-Class Alliances, and Centralization of Industrial Relations in Denmark and Sweden." *World Politics*, 43(4): 513–44.

Swidler, A., 2009, November 2. "African Chiefdoms and Institutional Resilience: Public Goods and Private Strategies." Presented at Center for European Studies, Harvard University.

Swidler, A. 2010. "Return of the Sacred: What African Chiefs Teach Us about Secularization," *Sociology of Religion*, 71 no. 2.

Tendler, J. 1997. *Good Government in the Tropics*. Baltimore: Johns Hopkins University Press.

Tewari, M., & Pillai, P. 2005, June. "Global Standards and the Dynamcs of Environmental Compliance in India's Leather Industry." *Oxford Development Studies* 33(2): 245–67.

Thelen, K. 2004. *How Institutions Evolve: The Political Economy of Skills in Germany, Britain, the United States and Japan*. New York: Cambridge University.

Timberland. 2007. Make It Better: Brief on Working Hours Version 1.0. Retrieved from http://responsibility.timberland.com/wp-content/uploads/2011/07/Make_It_Better_Brief-Working_Hours.pdf.

Trubek, D. M., & Trubek, L. G. 2007. "New Governance & Legal Regulation: Complementarity, Rivalry, and Transformation." University of Wisconsin Law School, Legal Studies Research Paper Series, 1047.

Trumbull, G. 2006. *Consumer capitalism: politics, product markets and firm strategy in France and Germany*. Ithaca, NY: Cornell University Press.

Trumbull, J. G. 2011. "Consumer Credit in Postwar America and France: The Political Construction of Economic Interests." New York: Cambridge University Press, forthcoming.

United National Conference on Trade and Development. 2004. World Investment Report. The Shift Towards Services. Geneva: United Nations Report.

United Nations High Commision for Refugees. 2006. "Interim report of the Special Representative of the Secretary-General on the issue of human rights and transnational corporations and other business enterprises" Geneva: UNHCR (Report E/CN.4/2006/97).

Utting, P. 2005. "Rethinking Business Regulation: From Self-Regulation to Social Control." *UNRISD Technology, Business and Society Programme Paper* (15).

Valkila, J., & Nygren, A. 2010. "Impacts of Fair Trade Certification on Coffee Farmers, Cooperatives, and Laborers in Nicaragua." *Agriculture and Human Values*, 27(3): 321–33.

Vietnam Chamber of Commerce and Industry. 2008. "Final Report: Factory Improvement Programme." Presented Hochiminh City, February, 2008.

Verité. 2004, September 7. "Excessive Overtime in Chinese Supplier Factories: Causes, Impacts, and Recommendations for Action" (pp. 1–30). Amherst, MA: Verité Research Paper. Retrieved from http://www.verite.org/news/Excessiveovertime.

Vogel, D. 2005. *The Market for Virtue: The Potential and Limits of Corporate Social Responsibility*. Washington, DC: Brookings Institution Press.

Vogel, D. 2008. "Private Global Business Regulation." *Annual Review of Political Science*, 11: 261–82.

von Hippel, E. 1987. "Cooperation between Rivals: Informal Know-How Trading." *Research Policy*, 16(6): 291–302.

Walton, R. E., Cutcher-Gershenfeld, J. E., & McKersie, R. B. 2000. *Strategic Negotiations: A Theory of Change in Labor-Management Relations*. Ithaca, NY: Cornell University Press.

Ward, J., Coe, N., & Johns, J. 2005. The Role of Temporary Staffing Agencies in Facilitating Labour Mobility in Eastern and Central Europe. Vedior Working Paper. Retrieved from http://ciett.org/fileadmin/templates/ciett/docs/The_role_of_temporary_staffing_agencies_in_facilitating_labo.pdf.

Ward, J., Zhang, B., Jain, S., Fry, C., Olavson, T., Mishal, H., Amaral, J., Beyer, D., Brecht, A., Cargille, B., Chadinha, R., Chou, K., DeNyse, G., Feng, Q., Padovani, C., Raj, S., Sunderbruch, K., Tarjan, R., Venkatraman, K., Woods, J., & Zhou, J. 2010. "HP Transforms Product Portfolio Management with Operations Research." *Interfaces*, 40(1): 17–32.

Weick, K. E. 1999. "Quality Improvement: A Sense-making Perspective." In R. E. Cole & W. R. Scott (Eds.), *The Quality Movement and Organizational Theory* (pp. 155–75), Thousand Oaks, CA: Sage.

Weil, D. 1991. "Enforcing OSHA: The Role of Labor Unions." *Industrial Relations*, 30(1): 20–36.

Weil, D. 1996. "If OSHA Is So Bad, Why Is Compliance So Good? "*The RAND Journal of Economics*, 27(3): 618–40.

Weil, D. 2005. "Public Enforcement/Private Monitoring: Evaluating a New Approach to Regulating the Minimum Wage." *Industrial and Labor Relations Review*, 58(2): 238–57.

Weil, D. 2010. "Improving Workplace Conditions through Strategic Enforcement." Report to the Wage and Hour Division, May 2010.

Wetterberg, A. 2011. "Public-Private Partnership in Labor Standards Governance: Better Factories Cambodia." *Public Administration and Development*, 31: 64–73.

Whitman, J. Q. 2007. "Consumerism Versus Producerism: A Study in Comparative Law." *The Yale Law Journal*, 117: 340.

Wilson, J. Q. 1968. *Varieties of Police Behavior: The Management of Law and Order in Eight Communities*. Cambridge, MA: Harvard University Press.

World Bank. 2003. World Development Report, *Sustainable Development in a Dynamic World*. Retrieved from http://www.dynamicsustainabledevelopment.org/.

Yu, X. M. 2008. "Impacts Of Corporate Code Of Conduct On Labor Standards: A Case Study Of Reebok's Athletic Footwear Supplier Factory In China." *Journal of Business Ethics*, 81: 513–29.

Zadek, S 2004. "The Path to Corporate Responsibility." *Harvard Business Review*, 82:12 (Dec. 1): 125–32.

Index